Ceramics for the Home

during the Celtic Revival

First published by Wordwell Books, 2025
Dublin, Ireland
www.wordwellbooks.com

Wordwell Books is an imprint of the Wordwell Group

Wordwell Books
The Wordwell Group
Suite 5, Hub 17, Corrig Road, Sandyford,
Dublin, Ireland

The Wordwell Group is a member of Publishing Ireland,
the Irish Book Publishers' Association

ISBN: 978-1-913934-97-2 (hardback)

Copyedited by Emer Condit
Design by Fiachra McCarthy
Printed by Sprint Books, Ireland

General Product Safety Regulation (GPSR): For any safety queries, please contact us at productsafety@wordwell.ie

British Library Cataloguing in Publication Data.
A catalogue record for this book is available from the British Library.

This publication has received financial support from the National Museum of Ireland

museum Ard-Mhúsaem na hÉireann National Museum of Ireland

Ceramics for the Home during the Celtic Revival

Irish Art Pottery in the National Museum of Ireland

AISLING MOLLOY

Ard-Mhúsaem na hÉireann
National Museum of Ireland

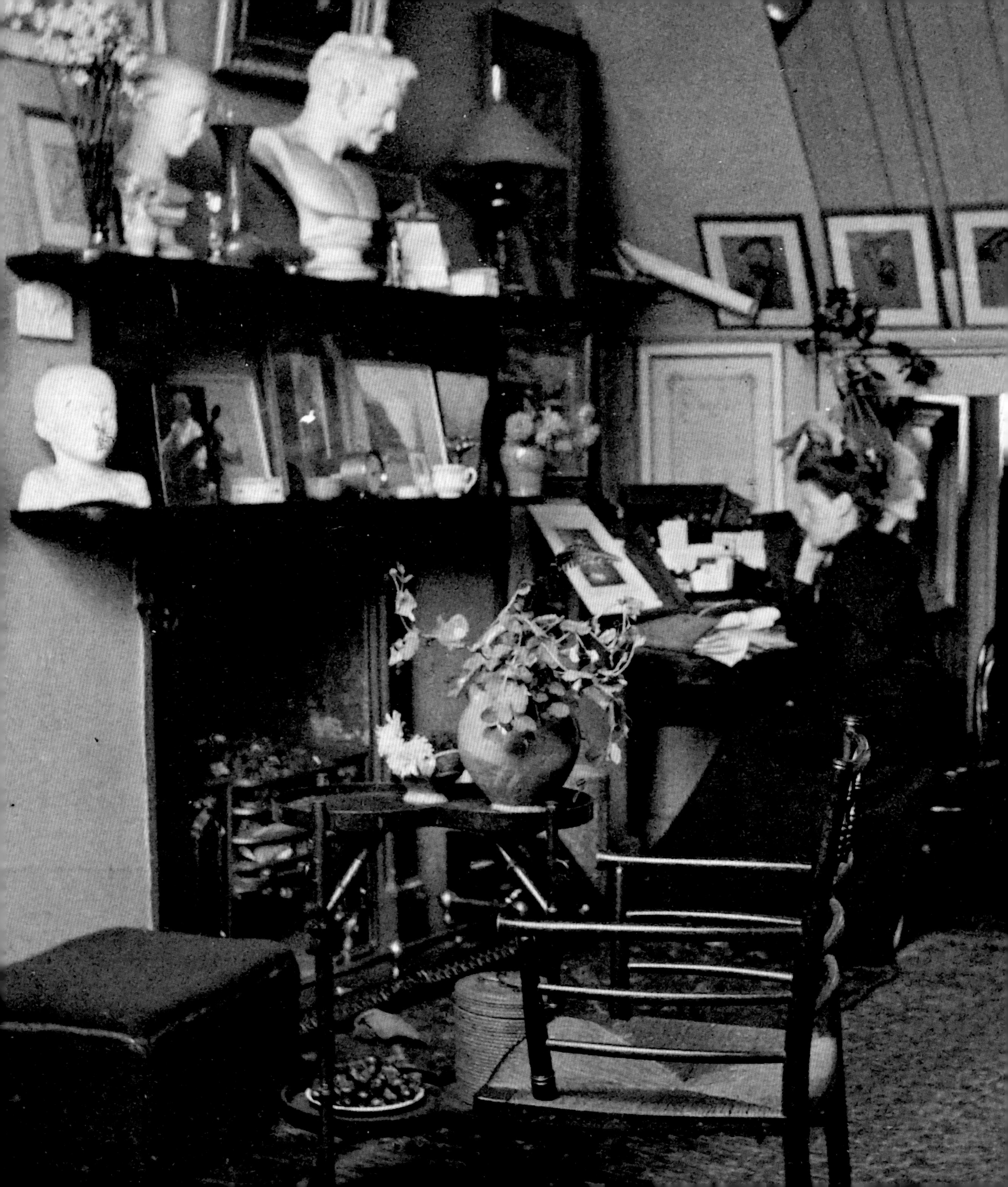

Summary

Fig. 1—Interior, Dublin, *c.* 1890. Photograph by T.F. Geoghegan (detail of Fig. 39). From *Photographs of Irish scenery* by T.F. Geoghegan, 8 Lower Sackville Street, *c.* 1890. Courtesy of the National Library of Ireland, ALB 8:40.

Summary

Art pottery was made in Ireland during the nineteenth century in response to a demand for art industry products from consumers influenced by the ideals of the Arts and Crafts movement. It also reflected developments in design education and the rise of national identity during the Celtic Revival. The story of 'Irish Art Pottery', made in Dublin during the 1870s and 1880s, opens a door onto a previously unexplored world—an artistic community where, against the backdrop of controversy about James Whistler's exhibition of paintings at the Dublin Sketching Club, social change led to the beginning of women's education and the recognition of artisans' rights.

During the 1880s, consumer demand in Dublin increased owing to suburban expansion and the growth of the middle class, giving rise to an increase in ceramic wholesalers and retailers and prompting Arnott's department store to open a separate premises for household furnishings. The introduction in the 1870s of ceramic education at the Queen's Institute, where classes were taught by Herbert Cooper and promoted by the retailer W.H. Kerr, reflected a trend in Ireland, and further afield in the United States and England, for hand-painted porcelain and single-glazed pottery in the home.

Following on from Kerr's retail of ceramics decorated by students at the Queen's Institute, Frederick Vodrey began to produce earthenware art pottery during the 1870s and 1880s. The Vodrey Dublin Pottery catered for an Aesthetic taste, reflecting the Art Nouveau style and emerging Modernist ideals. Vodrey's collaboration with artists like Mary Redmond and Charles Russell, and his association with curators at the National Museum of Ireland, provides valuable insight into cultural life in late nineteenth-century Dublin.

This catalogue documents the National Museum's collection of Vodrey Dublin Pottery and the ceramics hand-painted by Herbert Cooper and his students at the Queen's Institute. It includes a small number of objects from the Ulster Museum, part of an original acquisition of Vodrey Dublin Pottery by the Department of Science and Art in Dublin during the 1880s. These functional and

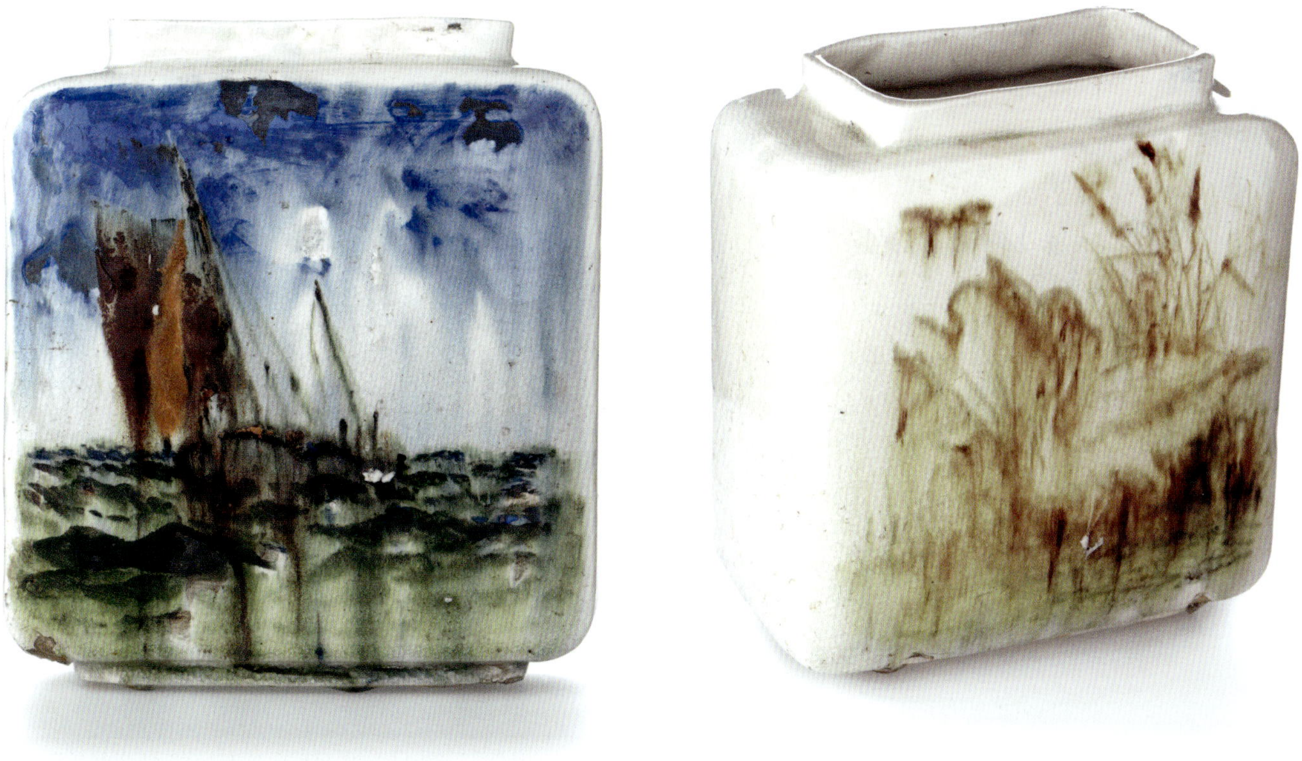

Figs 2 and 3—Vase, painted with ship on a stormy sea on one side, with reeds and grasses on the reverse side, 1880s; 'Dublin' written indistinctly on the underside; 19cm x 16.5cm; attributed to the Dublin Sketching Club. National Museum of Ireland, NMI 1913.14. Cat. 58.

ornamental objects range from tea and coffee sets, moustache cups and dessert plates to bulb pots, jardinières, vases and ornamental plaques, reflecting fashionable taste in home decoration among the middle and upper classes in Dublin during the late nineteenth century.

Author

Dr Aisling Molloy has lectured in Design History at the Limerick School of Art and Design (Limerick Institute of Technology), the University of Limerick and the Hunt Museum in Limerick, Ireland. She has published articles in the Irish Arts Review, History Ireland, *the* Journal of Design History, *the* Irish Studies Review *and* Ceramics Ireland. *She studied the History of Art at University College Dublin (BA, 1983; MA, 1992), and received a Ph.D (2007) in Design History from the Royal College of Art/Victoria and Albert Museum, London, for her doctoral thesis on the ceramic designer Frederick Vodrey.*

Contents

Acknowledgements

I offer my heartfelt appreciation to the descendants of Frederick Vodrey in Canada and the descendants of Jabez Vodrey, Ohio, for their invaluable co-operation and hospitality. My appreciation also extends to the descendants of Charles Russell, the late Paddy Healy and Peter Healy.

The support and assistance of the following curators at the National Museum of Ireland during many years of research was invaluable: the late Mairéad Dunlevy, Deirdre Power, Dr Audrey Whitty, Alex Ward, Dr Siobhán Doyle and Clare McNamara (photography department), Lynn Scarff, Dr Éimear O'Connor, Dónal Maguire, NMI Design and Photography departments.

Special mention must be made of Audrey Whitty's documentation of the Queen's Institute ceramics during her time as Curator of Ceramics and her encouragement for this publication.

I would like to thank the following individuals and institutes for professional support during my research:

- Ms Marcia Cuthbert (formerly conservation architect with the City of Toronto and descendant of Frederick Vodrey's wife Annie Cuthbert), Prof. Mary Daly, Dr Gordon Elliott, Dr John Turpin, Malcolm Haslam, Peter Lamb, Dairine Coffey (ceramic artist and descendant of George Coffey), the late Shirley Armstrong-Duffy, Ian Whyte (Whyte's auctioneers), Kieran Whitelaw (Ceramic Department, Limerick School of Art and Design), Mark Hickton (local historian, Stoke-on-Trent), Dr Elaine Sisson, Tom Scott and the late Dr Patricia McGloughlin (Dublin Sketching Club), Ruth Marshall (folklorist and writer), Dr Joseph McBrinn, Dr Janice Helland and Donna Gilligan (Scéal Heritage).

- Ulster Museum, Belfast: Kim Mawhinney (curator).

- East Liverpool Ceramic Museum, Ohio, US: former curator Sarah Vodrey-Hendrickson and Catherine Vodrey (descendants of the late Jabez Vodrey of Ohio).

- Stoke-on-Trent City Archives: Margaret Beard and Chris Latimer.
- University of Limerick: Dr John Logan (Emeritus Professor of History) and Ms Patti Punch (Humanities Librarian).

- Royal Dublin Society: Mary Kelleher (librarian).

- National College of Art and Design: the late Eddie Murphy (librarian).

- Staff of the National Library of Ireland: Berni Metcalfe, James Harte and Mary Broderick.

- Staff of Trinity College, Dublin, Library.

- National Gallery of Ireland archives: Andrea Lydon and Ciara O'Brien.

- National Archives of Ireland: Mr Brian Donnelly.

- Limerick City Library: Marie Stakelum (librarian).

This project received financial support from the following organisations, to which I would like to express my thanks:

- the National Museum of Ireland

- the Ireland Canada University Foundation;

- the Cumming Ceramic Research Centre, Canada;

- the British Association of Irish Studies;

- the Arts Council of Ireland.

Abbreviations

DSC	Dublin Sketching Club
IHIA	Irish Home Industries Association
IHMA	Irish Home Manufacturers Association
IIA	Irish Industries Association
NMI	National Museum of Ireland
QI	Queen's Institute of Female Professional Schools
RDS	Royal Dublin Society
RHA	Royal Hibernian Academy
RIA	Royal Irish Academy
VDP	Vodrey Dublin Pottery

Introduction

Production of art pottery in Ireland during the nineteenth century was influenced by Arts and Crafts ideals, based on concern for the welfare of the working classes combined with the promotion of Irish industry for economic revival. In the 1860s, writings by art critic John Ruskin and designer William Morris drew attention to 'the essential unity of the arts' and the close relationship between architecture and craftsmanship, resulting in a 'shift from a machine to a craft aesthetic'.[1] From the 1870s there was a popularisation and commercialisation of the craft ethos, when manufacturers specialised in 'both the production and retailing of "Art Manufactures"', including ceramics.[2] The interest in art pottery originated in a fashion for ceramics in the home, sometimes called 'Chinamania', which, influenced by *Japonisme*, created an awareness of the ceramic object as a means of artistic expression for both producer and consumer.[3]

Dunlevy's comprehensive survey of the history of Irish ceramics, *Ceramics in Ireland*, traces the early beginnings of a ceramic industry to the production of delftwares in Belfast and Dublin during the eighteenth century, and to the Royal Dublin Society's financial support for the production of fine earthenware 'commonly called Queen's ware or Paris ware'.[4] During the nineteenth century there was a renewed interest in the possibility of using Irish clays for ceramic manufacture, prompted by Sir Robert Kane's *The industrial resources of Ireland* (1844).[5] Kane's extensive survey of mineral resources in Ireland led to the founding of the Museum of Industry, the first publicly funded museum in Ireland, in the 1850s,

1 Naylor 1971, 120–1.

2 Ibid., 149. The author refers to the company Howell and James, whose exhibition of 'paintings on porcelain', some by talented amateurs, was admired at the 1878 Paris Exhibition.

3 Haslam 1975.

4 Dunlevy 1988, 22, 32.

5 Kane 1844.

during the same period as the creation of the Ordnance Survey of Ireland.[6]

Writing in the 1870s, the British ceramic historian Jewitt gave an extensive account of the Belleek Pottery and also referred to the Delamaine delftware produced in Dublin during the eighteenth century and the work of Donovan, who decorated imported blanks in the early nineteenth century.[7] Jewitt did not, however, mention either the Vodrey Dublin Pottery or the ceramics decorated at the Queen's Institute, possibly because these became active when he was writing. The earliest attempt to make fine ceramics from Irish clays, as distinct from the coarseware pottery made around the country since the seventeenth century,[8] took place at the Florence Court Brick, Tile and Pottery Works in County Fermanagh[9] and at the Worcester porcelain factory in England; this prompted further experimentation to develop Irish ceramics and create employment within the country. From the 1860s, porcelain and Parian ware were produced in Belleek, Co. Fermanagh, and in the 1880s earthenware art pottery marked 'Vodrey Dublin Pottery' was produced in Dublin city.

At the Dublin International Exhibition (1853) an English company, the Royal Porcelain Works in Worcester, received an award for a dinner service produced from Irish clays.[10] The manager at Worcester was W.H. Kerr, from a family of ceramic retailers in Dublin.[11] Like others in Ireland, Kerr was interested in experimenting with Irish clays for ceramic production, and he was helped by Robert Armstrong, an architect who later became art director at the new Belleek Pottery in Fermanagh.[12] When Kerr returned to live in Dublin *c.* 1862, he commissioned a dessert service, reportedly made with feldspar from Killiney Hill and gold from County Wicklow.[13] In the spirit of the Celtic Revival style, the bases were decorated with moulded Celtic interlace.[14]

In Ireland, the first instance of ceramic production for the home during the nineteenth century (aside from the utilitarian coarseware produced by several potteries around the country) occurred at the pottery in Belleek, situated in an area where clay with deposits of feldspar and kaolin, suitable for ceramic manufacture, were found.[15] The Belleek Pottery was founded in 1857 and employed trained potters from the Staffordshire pottery industry in England, who then trained local workers in Belleek, starting a tradition of skilled families working in the pottery over several generations[16] which continues today. The Belleek Pottery quickly progressed to producing domestic and functional ceramics for the

---

6 Bourke 2011, 173.

7 Jewitt 1878, 459.

8 Dunlevy 1988, 23.

9 *Ibid.*, 26. The author writes that the 'Florence Court factory for bricks, floor tiles and drainpipes (1840–70s)' was probably the first to produce 'artistic ranges'.

10 Langham 2001, 2–3.

11 Curry 1993. According to the author, Kerr worked as a manager of the Worcester factory in England from 1850 to 1862 and then returned to manage the family business at 114–115 Capel Street.

12 *Ibid.*

13 Curry 2001. According to the author the retailers Kerr and Binn exhibited Parian ware busts of Sir Robert Kane and William Dargan at the 1853 International Exhibition in Dublin.

14 *Ibid.*

15 Degenhardt 1993, 1–2.

16 *Ibid.*

home market, as well as fine ornate porcelain tablewares for export to prestigious clients amongst the royalty of Europe.[17]

The designs of the fine glazed Belleek porcelain and Parian statuettes were in a naturalistic style, popular during the mid-Victorian period. In the later nineteenth century, owing to the influence of the Aesthetic taste, a new style of ceramics for home decoration became fashionable. This created a demand for 'art ceramics', both hand-painted porcelain and earthenware art pottery with brightly coloured glazes. There are two known examples of the production of art ceramics in Ireland during the later nineteenth century: at the Queen's Institute and the Vodrey Dublin Pottery.

The Queen's Institute (QI) was set up to provide women with a range of practical skills so that they could earn an income.[18] From 1870 to 1883, female students at the QI painted porcelain wares with flowers and fruit, the blanks being imported from England.[19] The Painting on Porcelain School of the QI received patronage from aristocratic clients, who commissioned tea sets and dessert services.[20] The opening of a new studio for the teaching of a range of art subjects, including porcelain painting, was announced in 1878.[21] The students worked under the tuition of Herbert Cooper, manager of the Painting on Porcelain School; he had been encouraged to come to Ireland by Kerr, who financed the project.[22]

The other source of art ceramics in Ireland was the pottery of Frederick Vodrey, who took over the family retail business *c.* 1865, producing earthenware vases and jardinières glazed in bright colours and marked with the words 'Vodrey Dublin Pottery' (see Appendix). From *c.* 1872 to *c.* 1885 he produced art pottery behind his wholesale warehouse in Moore Street, Dublin, for which he won acclaim in Dublin society.[23]

Irish consumers interested in the Arts and Crafts movement and keen to support home industry purchased ceramics for the home from the Vodrey Dublin Pottery. However, while Vodrey's Celtic-style vases and jardinières catered for the growing interest in cultural revival, the range of styles produced also reflected international taste, revealing that Irish homes were decorated in a variety of styles, from mid-Victorian naturalism to Art Nouveau. Frederick Vodrey, who had a background in the English pottery industry (his father being a potter), was described as a 'Designer and Manufacturer'.[24] He worked with Irish artists (such as Mary Redmond and Charles Russell) as well as potters from Stoke-on-Trent.

The 'Irish Art Pottery' produced by Frederick Vodrey inspired an emerging national identity amongst the Anglo-Irish ruling class and the rising Catholic nationalist middle class who resided in the new suburbs. The term 'practical patriotism' was used frequently in newspapers, and consumers were encouraged to

---

17 Langham 2001, 2–3.

18 *Queen's Institute for the Training and Employment of Educated Women. Sixth Annual Report* (Dublin, 1868), 11.

19 Curry 1993.

20 *Ibid.*, 194.

21 An announcement of the opening of an Amateur Studio on 26 April 1878 appeared in *Saunders's News-Letter* on 23 April 1878: 'The Queen's Institute for the Technical Instruction and Queen's College for the Education of Women, School of Music, Art Industries, Female Schools of Art and Science (Under the Government of Science and Art), 25 and 26 Molesworth Street. A new Studio has been specially arranged for Lady students in the following ART SUBJECTS:—Porcelain Painting, Painting Wood Panels, Furniture &c., Photo Painting, Fan Painting on Silk, Satin, Ivory &c., Illuminating &c., Flower Painting from Nature, Wood Engraving, Wood Carving.'

22 Curry 1993, 193.

23 Frederick Vodrey's trade card (1885) is in the National Museum of Ireland (acquisition no. 1886:125).

24 *Irish Artisans' Exhibition Complete Official Catalogue* (2nd edn) (Dublin, 1885), 29. Frederick Vodrey was listed at his stand as 'F. Vodrey, Designer and Manufacturer'.

support Irish industries for economic revival. In terms of design, according to McBrinn, there was a 'systemic shift' in Irish identity at this time, which led to the democratisation of fashionable taste.[25] It was noticeable in dress and adornment, and by the end of the century jewellery, once a luxury largely confined to the upper class, was 'widely worn by every social class in the country and made in a distinctly Irish style'.[26] The consumption of ceramics was influenced by the same economic and cultural changes.

The increased prosperity of a predominantly Catholic nationalist middle class influenced the development of Irish national identity and was reflected in the production of material culture such as Vodrey's ceramics. Economic historians refer to the 'trickle-down theory', whereby the taste of aristocratic consumers influenced the consumption of the middle classes.[27] The latter theory has been applied to ceramic production from the eighteenth century onwards. It was reflected in the spread of the Aesthetic taste from the artistic élite to widespread production by home industry workshops for a broader range of middle-class consumers in Britain, the United States and Ireland. The spread of the Celtic Revival style and interest in Arts and Crafts to a wider range of social groups in Irish society demonstrates this social and economic evolution.

Study of the objects produced by the Vodrey Dublin Pottery reveals a close collaboration between the National Museum and Frederick Vodrey during the 1880s. The Museum purchased art pottery from Vodrey in 1884 and 1886, during the period of his success at the Art and Industry exhibitions in Cork and Dublin. The curator of ceramics was Thomas Longfield, who, along with other members of the Dublin Sketching Club (DSC), made and exhibited ceramics during the same period. Vodrey's entrepreneurial spirit is shown by the fact that he offered the facilities and materials in his art pottery workshop for use by the DSC members. His interaction with the DSC, which had most of the prominent artists in Dublin among its membership, gives new insight into the artistic community in Dublin during the late nineteenth century, showing that art pottery was appreciated and understood as an expression of the Arts and Crafts ideals, which gave rise to the Aesthetic taste. The Aesthetic taste was the expression of ideas, both social and artistic, based on literary sources. It influenced art and design in Britain, Europe and the United States from the 1860s to the early twentieth century. Aestheticism has been described as 'not in reality a "movement" with "a programmatic set of aims", but more "a loose association of the sometimes-shared aims, enthusiasms and ideals of a shifting cast of characters united for the most part by ties of comradely friendship"'.[28]

This catalogue documents the range of ceramics made or decorated in Dublin during the later nineteenth century and illustrates both the art pottery produced at Frederick Vodrey's workshop and ceramics hand-painted by female students at the Queen's Institute under the tuition of Herbert Cooper. These functional and ornamental wares, which include dessert plates, tea and coffee sets, moustache cups, bulb pots and jardinières, vases and plaques, were produced for the Aesthetic interior and are evidence of the existence of this style in Dublin.

---

25 McBrinn 2009, 211.

26 *Ibid.* The author refers to McCrum 1993.

27 Fine and Leopold 1998, 138–40.

28 Calloway and Federle Orr 2011, 13–14.

Foreword

July 2025

When Frederick Vodrey (1845-97) donated 47 of his ceramics to the Museum of Science and Art in 1886, it marked a very generous gesture by a living maker to a cultural institution in its infancy. Since then, the National Museum of Ireland has built upon Vodrey's donation to create a collection of Irish art pottery that reflects the varied repertory of shapes and styles produced by makers right up to the present day. The National Museum of Ireland's ceramics collection has been a valued resource for researchers and has also played a key role in exhibitions since the Museum's inception in 1877. The visual appeal of this collection, at times stunningly beautiful and technically exquisite, stimulates both the passion to collect ceramics and the interest to study them.

The Museum owes a great debt to many of the custodians of the ceramics collection, who have augmented, curated, documented, conserved, researched, photographed, published and displayed the collections. Their dedication and enthusiasm for ceramics has enriched the Museum's collection immeasurably. Close co-operation with Aisling Molloy has resulted in a publication which will take its place among the Museum's scholarly works which disseminate information about our collections to an international public and to researchers worldwide.

In a General Guide to the Art Collections published in 1907, the Director of the Science and Art Museum G.T. Plunkett (1851-1948) wrote that, to acquire a knowledge of pottery, 'the student must see typical examples of different kinds as shown in the Museum collections, but he should also make use of information gathered by experts and collectors; and given in the many books published on this subject'. This book, as a comprehensive and visually impressive guide to Irish Art Pottery in the National Museum of Ireland, adds importance to Plunkett's words on the value of research and learning through collections.

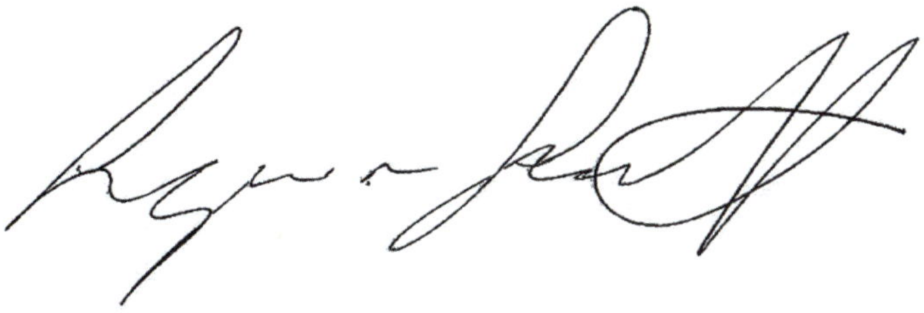

Lynn Scarff
Director, National Museum of Ireland
July 2025

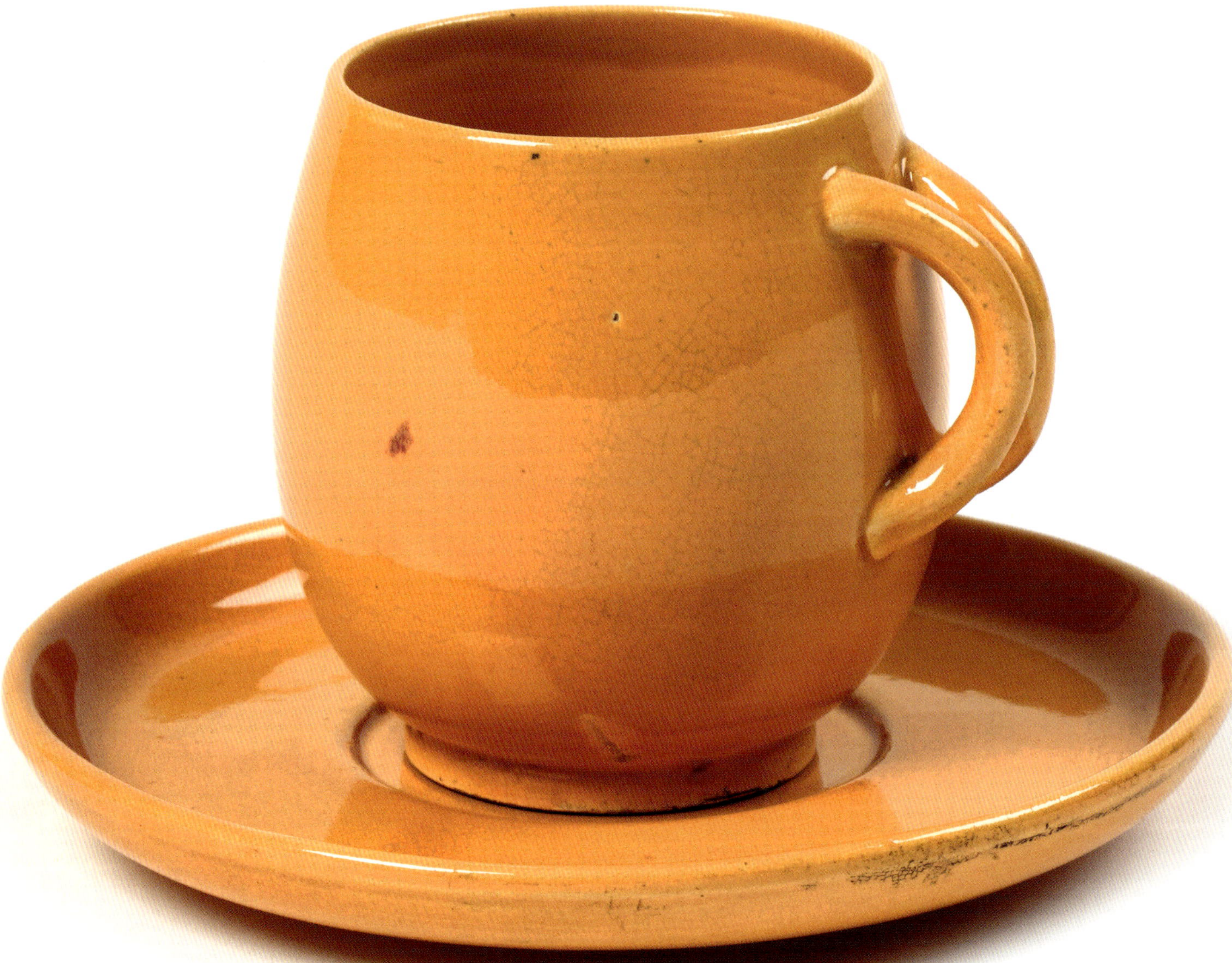

Fig. 4—Coffee cup and saucer, c. 1886; impressed mark 'DUBLIN POTTERY VODREY'; height 6.5cm, diameter 11cm. NMI 1886.103. Cat. no. 25.

CHAPTER 1

Home industry and economic revival

Home industry and economic revival

As in Britain and Europe during the late nineteenth century, art pottery in Ireland was one of several art industries catering for home decoration and started in response to the popularisation of design ideas spread by the Arts and Crafts movement. There was also a growth in small-scale producers of crafts in a variety of media, such as furniture, metalwork, textiles and ceramics.[1] The Irish Arts and Crafts Society was founded in 1894 and held exhibitions from 1895 to 1925.[2] Paul Larmour was the first to comprehensively document the Arts and Crafts movement in Ireland, which was based on 'the English model' of the Arts and Crafts Society founded in the 1880s.[3]

Irish home industries were begun in response to calls for economic revival and were an integral part of the Arts and Crafts movement.[4] There were parallels between the support for economic revival in Ireland and similar home industry ventures in other European countries. Nicola Gordon Bowe was the first to highlight the links between Irish design and the emergence of national identity as part of social and economic change in Europe.[5] The rising interest in Irish national identity was part of a Europe-wide interest in cultural origins 'amongst intellectual circles'.[6] The social historian Tony Farmar further elaborated on the shared experience of Ireland and other European countries in the late nineteenth century, pointing out that the 'class revolution' that occurred in Ireland was 'the Irish aspect of a larger continental movement'.[7]

From the 1880s, Irish consumers' interest in crafts led supporters of home industries to encourage the training of young girls in lacemaking and embroidery, with a dual purpose: to create employment and to

---

1 Aslin 1981.

2 Gordon-Bowe 1990, 133.

3 Larmour 1992, 5.

4 *Ibid.*, 3, 49–55.

5 Gordon-Bowe 1993, 7–14.

6 *Ibid.*, 7–8.

7 Farmar 2010, 3.

meet the demand for household goods and fashion accessories.[8]

The growth of suburbs around Dublin city from the 1860s[9] led to an increase in population, which 'nearly doubled' between 1851 and 1891.[10] Rains's research has confirmed the existence of a vibrant commodity culture in late nineteenth-century Dublin and revealed the 'growing infrastructure and social patterns necessary for development of middle-class life and identity, such as transport, housing, and fashions in home décor'.[11] During this time department stores advertised and promoted home industries such as furniture and lace, to the degree that consumption of 'Irish manufactured goods' was 'both politically symbolic and socially fashionable in Dublin by the early 1880s'.[12]

Despite Ireland's history of political strife and economic distress, there was significant economic prosperity and a growth of the middle classes during the nineteenth century,[13] giving rise to a consumer culture characterised by shoppers from 'redbrick villas' travelling by rail and tram to the 'Monster Stores' and new department stores.[14] Some of the Dublin department stores, including Arnott's, were founded at this time, while others, like Brown Thomas, McBirney's and Todd Burns,[15] expanded to supply a wider range of goods in response to increased demand for household furnishings, including ceramics.

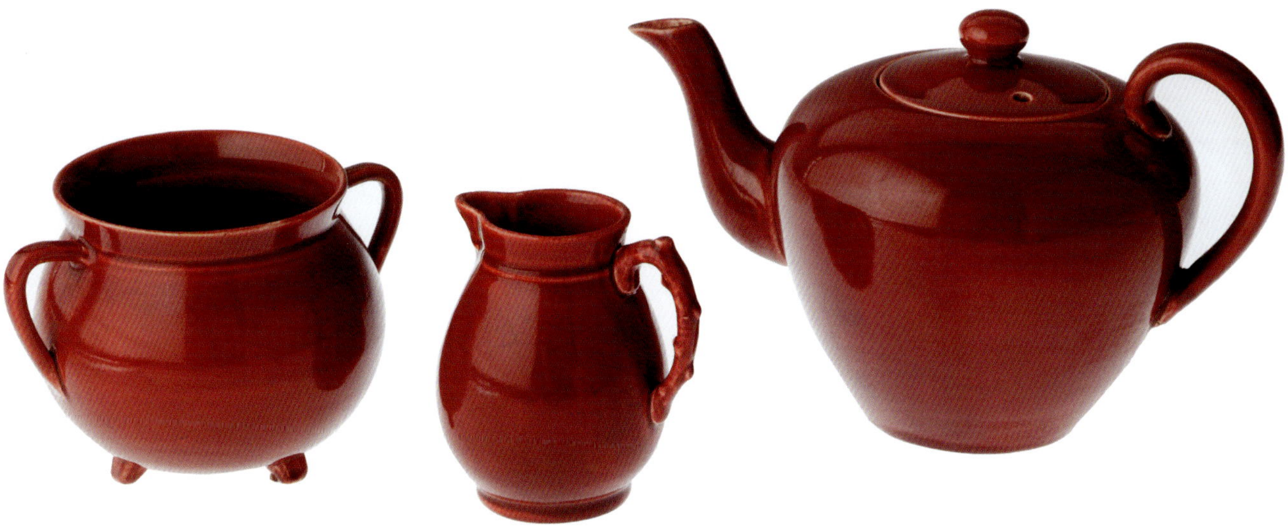

Fig. 5—Teapot, cream jug and sugar bowl, ruby-red glaze. Dimensions: 22cm x 24cm; 9.5cm x 6cm; 9.5cm x 9.5cm. Impressed mark 'VODREY DUBLIN POTTERY', 1880s. NMI.DC: 2023.49/50/51. Cat. nos 46, 47 and 48.

8 Helland 2007, 54, 82–3. The author refers to the Kells Embroidery Cottage, Florence Vere O'Brien's embroidery project in County Clare and the Irish School of Art Needlework, which made Celtic-style dress for Lady Aberdeen, the Viceroy's wife.

9 Daly 1998, 3–8.

10 Rains 2010, 3.

11 *Ibid.*, 5.

12 *Ibid.*, 96–7.

13 Bielenberg 2018.

14 Rains 2010, 5, 13–15.

15 *Ibid.*, 13–15, 26, 45–9.

Arnott's department store advertised the opening of a separate premises for these goods at No. 50 Henry Street in 1878.[16] The advertisement listed ceramics, including china dinner and dessert services 'comprising many exquisite specimens from the German, French and Home Manufacturers', and detailed other household furnishings such as 'ironmongery, electroplated goods, and table cutlery'.[17] The increase in the number of ceramic retailers could also have been caused by the abolition of customs tariffs between England and Ireland owing to the Act of Union, which took effect in the 1840s and would have made it favourable to import and sell Staffordshire ceramics in Ireland. In spite of the reported economic recession in the 1870s and 1880s, the development of a consumer culture coincided with a noticeable increase in ceramic wholesalers and retailers in Dublin's shopping district adjacent to O'Connell Street. According to *Thom's Street Directory*, in 1875 Frederick Vodrey was the only ceramic dealer in Moore Street; by 1881 there were seven others, and this had increased to nine in 1885.[18]

---

16 In *Saunders's News-Letter and Irish Daily News*, Saturday 29 June 1878, an advertisement announced the opening of the outlet at 50 Henry Street for 'Arnott and Company, Dublin Ltd. General House Furnishing Ironmongers China, and Glass Merchants'.

17 *Ibid.*

18 Molloy 2007. Examination of *Thom's Directory* from 1860 to 1890 shows a marked increase in the number of ceramic wholesalers and retailers in the Henry Street and Moore Street area. Analysis of nineteenth-century street directories over a period of twenty years at five-year intervals revealed that at first there was a predominance of victuallers (13) and bread- and biscuit-makers (6), there being only two china and delft dealers, including Vodrey, in 1865 (Appendix III). During the period 1875–85, however, there was a dramatic increase in ceramic retailers in Moore Street (Appendix IV); the ceramic merchants gradually occupied a section of the street and were situated beside one another.

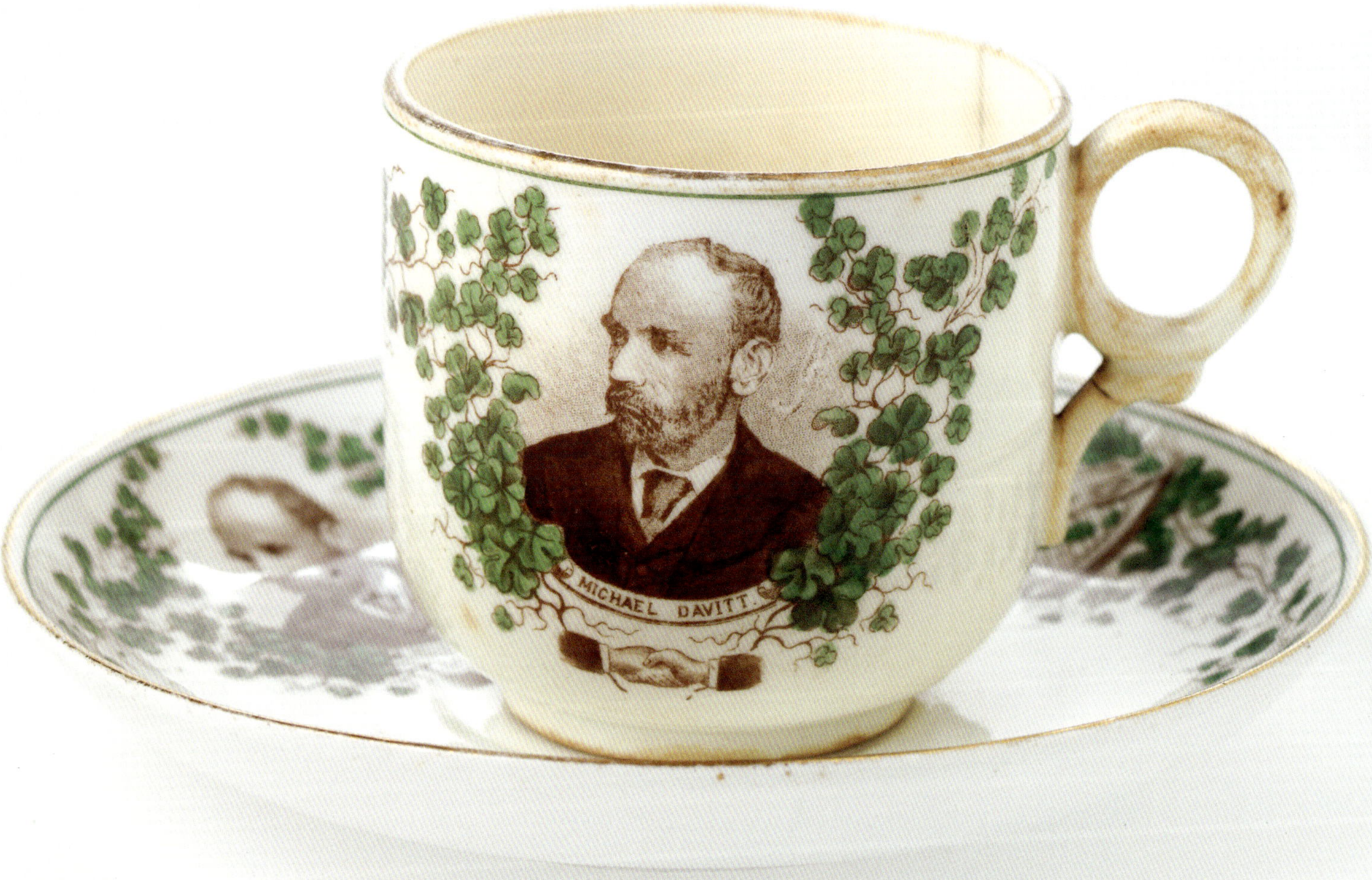

Fig. 6—Celtic Revival design, portrait of Michael Davitt bordered by shamrocks. NMI register DC: 1971.49;DC: 1971.51.

CHAPTER 2

Design during the Celtic Revival

Design during the Celtic Revival

Writers on the Irish home in Victorian Dublin indicate that home-owners' interest in both the Arts and Crafts movement and the Celtic Revival was reflected in household furnishings.[1] The production and consumption of design in Ireland at this time reveal the development of a consumer culture amongst the middle class, underpinned by social and political change. The influence of the Celtic Revival on Irish taste and design in the nineteenth century was first documented by Jeanne Sheehy.[2] The Revival influenced the production of ceramics, from the Belleek Pottery statuette of 'Erin Unveiling her First Pot' to Frederick Vodrey's 'Irish Art Pottery' in the Celtic style, both catering for a growing interest in cultural revival. In 1886 Frederick Vodrey's Celtic designs for ceramics were praised for offering new possibilities for Irish design and industry.[3]

The Celtic Revival in Irish society was first evident amongst the Anglo-Irish ruling class, the movement progressing to encompass many organisations promoting the revival of Gaelic culture.[4] In the 1850s the Celtic style was fashionable as a mode of personal adornment in dress and jewellery.[5] Embroidery of Celtic interlace patterns carried out by several women's projects, including the Royal Irish School of Needlework and the Kenmare Convent, generated income and was praised for its skill and high quality.[6] By the 1880s, Celtic style on all forms of craft and design was embraced by the upper-class establishment, most notably the British Viceroy's wife, Ishbel Aberdeen, who attended more than one State occasion in dress decorated with Celtic-style embroidery.[7]

---

1 Hearn 1998.

2 Sheehy 1980, 93.

3 Walker 1886.

4 Hutchinson 1987. The author discusses the influence of organizations such as the Gaelic League for language and sports, the Co-operative Movement for agriculture and Anglo-Irish literature.

5 McBrinn 2009, 209.

6 Larmour 1992, 12–15.

7 *Ibid.*, 13, 50.

Helland's research shows the influence of the Celtic style on women's fashions, popularised among upper-class women in Dublin and London through illustrations in journals and much-publicised accounts of a garden party where Lady Aberdeen and other guests wore gowns with Celtic designs.[8] The details of Lady Aberdeen's dress for the occasion demonstrated her commitment to the promotion of home industries and the use of Irish materials in the 'white poplin parasol trimmed with Limerick lace with a stick of "Irish yew"' and 'a handle in the shape of the famous "Tara brooch", an early eighth-century silver gilt brooch discovered in Co. Meath in 1850'.[9]

During her first period in Ireland, in 1886 Lady Aberdeen founded the Irish Industries Association (IIA), an 'umbrella organisation'[10] promoting several home industry projects. It provided information to workers and established depots for the sale of goods in Dublin and London, and as a result art needlework became 'a means of earning a "livelihood"'.[11] Helland suggests that whilst Ishbel Aberdeen 'embodied Irishness and epitomized Celtic revival with extravagance and splendour', her motives must be interpreted within the context of colonialism.[12] The way style in design is influenced by political motives is also evident in the early decades of the twentieth century. Research by Ward shows how the use of Celtic style in fashionable dress later became imbued with the idea of national costume and was associated with a more nationalist and separatist point of view.[13] Nevertheless, Ward states that 'Celtic costume was not adopted by the vast majority of the population and could never truly be viewed as part of mainstream fashion in Ireland'.[14]

Crooke points out the hierarchical nature of Irish society in the nineteenth century and notes that the association of the ruling class with the native Gaelic culture of the island could be interpreted as a means of asserting dominance and power.[15] Home industries were also, however, supported by the Catholic nationalist middle class, represented by Charles Dawson, MP and lord mayor of Dublin,[16] whose activities included the organising of the 1882 Art and Industry Exhibition. This exhibition, called the 'National Exhibition' in newspapers, was planned to coincide with the unveiling of the O'Connell monument. Dawson also wrote in support of Irish home industries and economic revival.[17] The advancement of Catholic middle-class businessmen and politicians like Dawson represented evolution in the Irish class structure. This was partly due to advances in education and the founding of a Catholic University in 1854.[18]

Since Catholic Emancipation (1829) there had been a significant change in Irish society, leading to the upward mobility of the Catholic population and reflected in church contributions from the wealthier

8 Helland 2007, 83–5.

9 Ward 2014, 200.

10 Helland 2007, 77–8. The Irish Industries Association (IIA) was distinct from the Irish Home Industries Association (IHIA) founded by Alice Hart and part of the English organisation of the same name. I am grateful to Janice Helland for her clarification of this point.

11 *Ibid.*, 93.

12 *Ibid.*, 104.

13 Ward 2014, 202–3.

14 *Ibid.*, 210.

15 Crooke 2000, 69, 96.

16 *Dictionary of Irish Biography* (dib.ie).

17 C. Dawson, 'Mr Charles Dawson on the Industrial Question', in Fitzpatrick 1886, 22–34.

18 McBride 1991, 19–22.

suburbs in Dublin city.[19] The establishment of the Catholic Commercial Club in 1881, which met at 42 Upper Sackville Street, demonstrated the strength of the Catholic community.[20] The Club included many prominent figures from the commercial and political spheres, such as Charles Dawson and Peter McSwiney (owner of McSwiney's department store, later Clery's), both of whom served terms as lord mayor during the 1880s.[21] The rise in power and prosperity of the Catholic middle class led to a demand for and trade in 'devotional artefacts' and a marked increase in the need for interior fittings used in churches.[22]

Daly's outline of the changing demographics in Dublin city during the nineteenth century established that suburban expansion, the rise of a Catholic middle class and nationalist politics were integrated.[23] The move to the suburbs was made first by upper-middle-class families, who lived in large red-brick villas to the south and west of the city, followed by families with more modest means, who lived in terraced houses.[24] There was similar suburban expansion in other Irish cities, Belfast, Cork and Limerick, the future investigation of which could provide new insights into the growth of the Irish middle class during the nineteenth century.

This social mobility resulted from the many economic and cultural changes that occurred in areas such as education and landownership during the later nineteenth century. As a result of advances in education amongst the Catholic middle class,[25] Catholics 'gained access to well-paid jobs in the professions, the civil service and in business', which contributed to their upward mobility and the suburban expansion.[26] The growth of the middle classes was also underpinned by changes in landownership in the rural areas as a result of the Land Act (1881), which 'transferred the land from the Ascendancy to the small farmers of Ireland',[27] leading ultimately to the rise of a 'strong farmer class'.[28] The latter occurred after a decrease in incomes of the landlord class owing to changes in global trade whereby their products were competing with products from the United States and the colonies, creating a situation where 'competition from "the new world" would upset the balance of the old world markets'.[29]

---

19 Farmar 1991, 25. The author referred to the lists of parish contributions to the Catholic diocese published in *The Freeman's Journal* in August 1907 as follows: 'Haddington Road in the Pembroke Estate—£59; St Andrews Church, Westland Row (Merrion and Fitzwilliam Squares)—£54; Ringsend—£6 (this was predominantly working-class); Two churches in Rathmines/Rathgar area—£30 and £39 and Beechwood Avenue—£42'.

20 Béaslaí 1958, 8–9, 14.

21 *Ibid.*, 10–11.

22 Godson 2003. The author notes that 'the *Irish Catholic Directory* carried numerous advertisements for church plate, vestments, and religious books'.

23 Daly 1984, 153–96.

24 Daly 1998, 17–19. The author writes that most houses in Dublin for the 'professional and upper middle classes' were built during the 1860s–early 1870s, except for Orwell Park in Rathgar, which was built after the 1870s. Later there was a demand for houses from 'clerks and those with modest incomes' that was catered for by 'small red brick houses' off the North and South Circular Roads and Drumcondra.

25 McBride 1991, 19–22. According to the author, the advancement of the Catholic middle class also resulted from changes in the administrative personnel of the civil service wrought by Gladstone's Liberal government and augmented by education for the civil service exams in Catholic schools. Despite these changes, there was still discontent amongst Catholic nationalists because the change only occurred at the lower levels of the civil service.

26 Daly 1998, 40.

27 Farmar 2010, 3–4.

28 Drudy 1982, 1–5, 55.

29 Farmar 2010, 32.

Hutchinson has shown that Irish cultural revivalism in the nineteenth century was founded on the development of political nationalism,[30] and Sheehy illustrated the relationship between Irish visual culture and political organisations such as the Young Ireland movement (1840s–60s)[31] evident in most aspects of material culture, including ceramics. The design of a tea set in the National Museum collection, decorated with portraits of key political figures (framed by shamrocks) such as Michael Davitt, leader of the Land League, and Charles Stewart Parnell, leader of the Home Rule movement, indicates the influence of political change on ceramic design during the nineteenth century.[32] Whilst the tea set was manufactured in England, the decoration and the use of national symbols around the borders reflect the strong interest in emerging Irish political identity during the 1880s. Strictly speaking, the design here does not use Celtic style, but the use of the shamrock, an important emblem of national identity, makes these ceramics an example of Celtic Revival design.

The use of Celtic motifs on all forms of craft was a distinctive feature of the Irish home interior during the nineteenth century:

> 'A neo-Celtic style of art, reviving forms and motifs from early Irish art, began to emerge about the 1840s. The impact was seen initially in metalwork and later in woodwork. Articles of furniture, including chairs, settles and cabinets, were carved or painted with interlaced patterns. In the late nineteenth century, the Arts and Craft movement, which was interested in handicrafts and design, gave neo-Celticism a new boost, and was responsible for the introduction of some elegant furniture into the Dublin home.'[33]

Celtic Revival design was inspired by the discovery of ancient Celtic artefacts and studies of the Gaelic language by members of the Royal Irish Academy (RIA).[34] In the 1840s a distinct national identity was evident in graphic illustration,[35] followed by the reproduction of Celtic jewellery in the 1860s[36] and the use of Celtic ornament on all forms of design, including ceramics, during the Arts and Crafts movement from the 1880s to the 1920s.[37] Whilst the reproduction of Celtic brooches from the 1850s was considered to be the first example of Celtic Revival objects, it has also been shown that distinctively Irish silver designs in the eighteenth century were based on ancient wooden vessels.[38]

30 Hutchinson 1987, 97.

31 Sheehy 1980, 36–40.

32 NMI Register, 21-52-1971: 'Composed of thirty-two pieces, china ware printed with portraits of Charles Stewart Parnell, Dr Croke, Michael Davitt, William O'Brien, John Dillon and W.E. Gladstone, each piece printed with one portrait and having the reverse printed with a harp and painted shamrocks. Mark S & P (Skelton and Plant, Longton, England) below the Registration Number 100761, Registered on the 15th of May 1888.' Purchased from Mrs Lindsay Cooper, 'Pant Glas', Boullysallagh H., Goleen, via Skibbereen, Co. Cork, on 22 April 1971 for £50.

33 Hearn 1998, 79.

34 McBrinn 2009, 211.

35 Crooke 2000, 74–5.

36 Sheehy 1980, 86–9.

37 Gordon Bowe and Cumming 1998, 39, 199. The authors discuss Holyrood pottery in Scotland and Vodrey Dublin Pottery in Ireland.

38 McBrinn 2009, 212–13. The author refers to Teehan 1995.

The artefacts discovered and collected by the RIA were later to become the basis of the National Museum collection of Celtic antiquities.[39] These include the Cross of Cong, the Tara Brooch, the Ardagh Chalice and the Broighter Hoard, and all had a significant influence on the development of Irish identity and design.[40] The production of Celtic Revival design was also greatly influenced by the writings of 'folklorists, linguists' and archaeologists.[41] The RIA collection provided sources for the art pottery produced by Frederick Vodrey from Charles Russell's designs, which were based on the study of objects in the collection of antiquities at the Royal Irish Academy and the Book of Kells. During the Irish Artisans' Exhibition (1885), the RIA collection was open to the public and artisans were expressly encouraged to visit.[42]

39 Crooke 2000, 105–6.

40 McBrinn 2009, 211.

41 *Ibid.*, 213, 216. The author refers to 'key publications' such as Henry O'Neill's *The fine arts and civilization of the ancient Irish (1863)* and Eugene O'Curry, *Manners and customs of the ancient Irish (1873).* He also notes the influence of the artist-archaeologist Margaret Stokes's publications, *Early Christian architecture in Ireland* (1878) *and Early Christian art in Ireland* (1886).

42 *Irish Artisans' Exhibition Complete Official Catalogue* (2nd edition) (Dublin, 1885), 114–15. Antiquities on display included the 'Brooch of Tara', the 'Cross of Cong', 'St Patrick's Bell' and the 'Ardagh Chalice'.

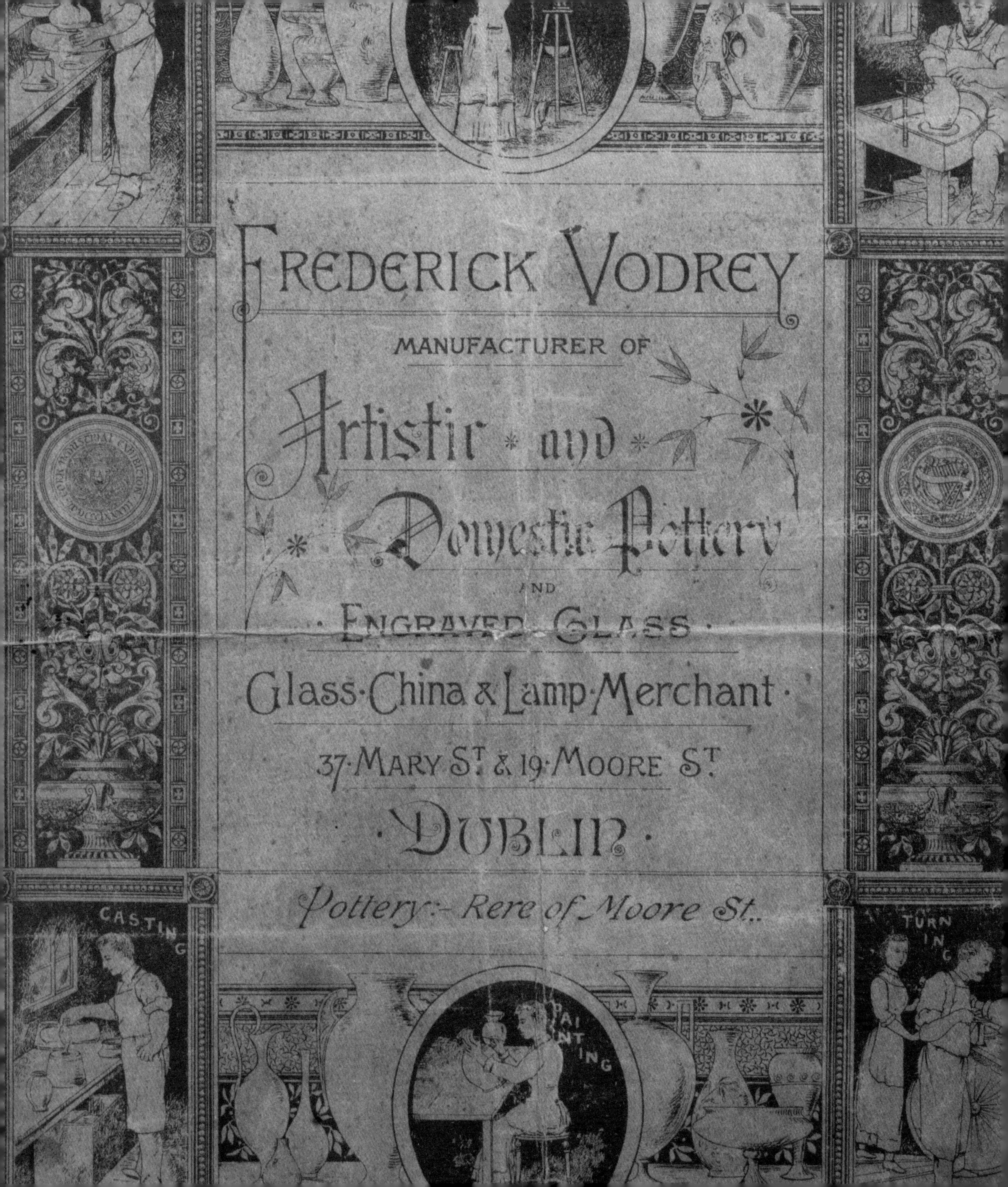
FREDERICK VODREY
MANUFACTURER OF
Artistic and Domestic Pottery
AND
· ENGRAVED GLASS ·
Glass·China & Lamp·Merchant·
37·MARY ST & 19·MOORE ST
·DUBLIN·
Pottery:- Rere of Moore St..
CASTING
TURNING
PAINTING

CHAPTER 3

Art pottery's origins in Arts and Crafts ideals – commercial art furnishings

Art pottery's origins in Arts and Crafts ideals—commercial art furnishings

During the later nineteenth century, the development of art pottery marked a change in ceramic production, leading to the growth of smaller potteries, organised along the lines of studio workshops.[1] The interest in ceramics for interior display originated with influential Arts and Crafts figures like William Morris and the painter D.G. Rossetti, who owned collections of Chinese blue and white ceramics. The most influential ceramic artists attached to the Arts and Crafts movement in England were William de Morgan and the Martin brothers. De Morgan was friends with leading figures of the movement and collaborated with them on decorative schemes for interiors.[2]

In contrast to the large-scale production in established potteries of the Stoke-on-Trent district, small potteries producing a different style of ceramics sprang up throughout Britain from the 1870s.[3] The imagery and text on Frederick Vodrey's trade card of 1885 (Fig. 7), along with the collection of VDP ceramics in the National Museum, indicate an awareness of Arts and Crafts ideals amongst Dublin consumers.[4] The demand for art ceramics prompted Vodrey to start producing art pottery in Dublin. The illustrations on the trade card show different stages of the pottery-making process and reflect the interest in craft revival at the time. These art potteries produced earthenware ceramics decorated with monochrome glazes and were inspired by Eastern ceramics. There was also a taste for ceramics decorated with hand-painted floral designs, such as those produced by the students at the Queen's Institute in Dublin. When it first started, the Vodrey Dublin Pottery produced similar hand-painted ceramics with applied floral decoration as well as Japanese- or Moorish-inspired forms. Vodrey's venture into producing art pottery began at a time when the *Pottery Gazette* noted a marked increase

1 Bartlett 1993.

2 McCarthy 2014, 59–61.

3 Haslam 1975.

4 Frederick Vodrey's trade card, 1885; Cahill Litho., Printers & Co., Dublin. National Museum of Ireland, NMI 1886.125.

in the production of art pottery in England,[5] so he was following a trend in the wider ceramic industry and responding to consumer demand.

Leading manufacturers such as Wedgwood and Minton adapted their production processes to include craft and hand-painted decoration 'in order to capitalise on the expanding market for artistic products in the late nineteenth century'.[6] There were also many small-scale producers in the United States who responded to the demand for hand-painted china.[7] In some cases art potteries were attached to art and design schools or to the larger industrial potteries in Stoke-on-Trent. Two notable examples in England were the art pottery studio run by the Minton factory and the Lambeth Pottery, connected with the Lambeth School of Art in London, owned by Doulton and Company.[8]

The Minton art pottery studio was based in London and employed students from the National Art Training School in South Kensington; they decorated pottery blanks brought from the factory in Stoke-on-Trent.[9] There were cross-influences between the training in art schools and the commercial potteries of Stoke-on-Trent. Creative input from painters and sculptors who used workshop facilities influenced the designs for large-scale production. Ventures such as the Minton art pottery studio were a model for Frederick Vodrey's collaboration with the Queen's Institute and the Dublin Sketching Club, and he operated along similar lines.

In other parts of Europe, art potters such as Theodore Deck in France (who became known for his experimentation with high-fired glazes from the Chinese tradition) contributed to the move away from industrial production. Deck's ceramics were highly praised when exhibited at the Paris Exhibition of 1884, being considered more advanced than other art pottery, which used majolica glazes on earthenware.[10] In England it wasn't until the early twentieth century that the Ruskin Pottery, founded in the 1890s, experimented with recreating the simplicity and beauty of high-fired Chinese ceramics.[11]

Late Arts and Crafts potteries like the Ruskin Pottery, founded by Edward Taylor and continued by his son William, laid a foundation for the studio potters of the twentieth century. Taylor was an art teacher and also had a family background in the Staffordshire pottery industry, and these dual influences reflect the mixed origins of art pottery. The concept of the ceramic object as meaningful artistic expression for both the maker and the collector was established at this time. Studio pottery further developed in response to new design concepts of Modernism and the influence of Bernard Leach, who drew upon the Japanese ceramic tradition.

Vodrey started by producing ceramics decorated with hand-painted flowers and applied decoration, and then moved on to produce ceramics with brightly coloured single glazes. Both styles met a demand for different aspects of fashionable taste. The latter designs were inspired by Japanese ceramics and were similar to ceramics from the Linthorpe art pottery, also produced in the 1880s, from designs provided

5 'Art Pottery', *Pottery Gazette*, 2 January 1888, 33.

6 Buckley 1990, 71.

7 Blaszczyk 1994.

8 Naylor 1971, 149–50.

9 Buckley 1990, 50–1.

10 'The Paris Ceramic Exhibition of 1884', *Pottery Gazette*, 2 March 1885, 324.

11 Atterbury and Henson 1993. The Ruskin Pottery was active from c. 1898 to 1935.

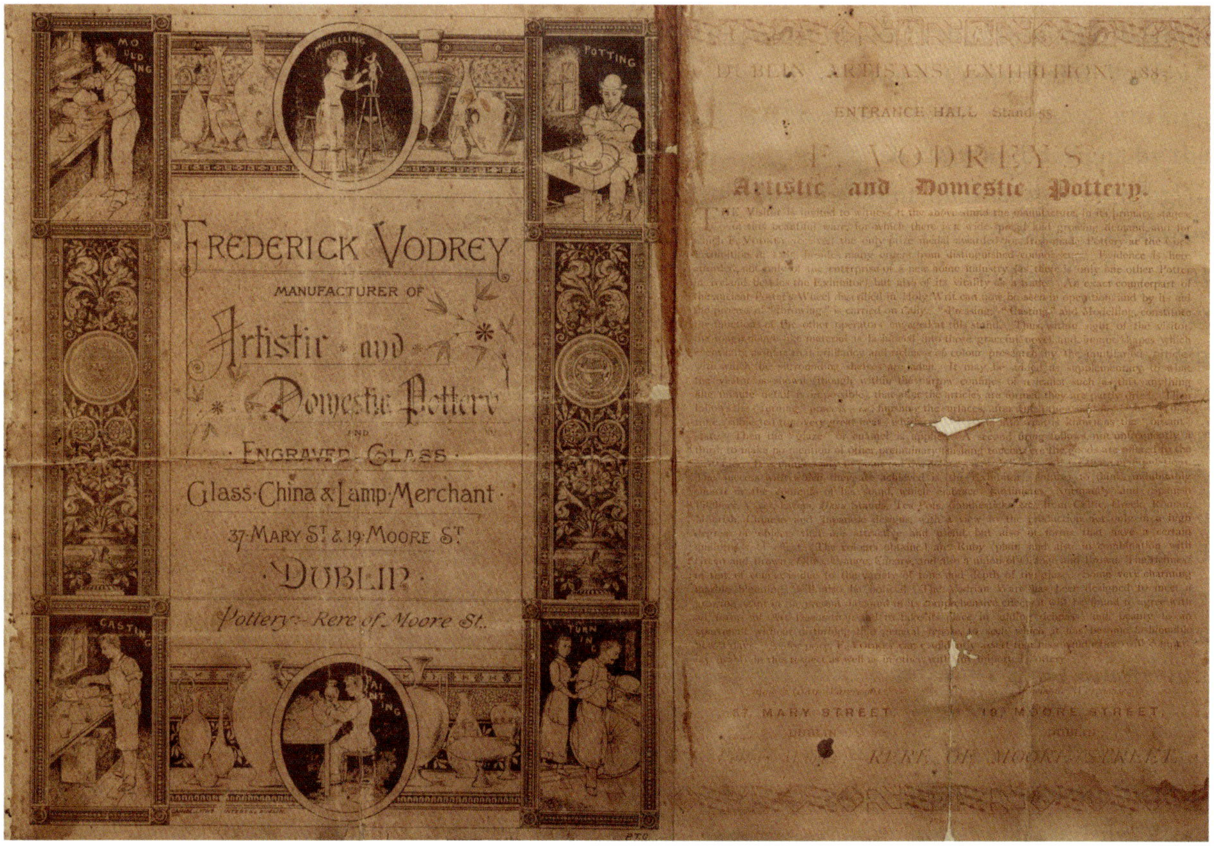

Fig. 7—Frederick Vodrey's trade card, 1885; Cahill Litho., Printers & Co., Dublin. Courtesy of the National Museum of Ireland, NMI 1886.125. The illustrations on the trade card show different stages of the pottery-making process and reflect the interest in craft revival at the time.

by Christopher Dresser.[12] Vodrey's trade card bears strong similarities to that of the Linthorpe Pottery.[13]

Potteries such as the Linthorpe Pottery were frequently started by philanthropists (often amateur or self-taught potters) who were motivated by the intention to create local employment. The Linthorpe Pottery produced designs that were entirely different from those produced by the larger potteries, such as organic Art Nouveau shapes and others based on both Japanese and Mexican forms in monochrome glazes. The interest in these forms influenced interior design in England and Ireland. The ceramic object was viewed as an art object that could convey the character and taste of its owner and was part of the Aesthetic style.[14] The art pottery produced by the Linthorpe Pottery in England and the Vodrey Pottery in Dublin catered for consumers who appreciated the new Aesthetic style and wanted to support philanthropic values. It was brightly coloured and decorated in single glazes or a fusion of two or three glazes.

In England, art industry was the commercialisation of Arts and Crafts taste by manufacturers and catered for consumers' demand for home decoration. Vodrey's art pottery could be regarded as part of this trend. Vodrey's trade card described the Vodrey Dublin Pottery as 'a new home industry'. There was a

12 Halen 1990.

13 'Linthorpe Art Pottery', *The Cabinetmaker and Art Furnisher,* 1 March 1883, 165–6.

14 Calloway and Federle Orr 2011, 124–52.

distinction between home industry and art industry in England,[15] where the term 'home industry' referred to the charitable craft projects set up by philanthropists to create employment in rural areas and was distinct from the more commercial art industries. These two terms overlapped in Ireland, and the term 'Irish Art Industry' was synonymous with the development of all home industries for economic revival, both commercial and philanthropic, as revealed by F.S. Walker's praise of Vodrey's art pottery.[16] In Ireland, the terms 'art industry' and 'home industry' referred to many craft projects in embroidery, lacemaking and furniture that were motivated by the ideals of the Arts and Crafts movement.

Vodrey's customers were influenced by two distinctly different organisations that promoted a 'Buy Irish' campaign: the Irish Home Manufacturers Association (IHMA) and the Irish Home Industries Association (IHIA).[17] The IHMA was a group of retailers and manufacturers who promoted the 'Buy Irish' ethos for their own interests.[18] The activities of the Irish Home Industry Association (IHIA) generated support for Irish crafts such as lacemaking, embroidery and furniture manufacture. Newspapers and journals called for a spirit of 'practical patriotism'[19] and urged the support of 'all creeds and classes'.[20] Whilst these words express what could be termed constructive Unionist sentiment, the 'Buy Irish' campaign was supported by all political viewpoints.

The encouragement and support for Irish industries from these two organisations influenced consumer demand during the 1880s. Whilst Frederick Vodrey's art pottery was a commercial enterprise, his comments to the Select Committee on Industries (1885) indicate that, like the organisers of other home industries, he was interested in the development of industry for the creation of employment and economic revival.[21] The designs of his ceramics indicate that the Aesthetic taste was popular in Dublin. His trade card advertised 'Artistic and Domestic Pottery', thereby catering for a demand for 'all forms of Art Decoration'.[22] ■

---

15 Harrod 2000, 13–14, 17.

16 Walker 1886.

17 Molloy 2013.

18 Royal Commission on Technical Instruction 1884, 118–19. Evidence given by Mr James Murray.

19 'The Industrial Exhibition and national wants', *The Irish Builder* 24 (15 August 1882), 231–2.

20 'The industrial prospect and new year', *The Irish Builder* 24 (1 January 1882), 1–2.

21 Select Committee on Industries (Ireland) 1885, 821.

22 F. Vodrey's trade card, 1885: Cahill Litho., Printers & Co., Dublin. NMI.1886.125.

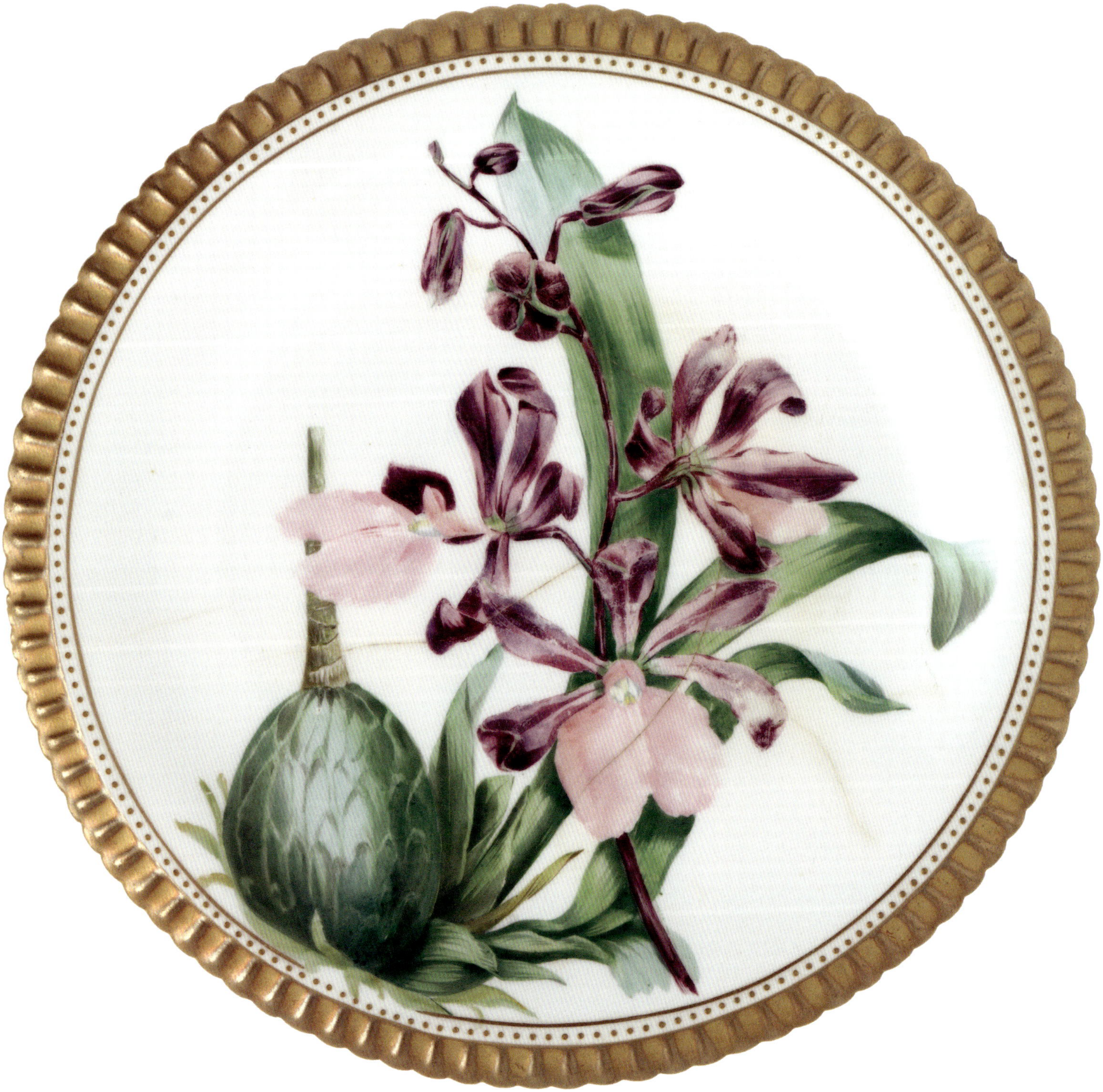

CHAPTER 4

Ceramic education for women at the Queen's Institute

Ceramic education for women at the Queen's Institute

The founding of the Queen's Institute (1861) in Dublin was in line with trends in England, where, to improve the standard of design, education for artisans was established in the 1840s, followed by a Female School of Design in 1842.[1] As the name suggests, the Queen's Institute in Dublin was supported by the viceroy and modelled on the lines of the London Queen's College, providing 'further education for young women seeking positions as governesses'.[2] The annual reports for the Painting on Porcelain School of the QI, based first in 43 Grafton Street and then 25 Molesworth Street, reveal determined efforts to provide education and income for women, and give important insight into plans and possibilities for design and the ceramic industry in Ireland. In 1868 the annual report of the Institute 'noted that there were newly established potteries in the north of Ireland and hoped that this would lead to artistic employment for its students'.[3]

The QI school for women's education was funded by membership and subscriptions,[4] and advertised classes in a range of skills from flower-drawing to telegraphy.[5] Students were accepted from the age of fourteen, and the curriculum was run under the direction of the Science and Art Department. The students' work was sent to London for examination, leading to a high standard and considered to be the reason why designs by QI students 'were purchased by English manufacturers'.[6] The 1868 annual report for the Queen's Institute optimistically expressed the intention that education and training provided by the QI would prepare

1 Buckley 1990, 46.

2 Armstrong-Duffy 1993, 12–14.

3 Dunlevy 1988, 29.

4 *Queen's Institute for the Training and Employment of Educated Women: Sixth Annual Report* (Dublin, 1868).

5 *Post Office Dublin Directory and Calendar 1873: advertisement for 'The Queen's Institute of Female Professional Schools for Improving the Education of Women of the Middle and Upper Classes, 25 Molesworth Street'.* In addition to art classes, there were also classes in languages, sewing, lacemaking, embroidery and telegraphy. The QI also advertised preparatory classes for the Trinity College examinations in Instrumental and Vocal Music.

6 *Queen's Institute of Female Professional Schools: Ninth Annual Report* (Dublin, 1871), 12 (NLI: Ir 3769 q1).

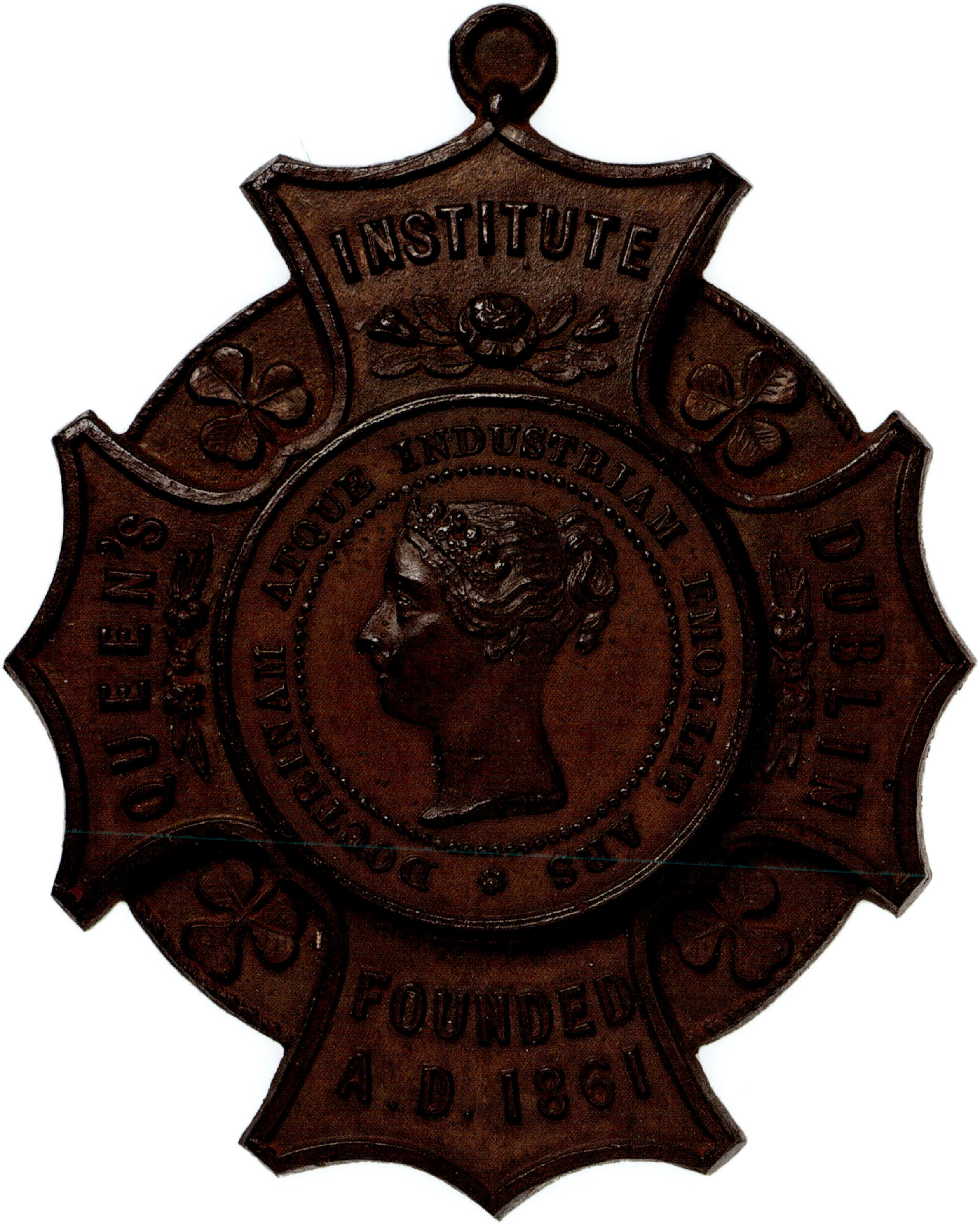

Fig. 8—Medal/badge of the Queen's Institute, bronze, 3.5cm x 3.2cm, by John Woodhouse, 1861. Inscribed with the words 'QUEEN'S INSTITUTE DUBLIN FOUNDED A.D.1861'. NMI HC RIA 131.

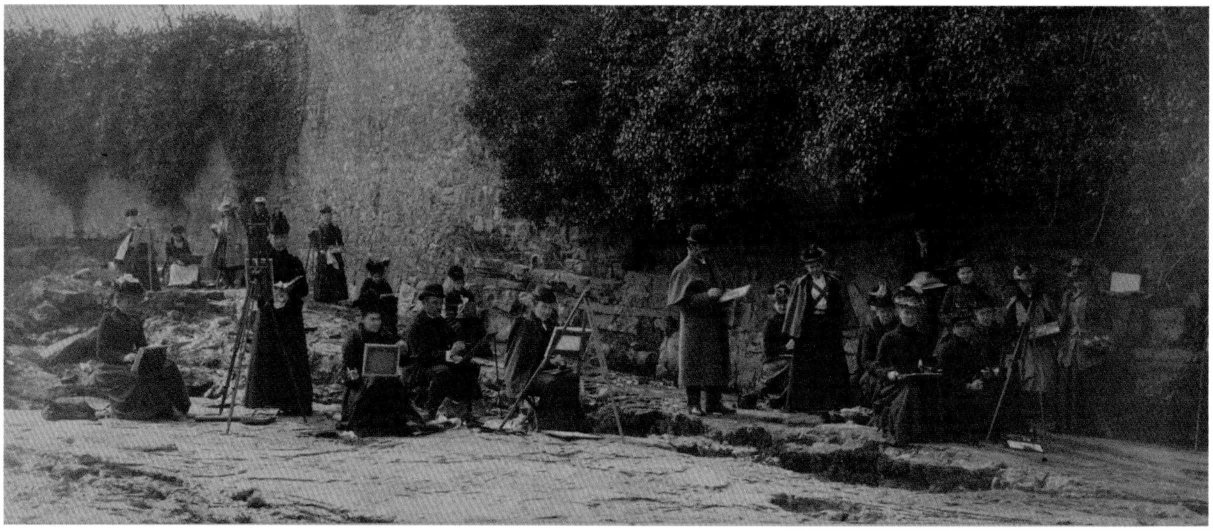

Fig. 9—A group of women and a man sketching outdoors; the latter could be the artist Richard T. Moynan, who gave art classes 'for ladies'. Photograph by T.F. Geoghegan, c. 1890. Courtesy of the National Library of Ireland.

women to do design and decorating work for the newly established potteries in Ireland.[7] This could only refer to the Belleek Pottery in County Fermanagh, and possibly the Coalisland Pottery. The students of the QI painted a service for the Belleek Pottery which was exhibited in the International Exhibition of 1872.[8]

Within the period of its existence from 1861 to 1883, the aim of the QI was to train women for employment in industry. According to the annual report for 1868, organisers hoped that 'With the extension of manufactures in Ireland it may be expected the prospect of employment will improve'.[9] The art classes were attended by two types of women: 'girls who went on to earn modest incomes illuminating, painting porcelain or colouring photographs' and 'gentlewomen who wished to pursue their interest in painting'.[10] The Queen's Institute closed in 1883 after ten years,[11] for reasons that are unclear. In her evidence to the Royal Commission on Technical Instruction, Miss La Touche, one of the QI organisers, indicated that the closure was due to mismanagement.[12]

According to Marie Bourke, the founding of the government Schools of Design in Ireland (1849) and the admission of women students to art education led to advances in women's education.[13] Before

---

7 *Queen's Institute for the Training and Employment of Educated Women: Sixth Annual Report*, 11. 'The establishment of potteries in the North of Ireland should open a field for artistic employment. The art of painting on china is one in which many ladies find employment in connection with the potteries in England, and the possibility of developing such a business in Ireland has become worth considering.'

8 *Queen's Institute of Female Professional Schools: Ninth Annual Report*, 12–13. This beautifully bound volume also contains a syllabus for the Queen's Institute and an address delivered by Alexander Parker at the annual meeting. It is noted that 'The Queen's Breakfast Service produced by Messrs Kerr to Her Majesty's order (models of form which have been designed by a lady connected with the Institute from the commencement) will be displayed in Belleek ware at the International Exhibition'.

9 *Queen's Institute for the Training and Employment of Educated Women: Sixth Annual Report*, 11.

10 Armstrong-Duffy 1993, 13.

11 Curry 1993.

12 Royal Commission on Technical Instruction 1884, 117. Evidence on the Queen's Institute was given by Professor Barrett, Miss La Touche and Miss Meyrick.

13 Bourke 2011, 180.

the government took charge of the Royal Dublin Society Schools and introduced the South Kensington system, women had either attended classes at the RDS since its beginning in 1731 or at one of several private drawing schools.[14] In the case of the RHA (begun in 1826), however, whilst women were permitted to enter their work in annual exhibitions and frequently entered subjects in 'the graceful and feminine department of fruit and flowers', they could not attend classes there, and many from privileged backgrounds chose to go abroad for art training in London or Paris.[15]

The Queen's Institute was central to changes in women's education and opportunities in Dublin during the late nineteenth century. Whilst some women had previously trained as artists to join a family business, there was limited employment for women in art and design, as well as a perception that painting and drawing were pastimes or a 'mere accomplishment' for upper-class women.[16] The QI art classes overturned this bias by creating opportunities for more women, offering training in practical vocational skills which could lead to employment in design and industry. In commissioning designs from the students at the QI, the Belleek Pottery followed the example of established manufacturers like Wedgwood and Minton, who adapted their production processes to include craft and hand-painted decoration 'in order to capitalise on the expanding market for artistic products in the late nineteenth century'.[17]

The benefits of education for women and their subsequent involvement in the pottery industry during the late nineteenth and early twentieth centuries are explored in separate studies by two ceramic historians, Buckley and Vincentelli. In England, the head of the new Female School of Design went to France and observed women 'artistes' in the Sèvres factory.[18] Since classes for women were held during the day, they were less accessible to the unskilled women in the potteries and more likely to be attended by middle-class women who trained and worked in the areas of painting and decorating.[19] There was the same student profile of middle-class women at the Queen's Institute in Dublin for whom 'the Art Pottery Movement created a suitable environment for women who wished to work as artist potters and as hand decorators'.[20]

From the eighteenth century, china-painting had been considered a respectable activity for middle-class women, a trend set by aristocratic women decorating their own porcelain.[21] In the nineteenth century china-painting became a useful skill for women, and one which could be used to earn an income if they remained unmarried or became widowed.[22] According to Buckley, this idea originated in the prevalent moral values and the hierarchical view of women as being more suited to working in areas of design close to their home-making skills and therefore the lesser decorative arts.[23] In line with these 'moral values',

14 Sheehy 1987, 7.

15 *Ibid.*, 9.

16 *Ibid.*, 8.

17 Buckley 1990, 70–1.

18 Vincentelli 2000, 88.

19 Buckley 1990, 70–1.

20 *Ibid.*

21 Vincentelli 2000, 89.

22 Buckley 1990, 48–9, 50–1.

23 *Ibid.*

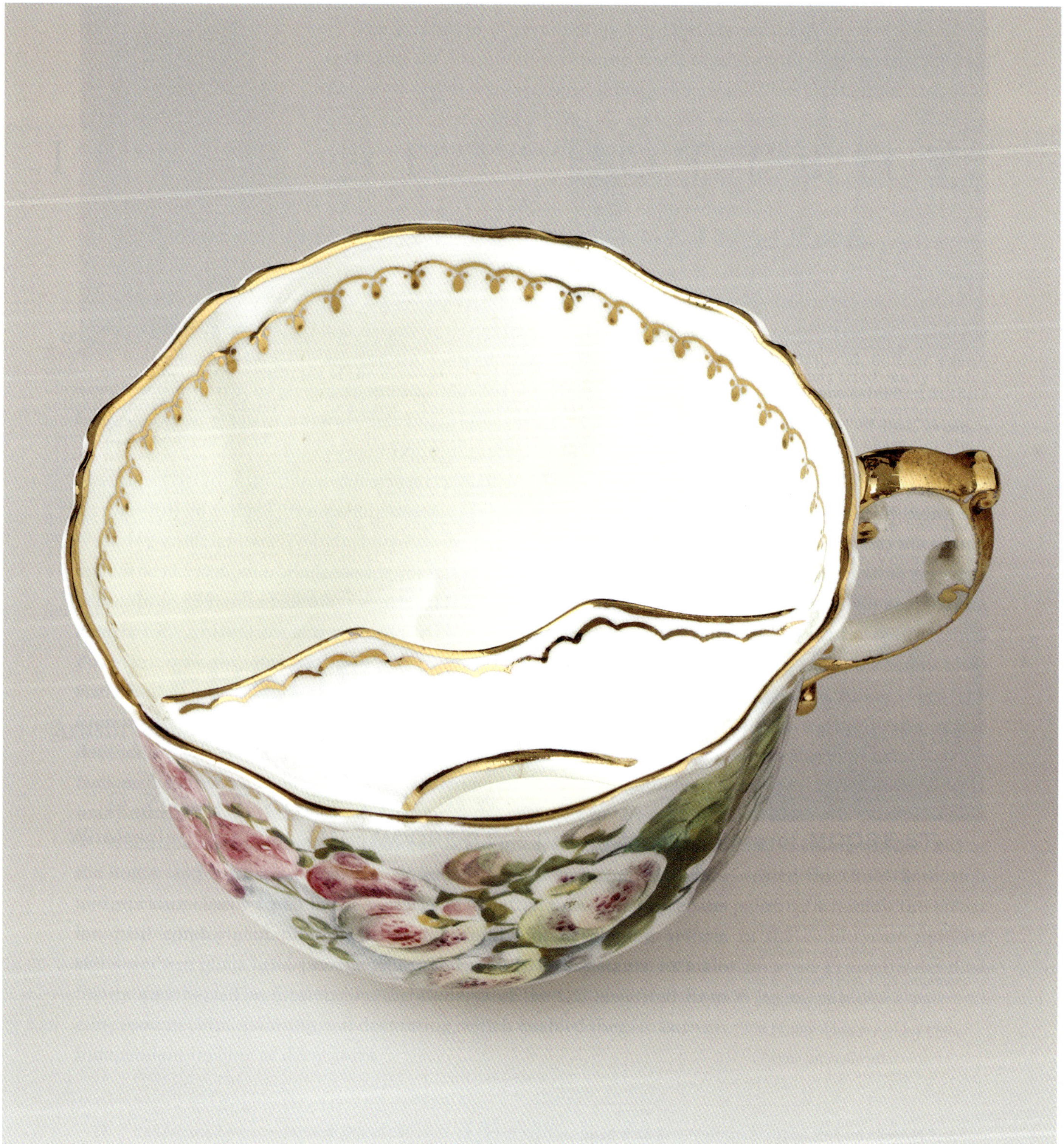

Fig. 10—Moustache cup, hand-painted with sweet pea flowers, 'H Cooper' painted in purple with registered design number underneath. NMI 1973.53. Cat. no. 82. The fact that the design was registered in 1891 by Hammersley and Co. in England indicates that this and other examples in the National Museum were painted in Cooper's own studio after the closure of the Queen's Institute.

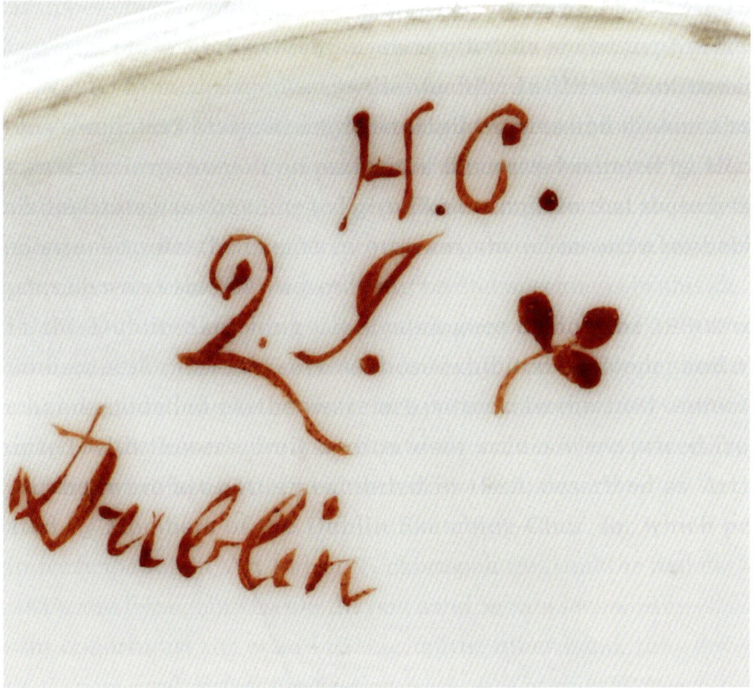

Fig. 11—Herbert Cooper's signature, 'H.C.', and 'Q.I. [Queen's Institute] Dublin', underside of a plate, c. 1872–83. NMI 1972.45. Cat. no. 79.

the aim of the Queen's Institute was primarily to assist 'Gentlewomen of limited means, by training them for the pursuit of suitable professions and occupations'.[24] In the tone of a charitable organisation, the QI organised employment for students 'to be carried out under the care of the Society'.[25]

The art classes at the QI included skills that were used in the decoration of ceramics[26] Dunlevy suggested that 'the training given to these lady students, helped by a popular hobby-interest in painting factory blanks, explains the quantity of hand painted china of the 1870s–1910s',[27] a curious example being the moustache cups, reflecting men's fashion in the nineteenth century (Fig. 10).

Students of the QI were employed on commissions, decorating a range of tea and dessert services for clients. The influence of the Celtic Revival style integrated with the Victorian taste for plant illustration is evident in the frequent use of the shamrock, symbol of Irish national identity since the mid-eighteenth century.[28] This was painted on the undersides of many QI ceramics, along with Herbert Cooper's initials and 'QI Dublin' when Cooper was still the manager of the Painting on Porcelain School (Fig. 11).

24 *Queen's Institute of Female Professional Schools: Ninth Annual Report*, 9–10.

25 *Ibid.*

26 *Post Office Dublin Directory and Calendar 1873:* advertisement for 'The Queen's Institute of Female Professional Schools for Improving the Education of Women of the Middle and Upper Classes, 25 Molesworth Street'. The advertisement listed the following: 'Flower Drawing, and Painting from Nature, Painting, Photography, Illuminating, Painting on Porcelain, Enamel, Gilding, Chasing, Drawing and Engraving on Wood, Lithograph, Drawing and Writing'.

27 Dunlevy 1988, 29.

28 Sheehy 1980, 11.

During the Celtic Revival, the shamrock, along with the wolfhound, 'round tower, the ancient Irish crown, and the harp', became a 'National Emblem';[29] it was sometimes the main subject of decoration painted on QI ceramics, along with other plant forms (Fig. 12).

The porcelain blanks hand-painted by Cooper and his students were imported from England, first from the Worcester Royal Porcelain Works in the 1870s (thanks to Kerr's connections with that company) and later from other Staffordshire factories such as Hammersley and Co., Liverpool, in the 1890s, the latter being bone china rather than the earlier porcelain. The decorated ceramics were fired in a muffle kiln, sometimes many times, colours being applied and fired separately in several stages.[30]

The Dublin ceramic retailer W.H. Kerr was one of the driving forces behind the founding of the Painting on Porcelain School on his return *c*. 1862 to take over the family business in Dublin, and after his time as manager of the Worcester Royal Porcelain Works. Kerr financed the QI classes in porcelain-painting and sold the ceramics in his shop; he organised fund-raising for a kiln and then donated the outstanding amount of £45 when contributions fell short.[31] According to the annual report in 1871, the china-painting at the QI had achieved a high level of expertise, and 'Mr Kerr's experiment with regard to Porcelain Decoration has been successful'.[32] It was reported that 'a kiln has been erected on the premises, which has proved to be of admirable construction, the firing being perfect'.[33] Following the introduction of the new kiln, the Institute had 'an extensive display at the Dublin Exhibition in 1872 of hand-painted items'.[34] In addition to the 'painting and gilding in flower subjects and ornament', the students also produced 'miniature subjects' and 'crests and arms on services', which 'were received with considerable favour by the public'. [35]

William Kerr used his connections with the English pottery industry to benefit the QI and presumably his own business interests, encouraging Herbert Cooper to take up the position of manager and sourcing porcelain blanks from the Worcester factory. This arrangement worked well until Kerr invited Cooper to work for him at his own premises in Capel Street, following which the two men had a disagreement.[36] Nevertheless, Cooper, originally from England, remained in Dublin, working as a successful decorator and teacher, first at the Queen's Institute until its closure in 1883, and then running his own studio until his retirement in 1907.[37]

According to Curry, the authority on the Queen's Institute ceramics, the porcelain and bone china decorated by Cooper and his students can be divided into three distinct periods:[38] 1870–1, during which W.H. Kerr was involved as financial backer and sold the ceramics in his shop; 1872–83, after Kerr

29 Crooke 2000, 74–5. The author shows an illustration entitled 'National Emblems' from the *Dublin Penny Journal of* 7 July 1832.

30 Curry 1993, 194.

31 *Ibid.*

32 *Queen's Institute of Female Professional Schools: Ninth Annual Report,* 12–13.

33 *Ibid.*

34 Dunlevy 1988, 29.

35 *Ibid.*

36 Curry 1993, 194.

37 *Ibid.*

38 *Ibid.*

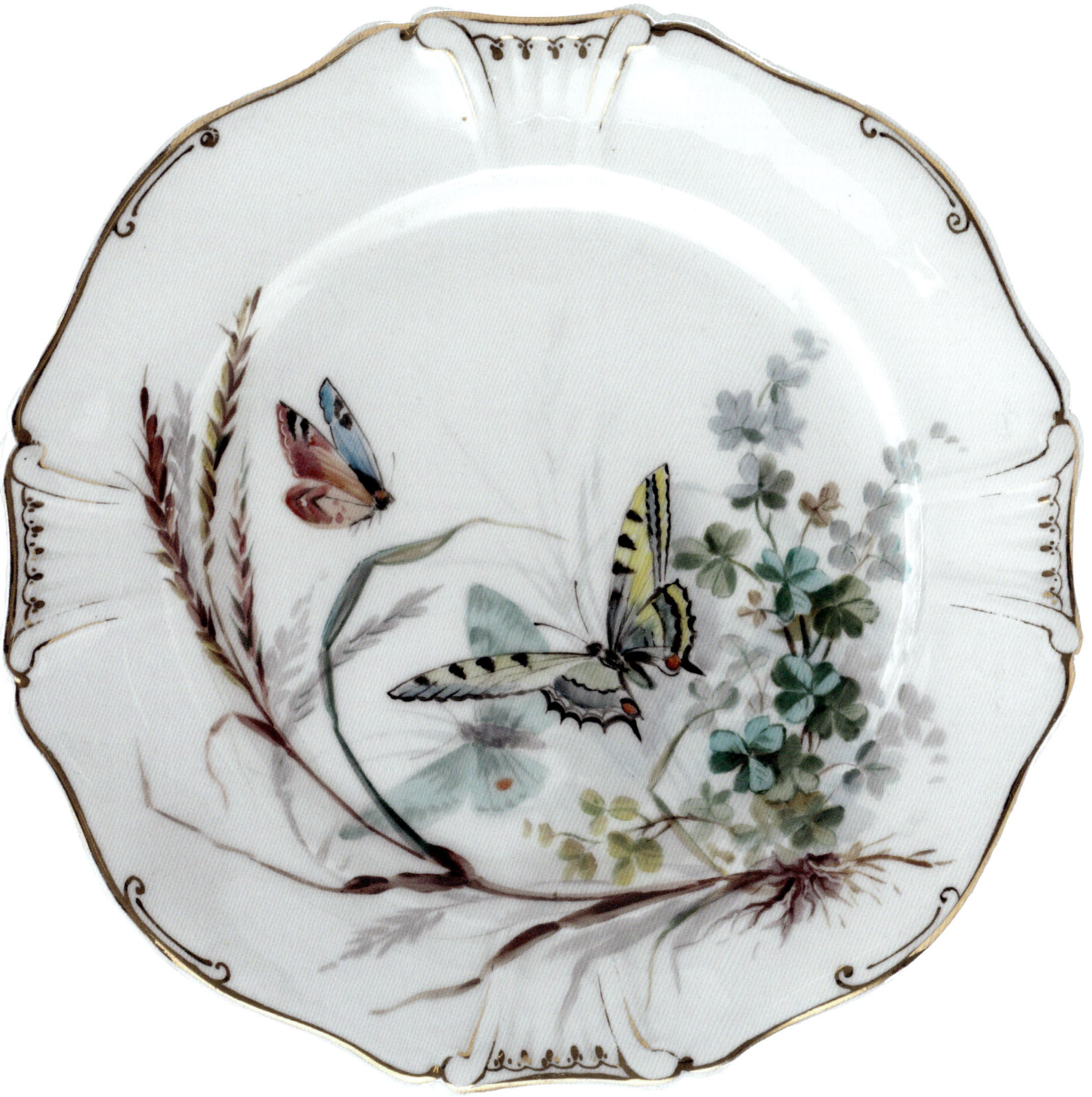

Fig. 12—Tea plate decorated with butterflies, shamrocks, and grasses. Signed 'H. Cooper' underneath. NMI 1974.41. Cat. no. 89.

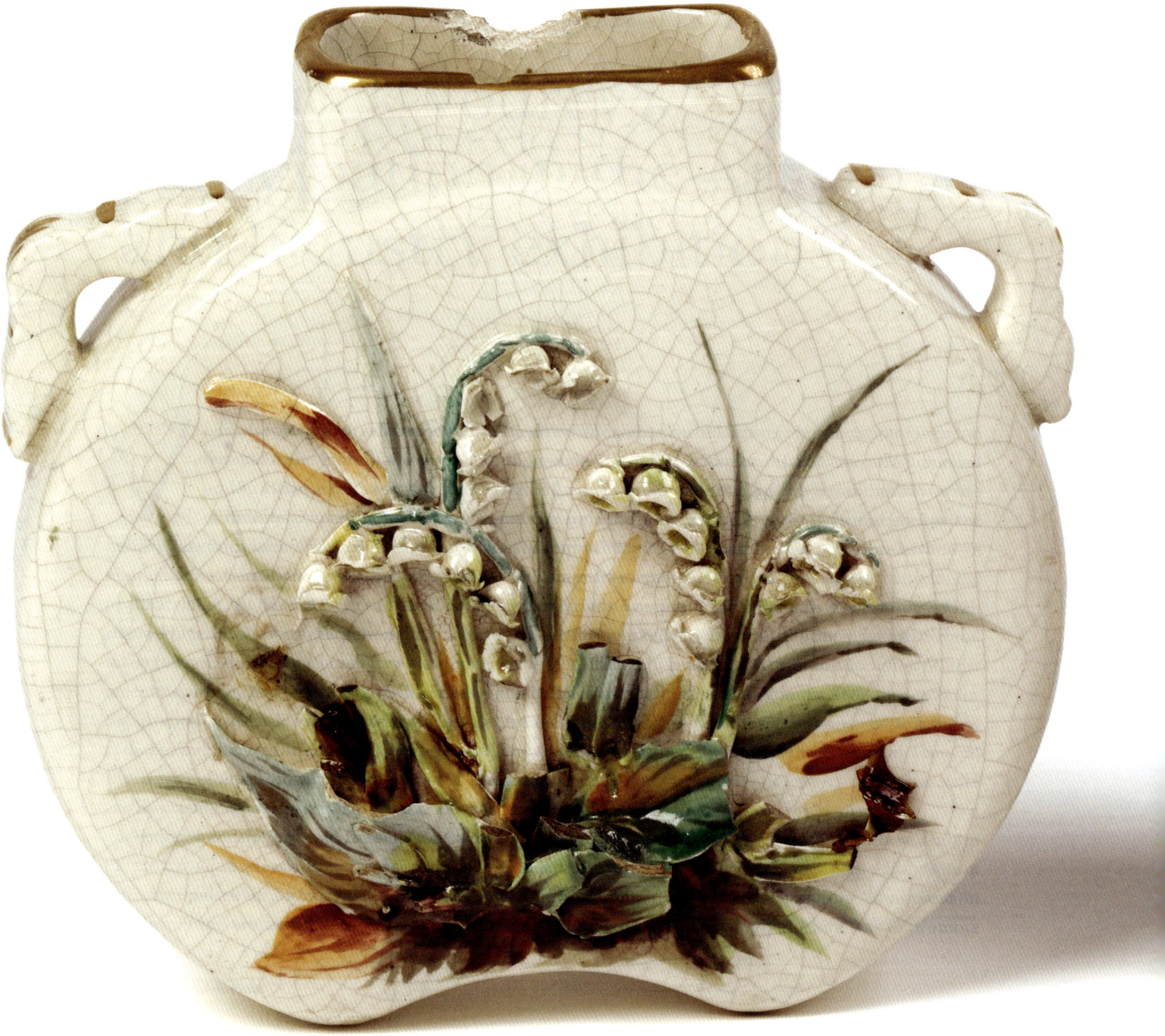

Fig. 13—A pair of vases/flower-holders, 1882, decorated with applied flowers in relief (lily of the valley and convolvulus), 13cm × 13cm. Mark underneath: 'VODREY DUBLIN POTTERY 1882'. NMI 1971.19 and 1971.20. Cat. nos 39 and 40.

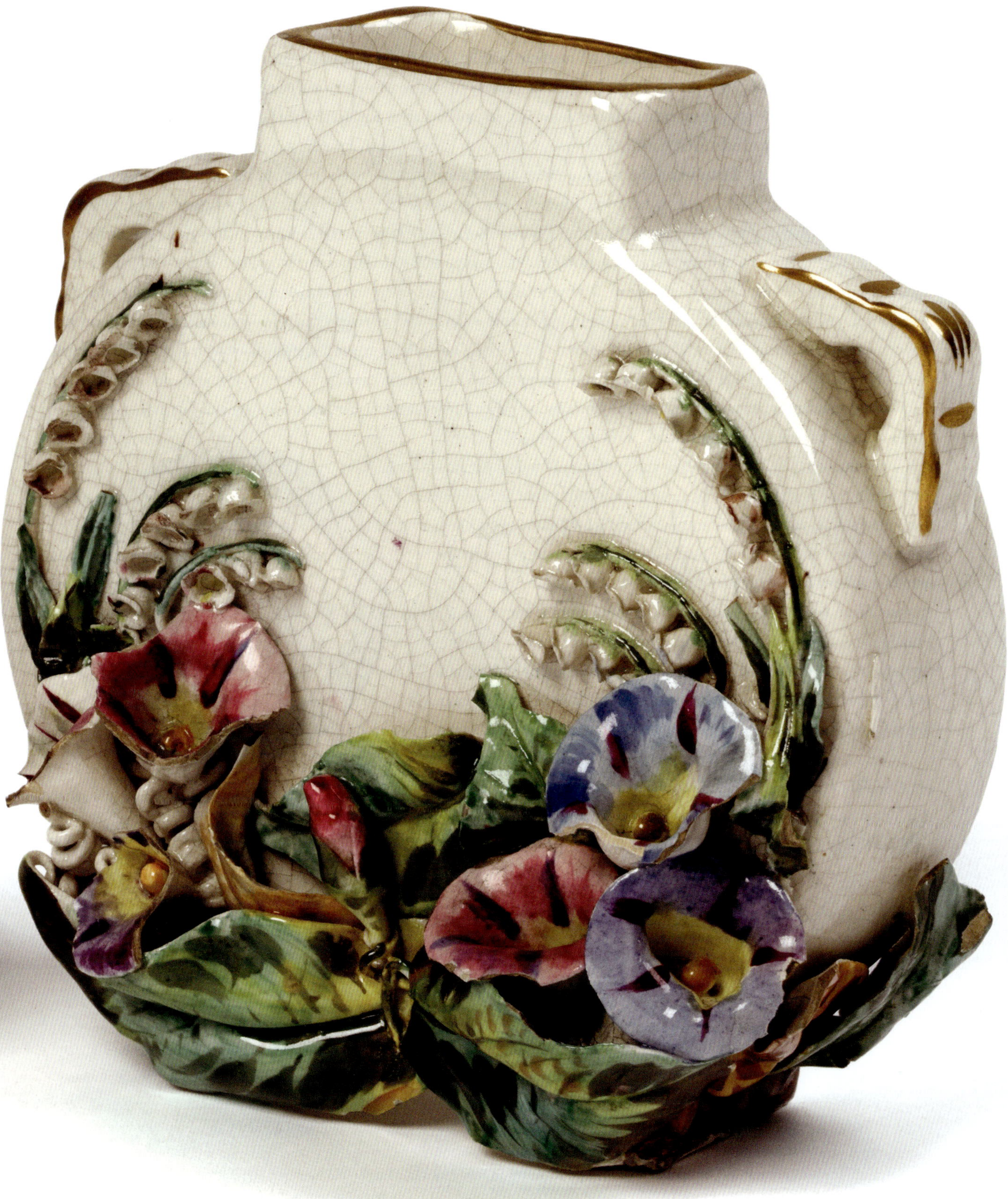

withdrew his involvement following a disagreement with Cooper (when many fine examples were produced until the QI fell into financial trouble); and 1883–1907, after the closure of the QI, when Cooper set up his own decorating business at 27 Molesworth Street, where he continued to train students, some becoming professional decorators with the studio.

The second period of QI painted ceramics, from 1872 to 1883, is when Herbert Cooper and Frederick Vodrey had a brief association, during which time Vodrey may have fired the ceramics painted by Cooper and his students or provided clays and facilities, as he did for the Dublin Sketching Club. The only indication that Vodrey and Cooper collaborated comes from Westropp, who, writing many years after both Vodrey and Cooper had ceased business, states that the two were in partnership for about twelve months, during which they made 'a small number of objects' using clay from Knockcroghery, Co. Roscommon.[39] Otherwise, the only indication of possible collaboration between Vodrey and Cooper is in the style of some of the ceramics produced by Vodrey at this time; the hand-painted floral decoration on white glazed earthenware marked 'Vodrey Dublin 1882' is similar in style to some of the Queen's Institute ceramics and could have been the work of QI students (Fig. 13).

The taste for hand-painted ceramics coincided with an interest in botanical illustration of newly discovered species, both native and colonial. The type of botanical illustration popular in the nineteenth century can be seen in the dessert plate illustrated below (Fig. 14). The collection and propagation of plants at the Royal Botanic Gardens in Dublin during the later nineteenth century was documented by two women artists, Lydia Shackleton (1828–1914) and Alice Jacob (1862–1921).[40] This influenced china-painting and the taste for botanical illustration, evident in several dessert plates in the NMI collection.[41]

Other items in the Museum collection signed by QI artists or by Herbert Cooper include cups and saucers with shamrocks, some examples painted and signed by Rose Skehan and Marie Skehan, talented amateurs who may have been sisters (cat. nos 102–5). There is also work by a third woman, Miss Plunket (Mrs Eastes), seen on two plates from a dessert service with a monogram,[42] possibly EP for her husband's family name (Eastes) and Plunket (cat. nos 76 and 77).

The ceramic objects in the NMI collection, painted by Rose and Marie Skehan and Miss Plunket (Mrs Eastes), confirm that, as elsewhere, some women who took classes in china-painting in Dublin did so in order to decorate their own tableware.[43] The names of two other artists who trained and worked with Herbert Cooper are known but not represented in the Museum collection: Alice Elwood, who studied with Cooper in the 1880s and produced 'exquisitely painted' work, and Fanny Moran, who studied there during the later years of Cooper's studio.[44]

---

39 Westropp 1913, 21–2. Westropp writes that 'Frederick Vodrey, a china and glass merchant in Moore Street, Dublin, became a kind of partner with Cooper for about twelve months, during 1873 and 1874, but after that, he worked on his own account in Moore Street'.

40 Butler 2000, 28-9, 30–1.

41 Figure 13 is one of a pair of plates with botanical illustrations that have the same design as another set of eleven dessert plates acquired by the Museum at a different time (cat. no. 90, NMI 1977.12.1–1977.12.12).

42 There may be a connection between Miss Plunket's work in the Museum collection and an album entitled *Wildflowers from nature in the collection of the Botanic Gardens*. The album, which contains drawings by Katharine Plunket (1820–1932) and her sister Florence (d. 24 February 1886), is described by Patricia Butler as 'a fine leather-bound volume of botanical watercolours' (Butler 2000, 63).

43 Blaszczyk 1994, 121–53.

44 Curry 1993, 195.

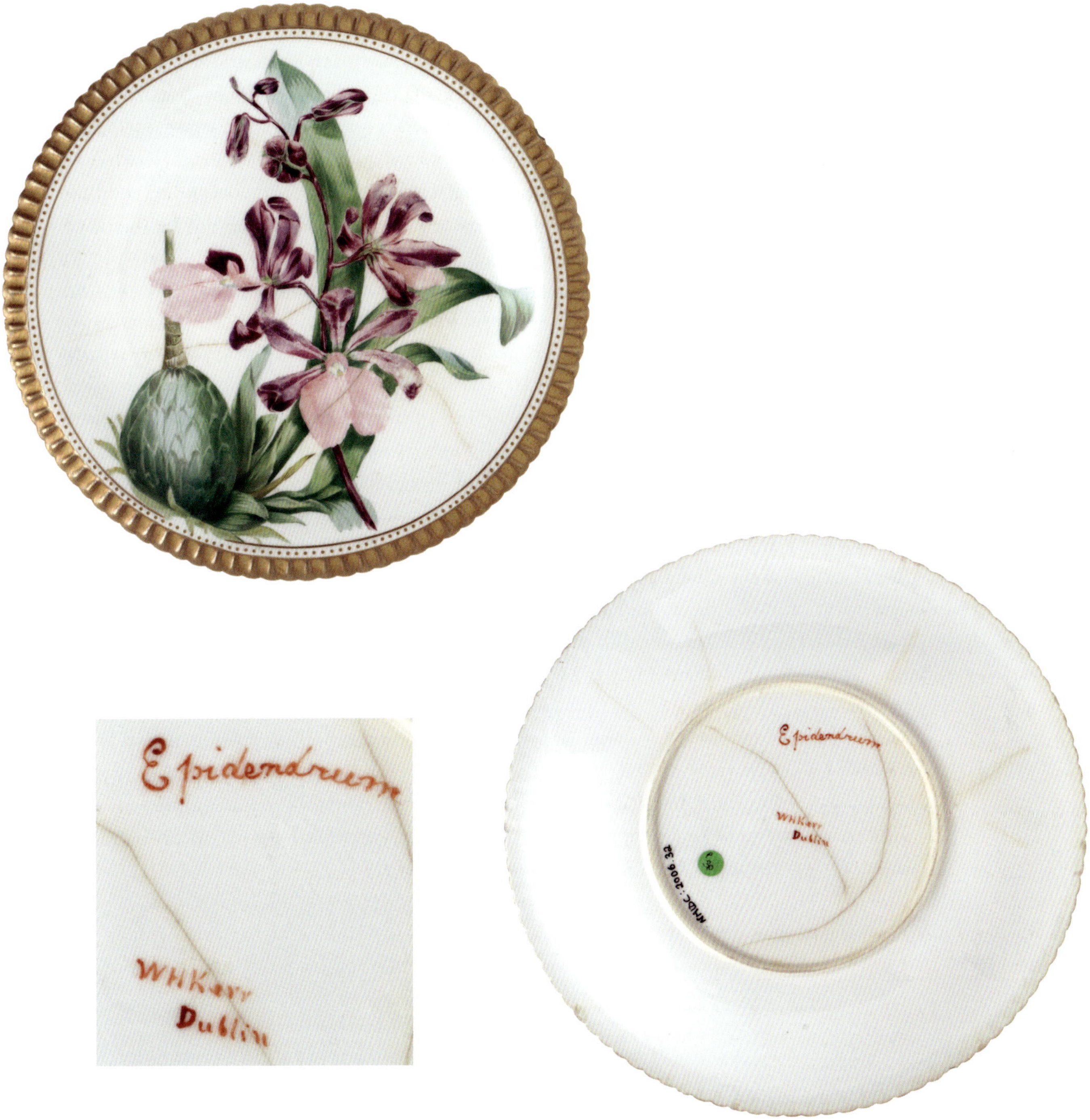

Fig. 14—Dessert plate painted with a botanical illustration of purple iris flowers, leaves and bulb. 'Epidendrum' (the Latin name of the flower) and 'WH Kerr' painted on the underside. NMI 2006.32. Cat. no. 99. This dessert plate is not dated and could be from the period when Kerr is known to have employed a decorator at his retail premises from c. 1872, after his association with the QI.

Evidence from documentary sources, family history and a specific object in the Museum collection suggests that there was some rivalry and possibly disagreement between Cooper and Vodrey.[45] Dunlevy notes that, in competition with Vodrey, Cooper began to make studio ceramics, working closely with Ballinphellig Pottery in County Cork, and claimed to use Irish clays and designs by the Dublin Sketching Club, but 'these pieces seem to have been of indifferent quality'.[46] According to Westropp, Vodrey only made ceramics from clays imported from Shelton in England, whereas Cooper made ceramics from Irish clays until 1875.[47] This, however, is contradicted by Pentland, writing at the time of Vodrey's successes. He clearly states that Vodrey used clay from Knockcroghery, adding 'ground flint and feldspar from the celebrated Belleek' to create a fine, 'creamy white' clay body, which is substantiated by examination of the objects.[48]

In the light of the above contradictions, it is significant that Cooper, although trained and working as a decorator, presented a curiously interesting vase to the Museum, bearing the original label with the words: 'Made of Pure clay found at Athlone and fired in a primitive kiln at the Queen's Institute 1882. Presented by H. Cooper' (cat. no. 96). This was the same year in which Vodrey was awarded prizes for producing ceramics made with Irish clays in the 1882 Dublin Exhibition, and subsequently at the 1883 Cork Exhibition. The object presented by Cooper is significant because it highlights the importance placed on efforts to produce ceramics from local Irish clays during the nineteenth century, and also confirms Dunlevy's assertion that Cooper was competing with Vodrey.

Reports of the Queen's Institute's annual exhibitions of 1875 and 1876 in both *The Builder* and *The Irish Builder* reveal that the QI training for women gave them new opportunities in the 'field of industrial design', with students receiving commissions from Irish manufacturers, including 'Pim's Silks design'.[49] The description of the exhibits displayed by Cooper's students gives details of the varied work and commissions undertaken by the QI students:

> 'There is a good display of tea and dessert services, and the pottery specimens are also good. There is an excellent breakfast service on view, prepared for a lady in Leeds. Some handsome vases evidence proficiency in painting on pottery, and we note some well painted fire tiles for a Belfast house. On the whole, the exhibition is very creditable to female talent.'[50]

Such evidence confirms that the Institute had succeeded in its original aim to train women for industries that were becoming important in the economy, most notably china-painting for the pottery

45 Conversation with Bruce Vodrey (grandson of Frederick Vodrey), Canada, 2003. A family story tells of how Frederick was let down by a partner (unnamed) 'who ran away with the money'. This story could refer to either Herbert Cooper or a later partnership which Vodrey had with two brothers in the Abbey Pottery, Stoke-on-Trent.

46 Dunlevy 1988, 29.

47 Westropp 1913, 21–2.

48 Pentland 1885, 35.

49 'The Queen's Institute Exhibition', *The Builder,* 1 January 1875, 4.

50 'The Queen's Institute Exhibition', *The Irish Builder,* 1 January 1876, 4, 9.

industry and lithography and engraving for illustration in books and newspapers.[51] Moreover, the Institute noted that:

> 'A number of illustrated periodicals are now published in Dublin and our Wood Engraving School obtains a portion of this illustrating. It may be remarked that but for the existence of this society much of this work would be of necessity sent to London instead of being executed at home.'[52]

After the opening of the new art studio for the Queen's Institute, with expansion to include the premises next door at No. 26 Molesworth Street announced in 1878,[53] the QI continued to thrive for several years until its abrupt closure in 1883, reportedly owing to financial difficulties. For some twenty years, the Institute had played a significant role in the education of women and had established links between early design practice and industry in nineteenth-century Dublin. ■

51 *Ibid.*, 14. 'In London some lady artists readily earn £10 a week; and where the gift of genius exists, this becomes the premier branch of industrial art.'

52 *Queen's Institute of Female Professional Schools: Ninth Annual Report, 12–13.*

53 *Saunders's News-Letter,* 23 April 1878, 1. Announcement of the opening of an Amateur Studio on 26 April 1878: 'The Queen's Institute for the Technical Instruction and Queen's College for the Education of Women, School of Music, Art Industries, Female Schools of Art and Science (Under the Government of Science and Art), 25 and 26 Molesworth Street'.

CHAPTER 5

Vodrey Dublin Pottery – success for an Irish home industry

Vodrey Dublin Pottery—success for an Irish home industry

In the late nineteenth century, Irish retailers and customers alike were influenced by the spirit of a 'Buy Irish' campaign and the promotion of economic revival by leaders in business and politics. Both Kerr and Vodrey are examples of ceramic retailers who became involved in the production of Irish products. When Vodrey began to experiment with making ceramics from Irish clay sometime in the early 1880s, the art pottery, although very different, was compared favourably with Belleek pottery,[1] already known since the 1860s for the success of its designs and the development of ceramics using local clays.[2] Whilst previous publications have acknowledged Frederick Vodrey's art pottery in the history of Irish ceramics,[3] and Westropp, an early source, wrote that Frederick Vodrey 'turned out ornamental ware with coloured glazes',[4] he remained an obscure figure in Irish design.

Writings by Vodrey's contemporaries, however, indicate that the art pottery achieved success in his own lifetime and was praised for contributing to economic and cultural revival.[5] The minutes of the Irish Home Manufacturers Association (IHMA), an organisation that drove the 'Buy Irish' campaign and encouraged consumers to buy Irish goods,[6] singled out and praised retailers like Vodrey for selling Irish products, describing Vodrey as a good employer who gave work to young Dublin girls.[7] After the VDP art pottery won prizes at the Art and Industry Exhibitions in Dublin (1882) and Cork (1883), a short section entitled 'Ceramic Art' in *Existing manufactures of Ireland* (1886), a book on Irish home

1 Dennis 1887, 113.

2 Bloomfield 1882–3.

3 Wallace and Kenny 1970, 16–17; Dunlevy 1988, 30–1.

4 Westropp 1913, 21–2.

5 The two main sources for this information are Pentland 1885 and O'Sullivan's report in *Cork Industrial Exhibition 1883. Report of the Executive Committee, Awards of Jurors and Statement of Accounts* (Cork, 1886).

6 MacLeod 1972, 9. According to the author the IHMA was founded in August 1881 and held weekly meetings on Tuesdays at 29 Upper Sackville Street (O'Connell Street), an account of the proceedings being published in the *Freeman's Journal* on Wednesdays.

7 *Freeman's Journal*, 27 December 1882.

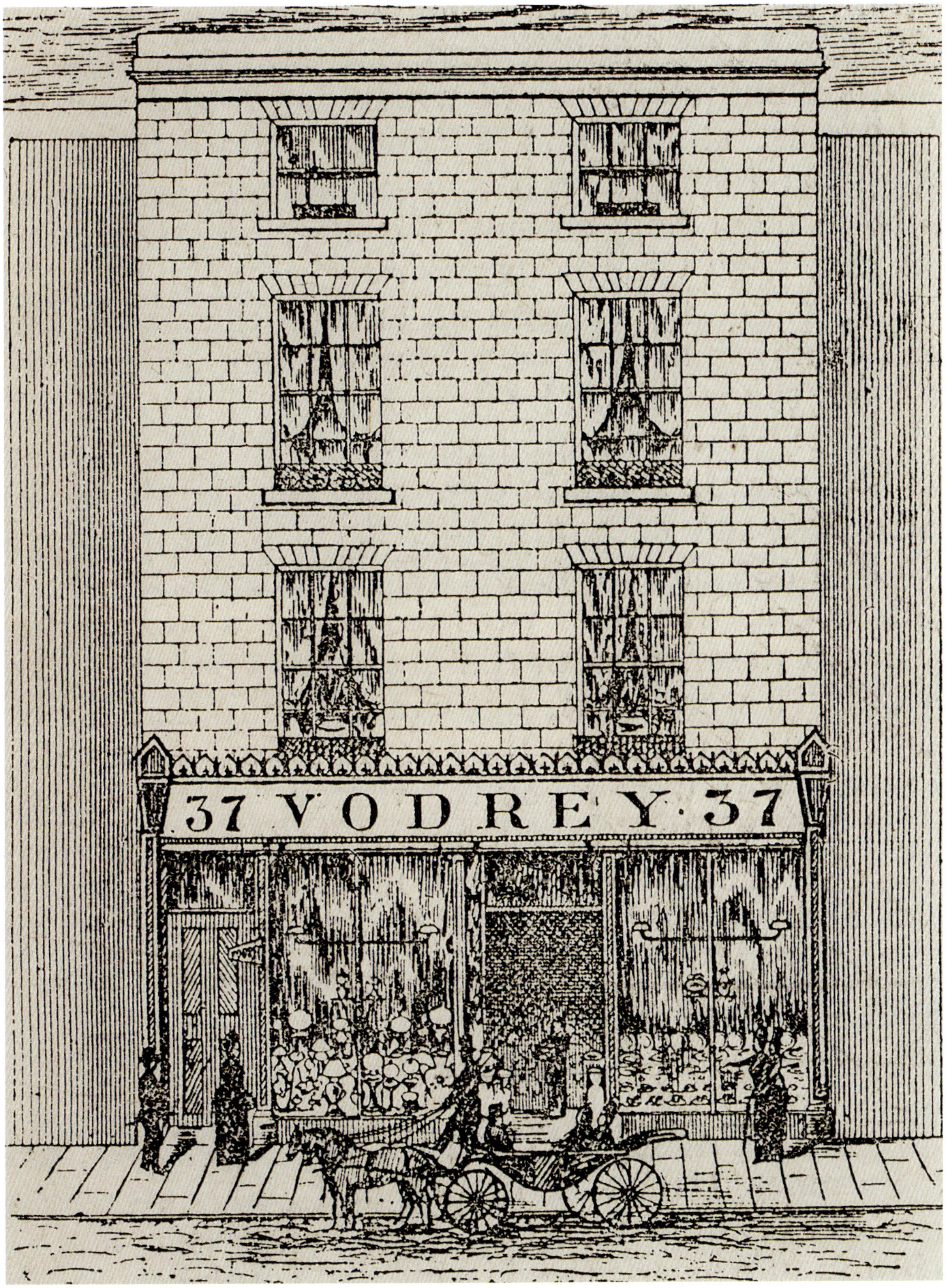

Fig. 16—Frederick Vodrey's shop at 37 Mary Street as it was illustrated in *Industries of Dublin* (Anon. c. 1888). Courtesy of the National Library of Ireland.

industries, praised the quality of objects produced by Vodrey as equal to Belleek pottery.[8] Some years later, in 1888, another writer on Irish industries suggested that Vodrey's success showed possibilities for the development of an Irish pottery industry.[9]

In 1880 Frederick Vodrey opened a shop on 37 Mary Street, an extension of the shopping district in Henry Street; it was illustrated in *Industries of Dublin* (Fig. 16).[10]

These premises were Frederick Vodrey's retail outlet during the 1880s, when he achieved success with his art pottery. According to Vodrey's trade-card, the art pottery workshop was situated nearby, at the 'rere of Moore Street', where he had a wholesale warehouse at number 19.[11] Frederick continued to expand to No. 18 Moore Street, further indicating that there was a high demand for ceramics in Dublin at this time, also shown by the marked increase in china merchants listed in Moore Street over a twenty-year period from *c.* 1860 to *c.* 1880.[12]

At the shop in Mary Street Vodrey sold imported tablewares from Staffordshire, England, and from factories in France and Germany, advertising in the *Freeman's Journal*, *Saunders's News-Letter*, the *Irish Times* and Hackett's *Dublin Illustrated Family Almanack*. He aimed to attract clients from different social groups and incomes, listing tea sets and dinner services in a range of prices for the predominantly middle- and upper-class shoppers.[13] The Vodrey family's background in the Staffordshire pottery industry, where their father William worked as a potter,[14] enabled them to set up an art pottery, in which Frederick's younger brother Thomas worked.

The exact location of Vodrey's art pottery is not evident on the Ordnance Survey map (1888) for Moore Street (Fig. 17) and can only be determined by future archaeological investigation.[15] Owing to the fact that Vodrey also leased a second premises on Moore Street, No. 18, the art pottery could have been located behind either No. 18 or No. 19.[16]

---

8 Fitzpatrick 1886, 88.

9 Dennis 1887, 113. 'The other manufactory of artistic pottery is in Dublin and was established there some years ago by Mr F. Vodrey, who says he has a rapidly growing demand for his ware and is exporting to the United States and Canada. That proves the practicability of making pottery a large and paying industry in Ireland.'

10 Registry of Deeds, Lease no. 1880, 44 105 1158. Frederick Vodrey took over the lease of 37 Mary Street from Thomas P. Torkington on 15 July 1880.

11 Frederick Vodrey's trade card, 1885, NMI 1886:125.

12 In *Thom's Street Directory* Frederick Vodrey is listed at 19 Moore Street from 1865 to 1896. In 1875 he took over another lease at No. 18 Moore Street. He advertised as 'Earthenware merchant, sole agent for Coalisland Pottery 18 and 19 Moore Street'. From 1870 to 1879 he is also listed at 23 Henry Street. In 1880 he took over the lease at 37 Mary Street. Frederick Vodrey is listed as consistently in business in 37 Mary Street and 18 and 19 Moore Street until he gave up the lease of Mary Street on 12 October 1896. Both his mother, Agnes, and his baby son Robert died in the same year. It seems that Frederick Vodrey may have ceased business the year before his own death on 26 October 1897.

13 Hackett's *Dublin Illustrated Family Almanack* (1881): 'Frederick Vodrey, Wholesale and Retail Glass, China, and Lamp Merchant'. Vodrey advertised a 50-piece dinner service priced at '15 shillings and 6 pence'. The advertisement also reveals that Vodrey catered for the higher end of the market, as he advertised 'Richly Gilt and Enamelled Dinner Services, from 10s. to £10'. The prices for 'China tea services ranged from 9s. 6d. to £5', and 'China Breakfast Services from 21s. to £10'.

14 The 1851 Census recorded the occupation of Frederick's father William as 'Potter Handler'.

15 Ordnance Survey, OS 146/Dublin City/11, sheet 47 (an 1888 map).

16 *Thom's Street Directory* records Frederick Vodrey at 18 Moore Street from 1879 to 1882. In 1875 Frederick Vodrey took a lease for 18 Moore Street (Griffith's Valuation Books Lease Ref. 12 61 327: memorial of mortgage for 17 March 1875). The lease-holder had previously been a Michael Rooney, also a dealer in china and glass. The valuation was £20 in 1863 and there was no change from 1882 to 1890.

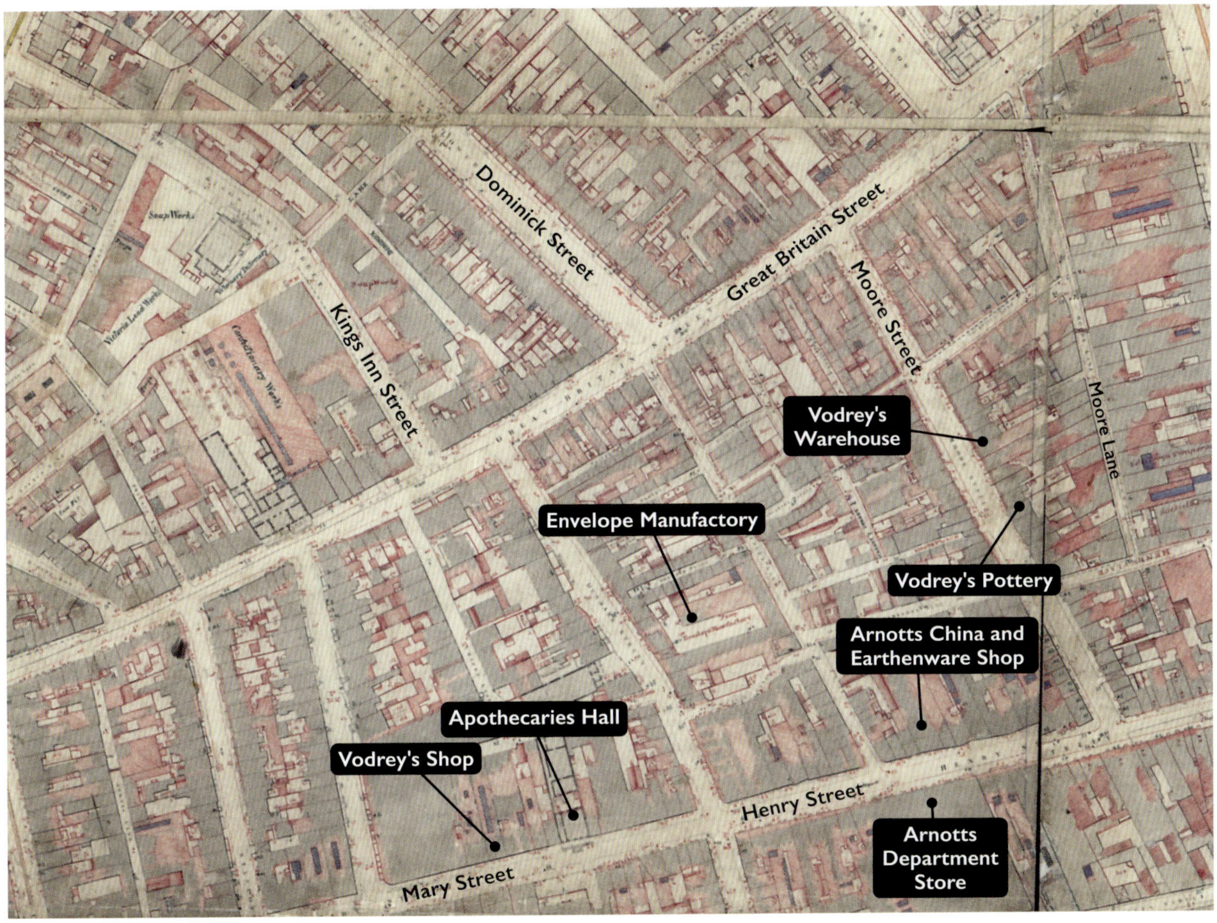

Fig. 17—Ordnance Survey map of the Henry Street and Moore Street area, 1888 (OS 146/Dublin City/11, sheet 47). Courtesy of the National Archives of Ireland.

The art pottery produced in Moore Street was advertised separately from the imported tablewares as 'Irish Art Pottery' made from Irish clays, and the advertisements appeared exclusively in the *Dublin University Review*, appealing to customers with an informed artistic taste who were keen to support Irish home industries (Fig. 18).[17]

The Museum's 1884 acquisition list records three art pottery vases purchased from F. Vodrey (one for 2s. 6d and two for 3s. 6d each). These prices indicate that Vodrey's art pottery was a luxury item and could only be afforded by the middle-income and mainly upper-middle-income groups. The daily wage of the cottier class at this time was 6d, and the rent for a cabin and one acre of ground was 50–55 shillings per year.[18] Further up the income scale, the civil servant earned £7–£8 per week.[19] It could be deduced that Vodrey's clients were amongst the professional middle class whose incomes were £700 a year or £15 a week.

17 Advertisement for 'Irish Art Pottery' in *Dublin University Review*, August 1885, 93.

18 Murray 1903, 785.

19 The Victorian Web (https://www.b.uk).

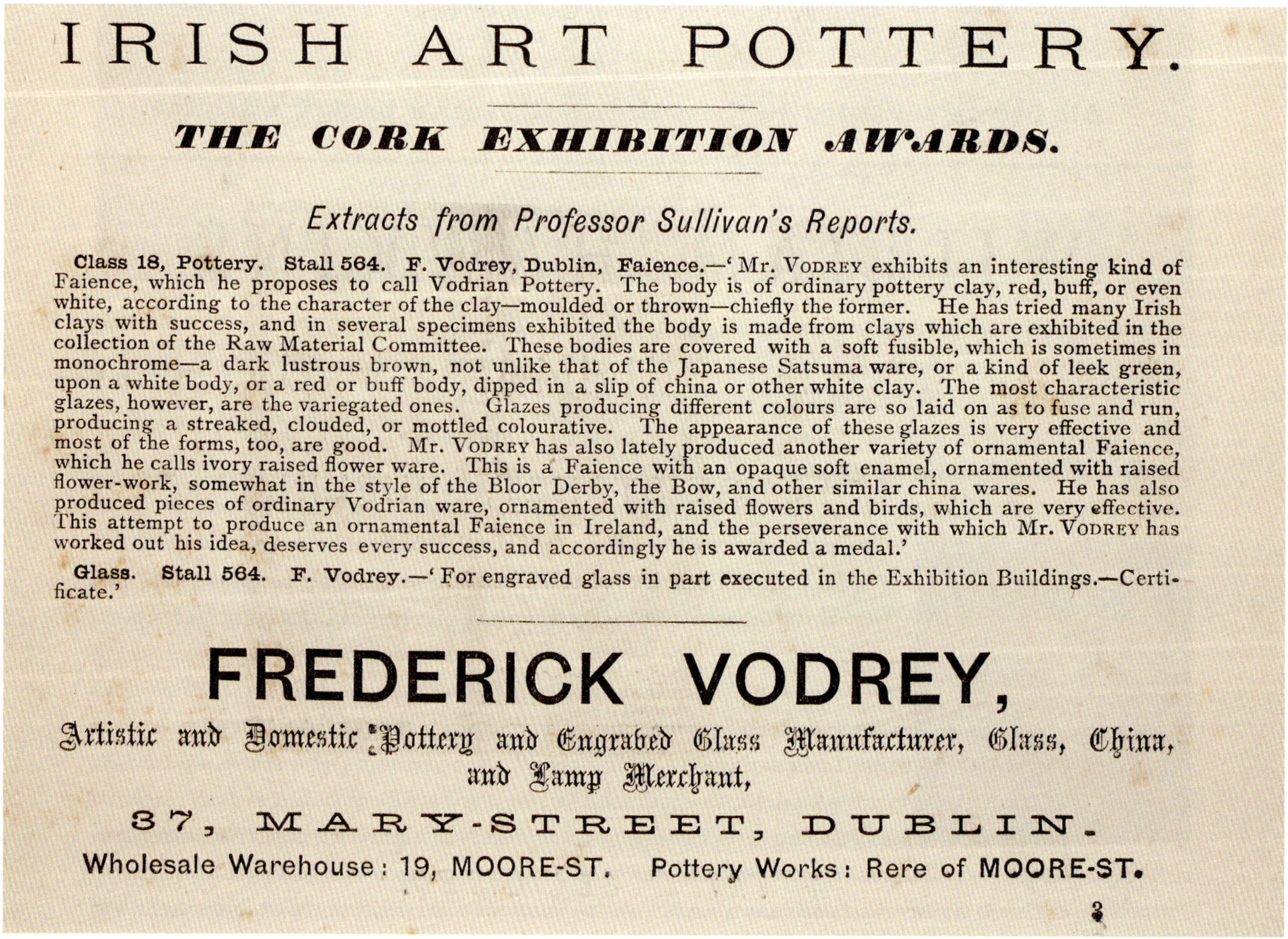

IRISH ART POTTERY.

THE CORK EXHIBITION AWARDS.

Extracts from Professor Sullivan's Reports.

Class 18, Pottery. Stall 564. F. Vodrey, Dublin, Faience.—'Mr. VODREY exhibits an interesting kind of Faience, which he proposes to call Vodrian Pottery. The body is of ordinary pottery clay, red, buff, or even white, according to the character of the clay—moulded or thrown—chiefly the former. He has tried many Irish clays with success, and in several specimens exhibited the body is made from clays which are exhibited in the collection of the Raw Material Committee. These bodies are covered with a soft fusible, which is sometimes in monochrome—a dark lustrous brown, not unlike that of the Japanese Satsuma ware, or a kind of leek green, upon a white body, or a red or buff body, dipped in a slip of china or other white clay. The most characteristic glazes, however, are the variegated ones. Glazes producing different colours are so laid on as to fuse and run, producing a streaked, clouded, or mottled colourative. The appearance of these glazes is very effective and most of the forms, too, are good. Mr. VODREY has also lately produced another variety of ornamental Faience, which he calls ivory raised flower ware. This is a Faience with an opaque soft enamel, ornamented with raised flower-work, somewhat in the style of the Bloor Derby, the Bow, and other similar china wares. He has also produced pieces of ordinary Vodrian ware, ornamented with raised flowers and birds, which are very effective. This attempt to produce an ornamental Faience in Ireland, and the perseverance with which Mr. VODREY has worked out his idea, deserves every success, and accordingly he is awarded a medal.'

Glass. Stall 564. F. Vodrey.—'For engraved glass in part executed in the Exhibition Buildings.—Certificate.'

FREDERICK VODREY,

Artistic and Domestic Pottery and Engraved Glass Manufacturer, Glass, China, and Lamp Merchant,

37, MARY-STREET, DUBLIN.

Wholesale Warehouse: 19, MOORE-ST. Pottery Works: Rere of MOORE-ST.

3

Fig. 18—Advertisement for Frederick Vodrey's 'Irish Art Pottery' in the *Dublin University Review*, May 1885. It includes an extract from Professor Sullivan's report on Vodrey's 'Faience', which he proposes to call 'Vodrian Pottery' and for which 'He has tried many Irish clays with success, and in several specimens exhibited the body is made from clays which are exhibited in the collection of the Raw Material Committee'. Courtesy of the National Library of Ireland.

Whilst only the middle and upper classes could afford the prices of both the 'Irish Art Pottery' and the Staffordshire wares that Vodrey retailed, the range of prices shows that he aimed to provide for a variety of incomes within that social group, from the modest to the wealthy. In the case of the Staffordshire tableware that he retailed in his shop at 37 Mary Street, he stocked tea sets and dinner services costing from 10 shillings to £10.[20] To date, information on prices for the ceramics decorated by Herbert Cooper and the students at the Queen's Institute has not come to light. However, given that these sets were hand-painted and sometimes commissioned with the client's monogram, the prices were probably similar to and higher than the more expensive wares sold by Vodrey.

Price lists for ceramics in the Dublin Sketching Club catalogues during the 1880s confirm that china plaques painted with landscapes or flowers, such as those exhibited by Cooper and other artists, were priced higher than the hand-modelled earthenware art pottery. In the 1881 annual exhibition, china vases and plaques painted with flowers, fruit and outdoor scenes were priced from £1 to £1 15s.,[21] contrasting with the earthenware art pottery exhibited in 1882, described as 'Artistic Pottery Modelled, Fired and Decorated by Members of the Dublin Sketching Club', for which prices ranged from 5s. to 10s.[22] ■

20 *Dublin Illustrated Family Almanack* (1881). Advertisement for 'Frederick Vodrey, Wholesale and Retail, Glass, China, and Lamp Merchant, 37 Mary Street; Wholesale Warehouse—19, Moore Street, Dublin'.

21 *Dublin Sketching Club Catalogue*, Eighth Season (1881–2), 11–12. Of the china vases and plaques, Herbert Cooper exhibited twelve items, A. Williams five, T.H. Longfield one and E. Eagle two.

22 *Dublin Sketching Club Catalogue*, Tenth Season (1883–4), 18–21.

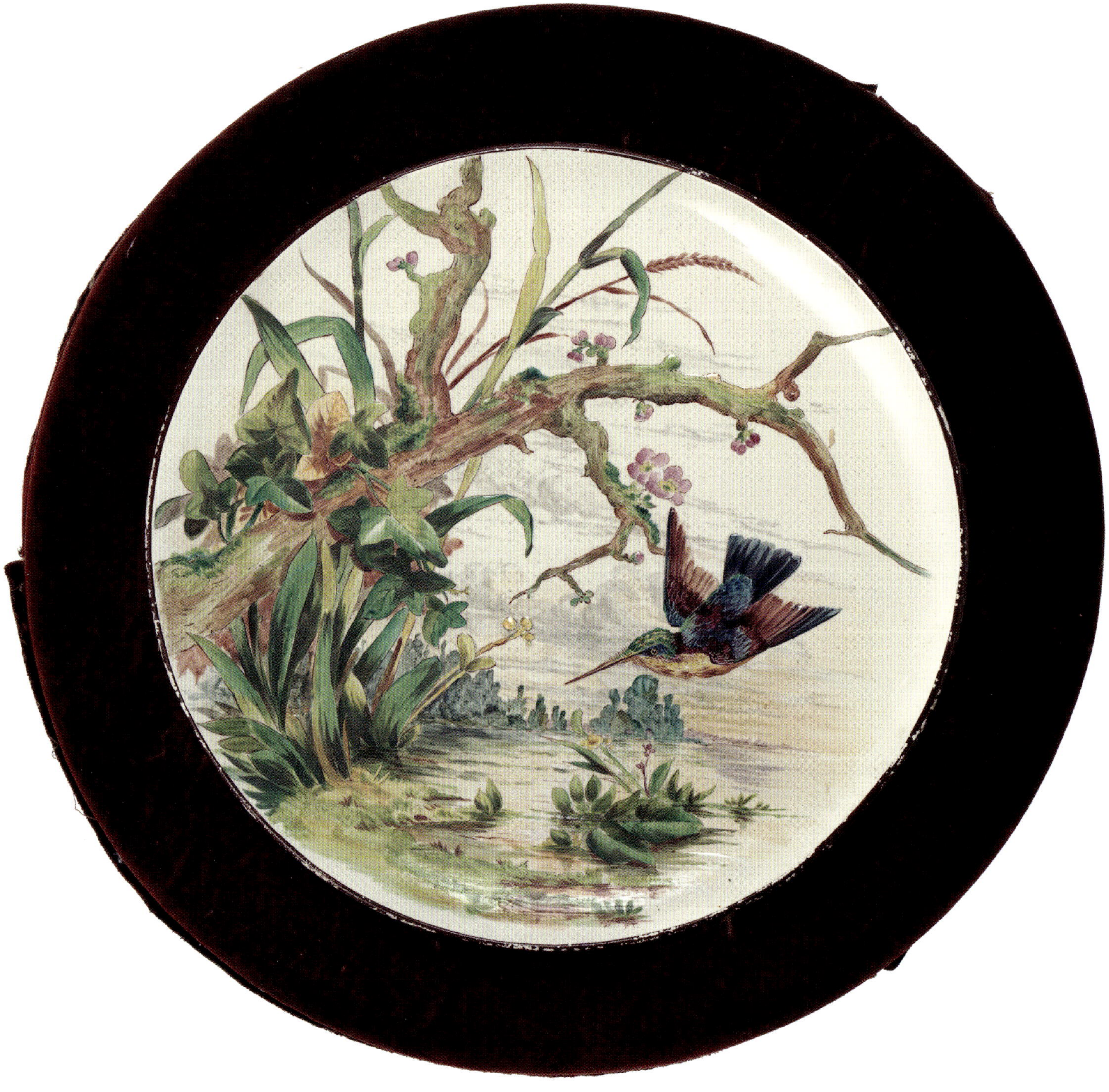

CHAPTER 6

Frederick Vodrey's participation in the Art and Industry exhibitions

Frederick Vodrey's participation in the Art and Industry exhibitions

Vodrey's role in Irish economic and cultural revival can be charted through his participation in the Art and Industry exhibitions held in Ireland during the later nineteenth century, and modelled on the Great Exhibition held at Crystal Palace, London, in 1851. The latter prompted a spate of industrial exhibitions in Europe and the United States, which drew crowds and excited the public.[1] The purpose of industrial exhibitions was 'to improve taste of the middle-class consumers 'inform manufacturers about mechanical improvements' and 'morally educate the working classes'.[2]

In Ireland, the first of many Art and Industry exhibitions was the Cork Industrial Exhibition (1852), followed by the Dublin International Exhibition (1853); the subsequent run of exhibitions held in Ireland throughout the nineteenth century culminated with the Irish International Exhibition in 1907. Whilst recent research has revealed the significance of the Dublin International Exhibitions in 1853 and 1872 for the promotion of Irish manufactures, including ceramics,[3] the importance of the Cork Industrial Exhibition of 1852 and its recognition of cottage industries and the 'Female Industrial Movement' is less well known.[4] The report of the exhibition by John Francis Maguire, lord mayor of Cork, listed producers of domestic and architectural 'coarse pottery' already established in many parts of Ireland.[5]

Vodrey's art pottery was first displayed and won prizes in the 'National Exhibition' held in Dublin in 1882 and the Cork Industrial Exhibition in 1883. During the 1880s there was less emphasis on international exhibitions, which included exhibitors from abroad, and a corresponding 'movement in public opinion towards the encouragement of home manufactures';[6] increasingly the aim was to promote

---

1 Greenhalgh 1988.

2 *Ibid.*, 18–19.

3 Rains 2010.

4 Maguire 1853, 183–5.

5 *Ibid.*, 35–6.

6 Turpin 1983, 50.

Irish industry and employment. The Irish Artisans' Exhibition in 1885, for which Vodrey's trade card was created, marked the peak of the VDP's exhibition success, which began in 1882 at the Irish Exhibition of Arts and Manufactures or the 'National Exhibition', as it was named in the newspapers.

Vodrey was represented in several sections of the 1882 exhibition, the division of exhibits into different sections being characteristic of such events in the nineteenth century.[7] He exhibited both as a retailer/agent of Coalisland ceramics in County Tyrone and as a producer of his own art pottery, described as 'an elaborate collection of Irish pottery ware, some of it from Belleek and some of it very excellent work manufactured by the exhibitors themselves',[8] for which he was awarded a certificate.[9] The catalogue of the 1882 exhibition does not give evidence of the exact type of designs displayed by Vodrey in the 'Artistic and Domestic Pottery' category, but an assessment of the chronological development of style and marks indicates that the Vodrey Dublin Pottery was producing a range of popular Victorian styles by this time. There is also evidence to indicate that Vodrey was producing art pottery in the Japanese aesthetic by this date.[10]

In addition to his own 'Artistic and Domestic Pottery', Vodrey displayed hand-painted ceramics by women of the Queen's Institute in the Fine Art section, indicating that he may have provided facilities to the QI students for a period of time and is further evidence of his association with the Institute.[11] Two large plaques in the Museum collection, similar to the descriptions of those displayed by Vodrey in the 1882 exhibition, show the Victorian taste for naturalistic floral decoration. These two plaques, one decorated with hand-painted flowers (on display in the Museum) (cat. no. 74) and the other with a Japanese-inspired design of kingfisher and pond (Fig. 18; cat. no. 97), are examples of the varied popular taste in decorative ceramics for the home produced by the Queen's Institute.

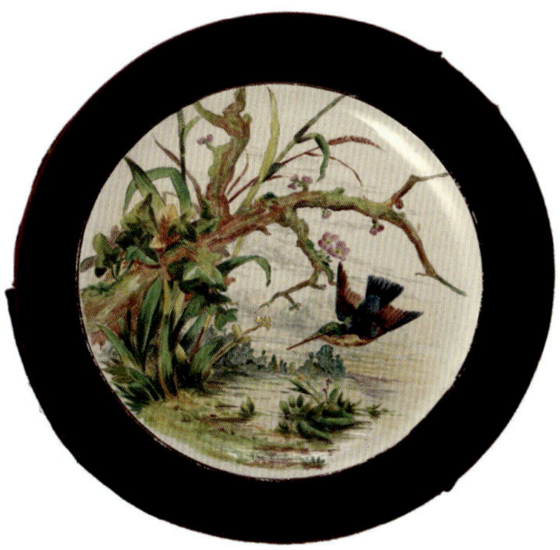

Fig. 18—Plaque in frame, with hand-painted decoration showing kingfisher, *Prunus* blossom, water lily and pond, c. 1871–83. Signed 'HC Queen's Institute', with a shamrock. Diameter 41cm. NMI 1996.6. Cat. no. 96.

Of the seven ceramic plaques exhibited in the Fine Arts section, all (aside from one) were lent by F. Vodrey;[12] the only other plaque, entitled 'Flowers' by Miss Leech, was lent by the lady mayoress, Mrs Charles Dawson.[13]

7 Greenhalgh 1988, 54.

8 *Irish Times*, 23 August 1882.

9 Certificate awarded to Frederick Vodrey at the Exhibition of Irish Arts and Manufactures, Dublin, 1882, for 'Vases, Jugs, teapots made from Irish clay and for Rich Painting thereon. Given at Dublin, the 30th Day of December 1882.' National Museum of Ireland; presented by the Vodrey family, Canada.

10 Appendix. A gourd-shaped 'purse vase' in a private collection has the mark dated 1882.

11 *Record of the Irish Exhibition of Irish Arts and Manufactures 1882* (Dublin, 1883), 68, 49.

12 *Ibid.*, 49. The plaques exhibited by F. Vodrey were numbered 676–682. They were listed as follows: '676 "Who are you?"—Miss F.J. White and Miss Wiesse 10s Lent by F. Vodrey; 677 Sunflowers (plaque)—Miss Wiesse 5s 0d Lent by F. Vodrey; 678 Winter Fruit (plaque) Miss Wiesse 5s 5d Lent by F. Vodrey; 679 Grapes (plaque) Miss F.J. White 3s 3d Lent by F. Vodrey; 680 Winter Fruit (plaque) Mrs Wiesse 2s 2d Lent by F. Vodrey.'

13 *Ibid.*

The names of the QI artists exhibited by Vodrey—Miss F.J. White and Miss Wiesse—were listed in the exhibition catalogue, but there are no pieces signed by them in the National Museum collection, indicating that the objects have not yet been identified and are in private ownership. Vodrey's display of these ceramic plaques, richly decorated with flowers and fruit, indicates his involvement with the Queen's Institute and his intention to gain social advantage by exhibiting within the context of Fine Art. By associating himself with Fine Art and, later, with the members of the DSC, Vodrey claimed cultural capital for his business and was elevated to the stature of public figures such as the lady mayoress of Dublin.

Other exhibitors of ceramics and glass at the 1882 exhibition included well-known merchants like the Pugh brothers and Whyte and Sons, Vodrey's competitors in the retail of ceramic and glass tableware. T. and R. Pugh exhibited 'Artistic and Domestic Cut and Engraved Glass', and Whyte and Sons were listed as displaying 'Glass and China'.[14] These two companies were the other main retailers of ceramic and glass tableware in Dublin city. The Pugh family were glass-engravers who had migrated from England;[15] they worked first in Cork and then established a glassworks in Dublin.[16] Whyte and Sons commissioned glass from Pugh's for sale in their shop and retailed imported ceramics; the company was in business into the twentieth century. Vodrey's intention to supply all the tableware needs of his customers, including engraved glass, shows his business acumen in recognising the demand for Bohemian-style engraved glass at the time.[17] The following year he employed a glass-engraver, Franz Tieze,[18] and won a prize and certificate for glass-engraving at the Cork Exhibition.[19] In addition, he was awarded a certificate and a medal for 'faience' (Figs 19 and 20).

During the months leading up to the opening of the Cork Industrial Exhibition (1883), reports in the *Irish Builder* indicated that its aims were to promote and improve design for industry.[20] The exhibits of Vodrey's art pottery reveal a further development in style from previous exhibits at the 1882 Dublin exhibition (Appendix). In the official report of the Cork exhibition, Dr Sullivan of Queen's College Cork compared 'Vodrian ware' designs favourably with those from English art potteries such as Linthorpe and Vallauris, and praised the use of Irish clays for ceramic manufacture.[21] Subsequently, in 1885, when Vodrey's art pottery achieved further success in the Irish Artisans' Exhibition, John Mahaffy Pentland,[22] a prominent figure in cultural and academic

---

14 Record of the Irish Exhibition of Irish Arts Manufactures 1882, 49. Vodrey was listed at stand 1156, Whyte and Sons at 1155 and T. and R. Pugh at 1159.

15 Boydell and Doyle 1994, 7.

16 MacLeod 1972, 3–5.

17 Boydell and Doyle 1994, 7.

18 There are three engraved glass pieces in the National Museum which were retailed by F. Vodrey (register no. 1883.873–5). The glass 'is probably English-produced' and was engraved 'by a Dublin-based Bohemian engraver, Franz Tieze'. I am grateful to Deirdre Power for this information.

19 *Cork Industrial Exhibition 1883. Report of the Executive Committee, Awards of Jurors and Statement of Accounts* (Cork, 1886), 392. The certificate won by Frederick Vodrey at the Cork Exhibition of 1883 is now in the NMI, presented by the Vodrey family. It reads: 'This Certificate of merit has been awarded to Frederick Vodrey Dublin for Glass Engraving'.

20 *Irish Builder*, January, February, March, and April 1883.

21 *Cork Industrial Exhibition 1883. Report of the Executive Committee,* 392, 395–6.

22 *Oxford Dictionary of National Biography,* Vol. 36, 151–3.

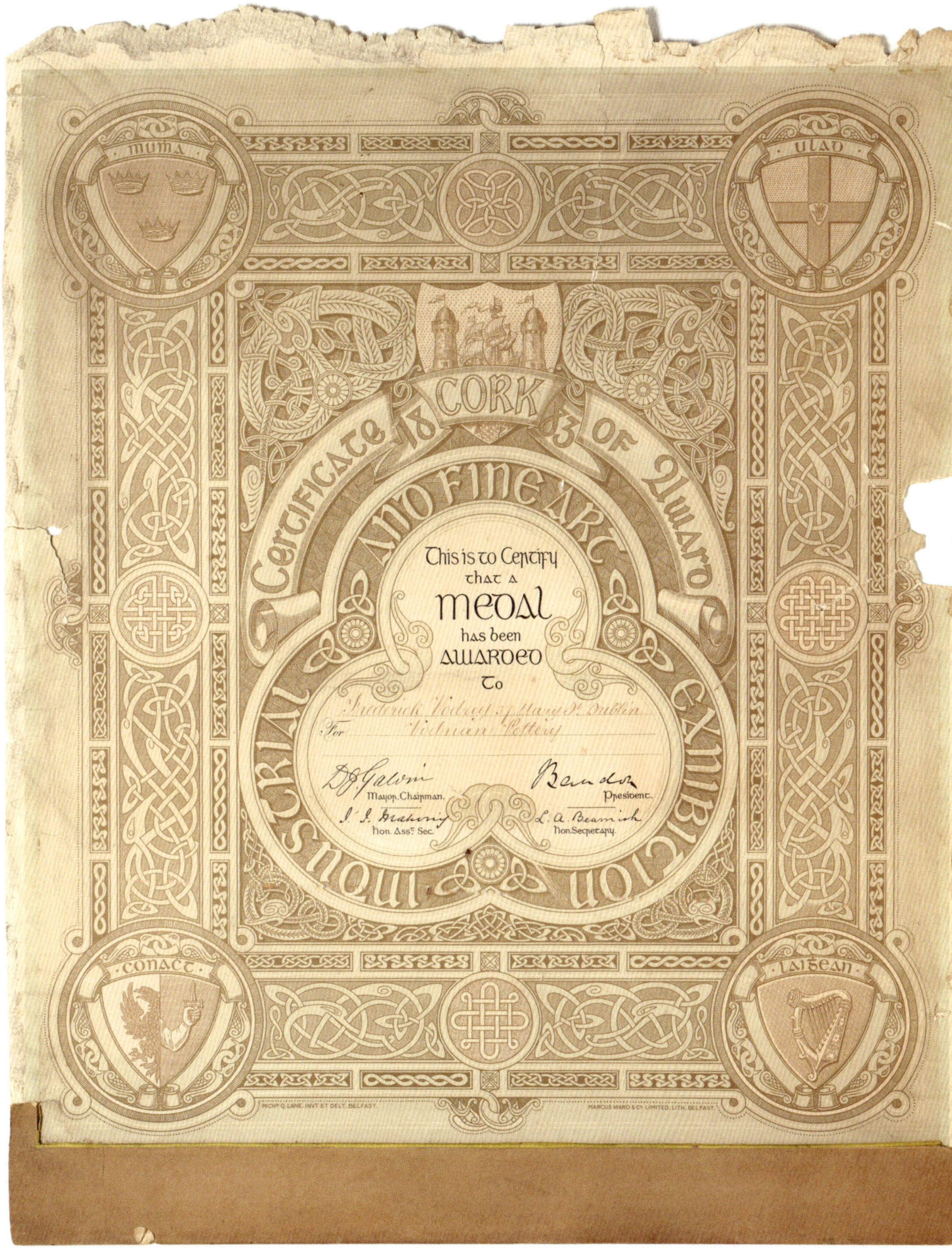

Fig. 19—The certificate awarded to Frederick Vodrey at the Cork Exhibition of 1883 reads: 'This is to certify that a medal has been awarded to Frederick Vodrey of Moore Street Dublin. For Vodrian Pottery'. Courtesy of the National Museum of Ireland; presented by the Vodrey family, Canada.

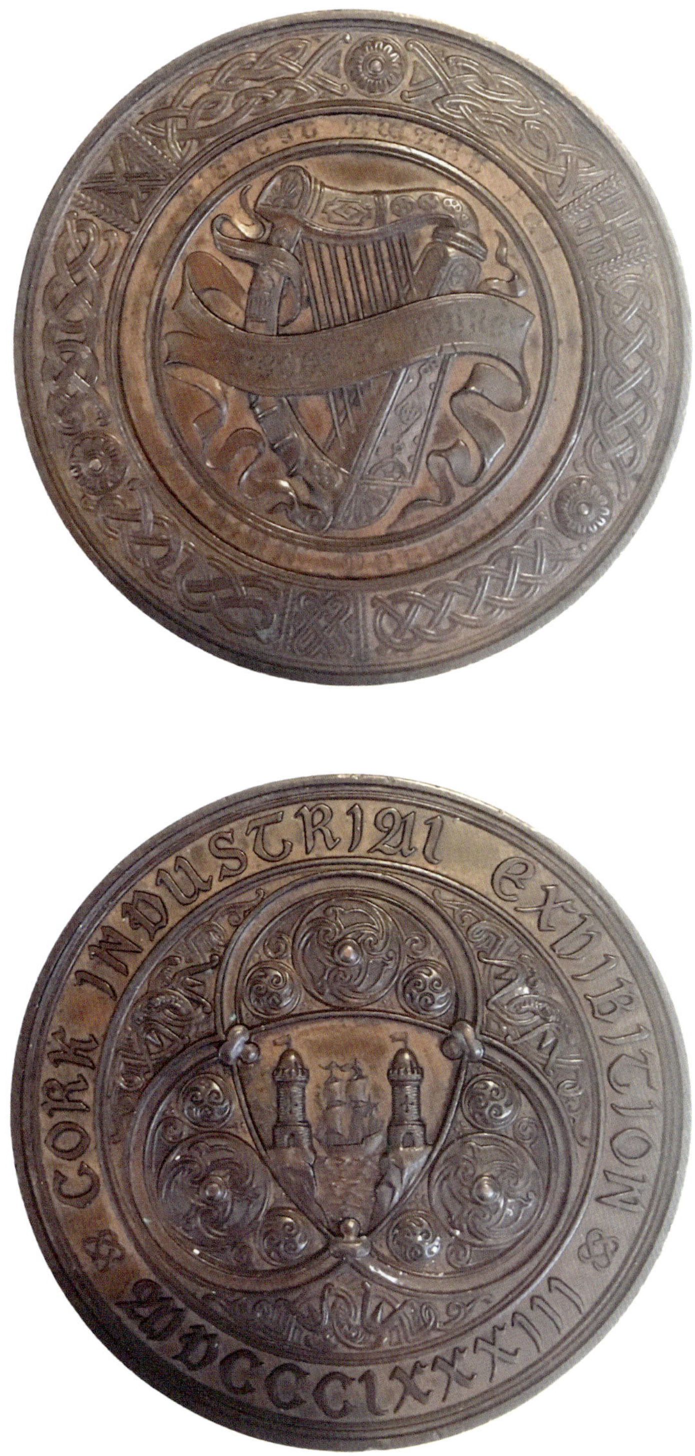

Fig. 20—Bronze medal from the Cork Industrial Exhibition, 1883; diameter 9.5cm. Side 1: harp in the centre, Celtic interlace on the borders, the words 'Frederick Vodrey' on the ribbon across the harp. Side 2: trefoil border framing Cork city emblem of a ship and two towers. Photo courtesy of the Vodrey family, Canada.

circles, described Vodrey's use of Irish clays and Celtic designs,[23] which the artist F.S. Walker claimed could offer great possibilities for Irish art industry.[24] Vodrey's mix of clays from Knockcroghery and Belleek created a clay body that was described as 'remarkably plastic and capable of the most delicate modelling', producing a 'beautiful creamy biscuit' owing to 'the presence of a small quantity of iron'.[25] Pentland, provost of Trinity College, an aesthete and mentor of Oscar Wilde (the Irish playwright who was one of the leading proponents of the Aesthetic taste in London), praised Vodrey for introducing a new, improved style and quality of ceramics to Dublin.[26] ■

---

23 Pentland 1885, 34–5. 'Mr. Vodrey, the manufacturer, was led into the venture for amusement's sake, and being successful in his experiments on home materials, established a pottery on a small scale at his Moore Street premises.'

24 Walker 1886.

25 Pentland 1885, 35.

26 *Ibid.*, 39.

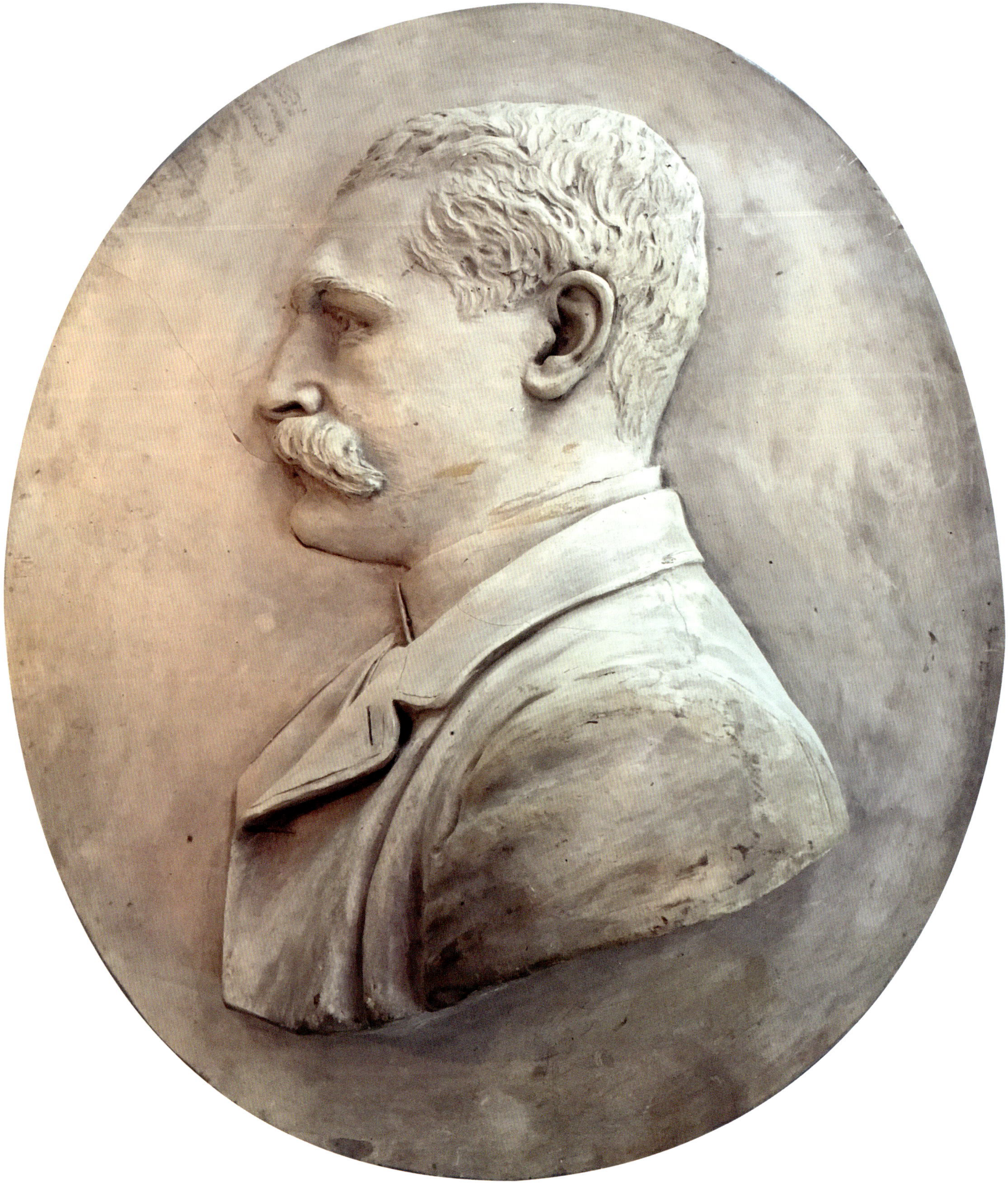

CHAPTER 7

The Irish Artisans' Exhibition, 1885

The Irish Artisans' Exhibition, 1885

Whilst the Great Exhibition in London (1851) was a display of empire, the main aim of subsequent exhibitions in Britain was the education of artisans, who were vital to manufacturing and the crafts.[1] In Dublin, reports about the organisation of the Irish Artisans' Exhibition (1885) indicate a similar focus.[2] The new, purpose-built building for the exhibition was in the centre of the city, with the main entrance on Exchequer Street and two other entrances on South Great George's Street and Trinity Lane.[3] The entrance hall contained an exhibition of sculpture and paintings by artists such as Aloysius O'Kelly and Charles Russell.[4] The upstairs gallery was reached by means of 'three spacious staircases'. The building, designed by J.J. O'Callaghan, was constructed of 'timber and glass, excepting the Picture Gallery', which was of brick.[5] The central hall was estimated to be 200ft long by 120ft wide;[6] it later became known as the South City Markets.

The Irish Artisans' Exhibition (1885) was praised in the *Irish Builder* for giving credit to the artisans for their work and was described as 'a new departure'.[7] It included a range of exhibits, from industrial manufacturers to crafts such as 'coloured and engraved glass' by T. and R. Pugh and 'a handsome bedroom suite, made of American walnut, with inlaid panels on satin wood ground' exhibited by furniture-maker T.R. Scott.[8] The organisers specifically encouraged entries from women and aimed to include many

---

1 Greenhalgh 1988, 21.

2 *Irish Artisans' Exhibition Complete Official Catalogue* (2nd edn) (Dublin, 1885).

3 *Ibid.*, 10.

4 *Ibid.*, 1.

5 *Ibid.*, 16.

6 *Irish Builder*, 15 June 1885, 179. The opening paragraphs of the exhibition catalogue give detailed dimensions of separate areas of the building.

7 *Irish Builder*, 1 July 1885, 180.

8 *Irish Artisans' Exhibition Complete Official Catalogue*, 31. T.R. Scott's exhibits at stand 129 included a 'Pair of mirrors (hand painted) by Miss Irwin' and a 'Rosewood Tea Caddy (Queen's style), designed and made by John Whitty'.

involved in the Home Industries movement.[9] It was clearly stated that manufacturers had to name both 'Artisans and Employers'. Lectures and concerts were held for the 'education of the artisan class',[10] and the Royal Irish Academy gave free admission to artisans. The exhibition was held in an environment of social change, in which contemporary writers and the exhibition organisers supported education and the recognition of craftworkers' rights.

According to the exhibition catalogue, Frederick Vodrey was assisted by several workers from Stoke-on-Trent, including his brother Thomas, who was a 'Mould-maker and Presser'.[11] Vodrey's art pottery was displayed near the Belleek pottery.[12] Vodrey listed nine workers, in contrast to the much larger Belleek Pottery, which listed 88 workers. Like the furniture-maker Scott, Vodrey was described as the designer of the exhibits; both were catering for the fashionable Aesthetic taste. Vodrey advertised his ceramics as 'Irish Art Pottery' and Scott advertised as 'Artistic Cabinet Manufacturers'.[13] Vodrey was subsequently praised for his contribution to Irish industry and for being a good employer:

> 'Belleek used to enjoy a monopoly of favour in the matter of pottery of attractive form and fashion, but in the presence of the enterprise of Mr. Vodrey, of Moore-street and Mary-Street, the fame of that celebrated district is in imminent danger of being eclipsed. Mr. Vodrey's busy hive at the rere of Moore-street is in the best sense of the word an artistic pottery, where the most beautiful things imaginable are manufactured. It is essentially a credit to Dublin and to Ireland, and of such a high-class nature are his goods, that they have not only forced themselves into Irish households but have invaded English and Scottish markets. Mr. Vodrey deserves well of his fellow citizen's (praise) being a genuine devotee of art in this, and a generous employer.'[14]

Vodrey's own evidence to the Select Committee on Industries in 1885 stated that there was 'a rapidly growing demand for my ware' and that he was 'exporting it to the United States and Canada'. He also declared that there were 'only two manufactories in Ireland that make glazed white body ware; these are the Belleek Pottery and myself'.[15]

Vodrey's trade card in the National Museum was produced for the Irish Artisans' Exhibition (1885). It is an amalgam of sources and images, some specific to Vodrey and others stock-in-trade images of the period (see Fig. 7).[16] For example, the imagery includes an illustration of the medal won by Vodrey at the 1883 Cork Exhibition, while the floral designs in the side panels are similar in style to those on

---

9 *Ibid.*, 11: 'In the Department of Home Industries and Art Workmanship, the work of Women is especially invited'.

10 *Ibid.*

11 *Ibid.*, 29.

12 *Ibid.* The Belleek Pottery exhibited at stall 50 and Vodrey's exhibit, entitled 'Potter's Wheel at Work', was at stall 55.

13 *Dublin University Review* 2 (April 1886).

14 Fitzpatrick 1886, 88.

15 *Report of the Select Committee on Industries (Ireland)*, 821.

16 F. Vodrey's trade card, 1885: Cahill Litho., Printers & Co., Dublin. NMI.1886.125.

the majolica tiles decorating the walls of the new Museum of Science and Art in Dublin.[17] Analysis and cross-referencing of the trade card with the list of workers' names in the catalogue of the Irish Artisans' Exhibition reveals the names of the many individuals involved in the production process, confirming Fitzpatrick's account of the Vodrey Dublin Pottery as a 'busy hive at the rere of Moore-street'. According to another textual source, Vodrey's pottery was referred to as 'his atelier', where 'beautiful articles of ornament and utility' were produced through a range of 'artistic skills' that included 'modelling', 'enamelling and glazing'.[18]

In the ceramic industry, the demonstration of different manufacturing techniques in practical manuals was common,[19] showing the division of labour within the industry.[20] The trade card illustrates the production process in Vodrey's art pottery, with images of potters and artists carrying out the various stages of the ceramic production process. The design of the card is in a format advertised by a printer in the *Pottery Gazette*[21] and bears a strong resemblance to an advertisement for the Linthorpe Pottery in England.[22] Whilst it is possible that the article on Linthorpe influenced Vodrey, both art potteries were active at the same time in the 1880s and could have purchased advertising images from the same printer.

The imagery and words on the trade card bring alive the activity at Vodrey's art pottery, giving us a glimpse of the workers' demonstration in the Irish Artisans' Exhibition (1885), where they showed the pottery-making process, from throwing and casting to firing and glazing, as follows:

> 'Thus, within sight of the visitor, the rough dough like material is fashioned into graceful, novel, and unique shapes which eventually assume that brilliancy and richness of colour presented by the multifarious articles with which the surrounding shelves are laden. It may be added as a supplementary to what the visitor is shown (though within the narrow confines of a leaflet, such as this, anything like minute detail is impossible), that after the articles are formed, they are partly dried. Then follows the "turning process"—i.e., finishing the surfaces, after which they are "fired" for the first time (subjected to very great heat) which converts them into what is known as the "biscuit" state. Then the "glaze" or enamel is applied. A second firing follows, not infrequently a third to make no mention of other preliminary touches ere the goods are offered to the customer.'[23]

17 Pearson 2002, 56. The author attributes the majolica panels of the door surrounds to Burmantoft's in Leeds.

18 This is from an article entitled 'Irish Art Pottery', from a newspaper cutting of unspecified origin in the Vodrey family papers (courtesy of the late Mr Jack Vodrey).

19 Elliott 2000, 13 and 296 (illus. 8). The author refers to a 'small booklet' entitled *A representation of the manufacturing of earthenware* (1827).

20 Forty 1986, 35.

21 *The Pottery Gazette*, 1 September 1892, 156: advertisement by printers J. Williams Benn, Finsbury Press, 42 City Road, London, EC. It read as follows: 'Special and Artistic Designs, suitable for Pottery Trade Circulars, Memorandum, Forms, Cards, Invoices, &c., can be had'. The imagery showed different aspects of the woodworking craft. It seems that the same concept was applied to the ceramic craft in Vodrey's trade card.

22 'Linthorpe Art Pottery', *The Cabinet Maker and Art Furnisher*, 1 March 1883, 165–6.

23 F. Vodrey's trade card, 1885: Cahill Litho., Printers & Co., Dublin. NMI.1886.125.

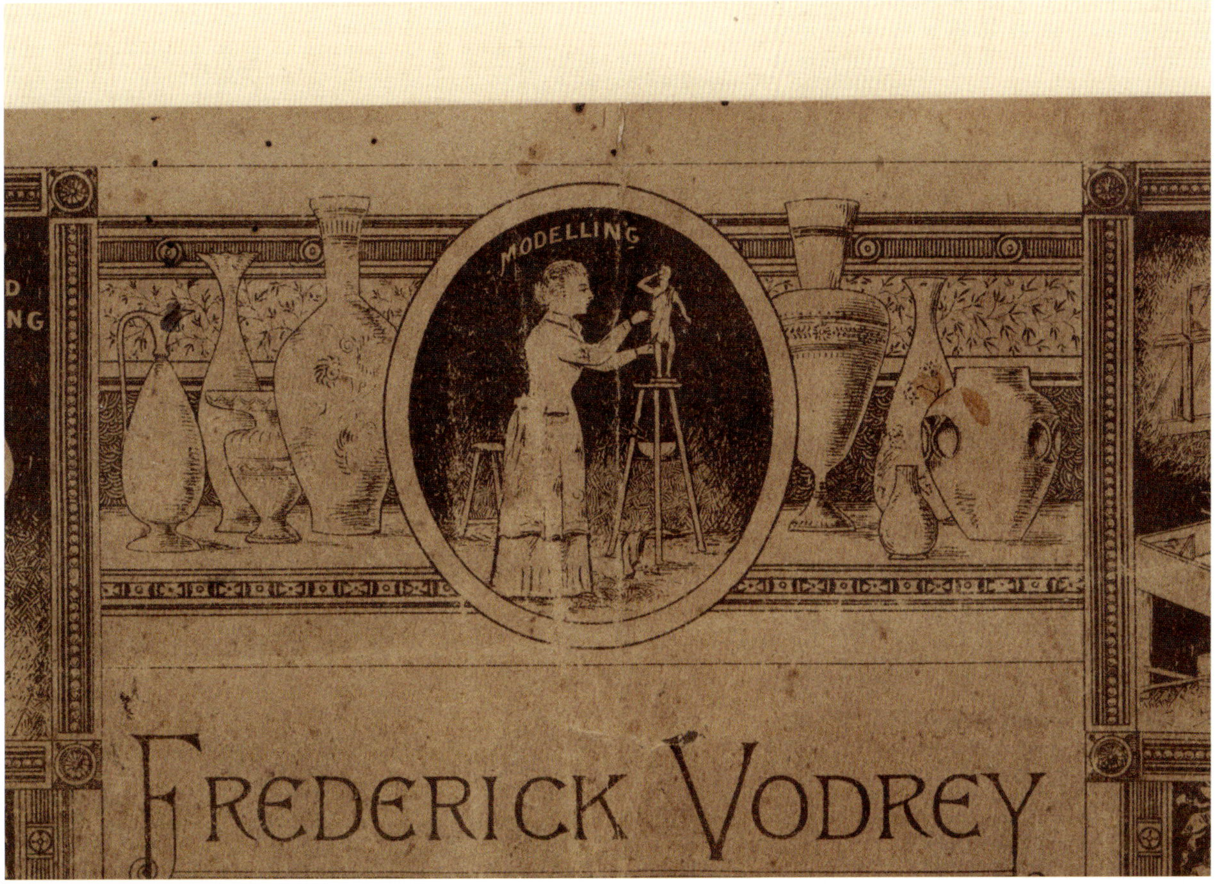

Fig. 21—Detail of Frederick Vodrey's trade card (Cahill Litho., Printers & Co., Dublin). The woman represents the sculptress Mary Redmond. Courtesy of the National Museum of Ireland, NMI 1886.125.

The description, alongside the illustrations, elevates the significance of the craft process, as it was admired by followers of the Arts and Crafts movement. The names of the workers listed at Vodrey's stand in the Irish Artisans' Exhibition catalogue can be matched with the activities illustrated in the trade card, but it has not been established whether or not they are exact portraits. For example, William Lucas, the 'Thrower (Potter on the Wheel)', is represented on the top right-hand side of the card, and Patrick Slevin, the 'Presser and Mould-maker', is on the top left-hand side.[24]

The woman illustrated as 'modelling' in the top medallion is not listed among the workers in the catalogue of the Irish Artisans' Exhibition, but it is most likely that she represents the talented sculptress Mary Redmond (1863–1930), who exhibited at the RHA and the Walker Gallery in London (Fig. 21). It is known that she 'worked at the decoration of Pottery for Frederick Vodrey' and 'gave lessons to ladies in Art'.[25] Redmond later went to study in Italy, where she lived for the rest of her life.[26]

24 *Irish Artisans' Exhibition Complete Official Catalogue*, 29.

25 Snoddy 2002, 551–2.

26 Murphy 2010, 152–3. Redmond trained in the Farrell Studio and the School of Art in Dublin, and the Tenerani and Romanelli studios in Rome and Florence.

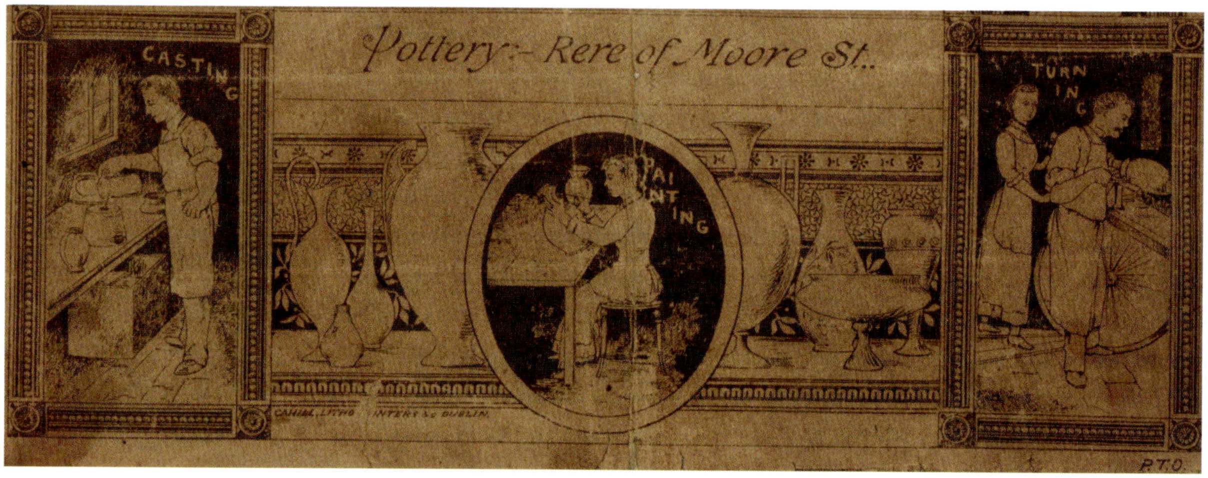

Fig. 22—Detail of Frederick Vodrey's trade card, 1885 (Cahill Litho., Printers & Co., Dublin). The man on the left represents Thomas Vodrey, Frederick's brother; the figure in the centre represents Mary Ann Carr. Courtesy of the National Museum of Ireland (NMI 1886.125).

The illustration in the lower central medallion shows Mary Ann Carr 'Painting and Glazing' (Fig. 22). On the lower left, the person represented is Frederick's brother Thomas or T. Vodrey, who was 'Pressing and Casting'.[27]

While the images of Redmond modelling and Carr decorating confirm that these roles were filled by women, the illustration of a third woman as assistant to the turner reveals the strenuous work frequently carried out by unskilled women in the pottery industry.[28] As a result of education such as that provided by the Queen's Institute in Dublin, there was an increased involvement of skilled women in the prestigious role of ceramic decoration, when 'tile painting, pottery decoration, and china painting became a source of income for a few women and an interesting hobby for many others'.[29]

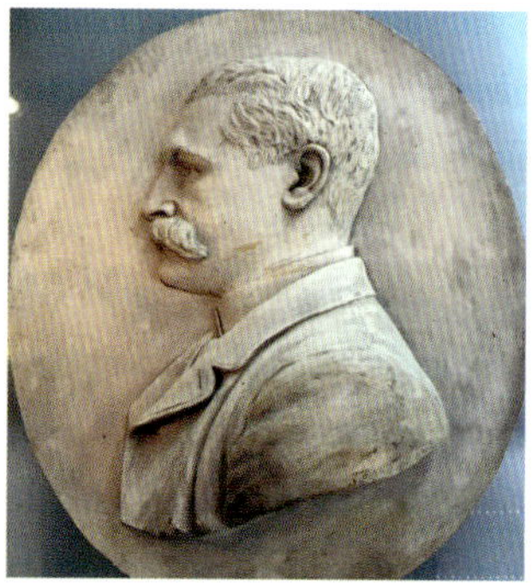

Fig. 23—Portrait of Frederick Vodrey, 'Designer and Manufacturer', bust profile in oval medallion, life-size, terracotta. Signed on the back 'M Redmond 1884' and 'F Vodrey Jany [January] 1st 1884'. Impressed mark: 'DUBLIN POTTERY VODREY'. Photo courtesy of the Vodrey family, Canada.

When considering the benefits of education in ceramics for women in the 1870s and 1880s, a distinction must be made between middle-class and working-class women in the potteries. The latter, for whom there 'was low-paid employment offering little opportunity for developing artistic skills and carrying little prestige',[30] worked mainly as assistants to male family members. The former, like the students of the QI, benefited from education in china-painting and decorating, which enabled them to earn an independent income as decorators.

27 *Irish Artisans' Exhibition Complete Official Catalogue*, 29. Other workers listed were Jane Norman, Assistant, William Norman, Fireman, and William Norman junior and P. Buckley, Thrower's Assistants.

28 Vincentelli 2000, 89.

29 *Ibid.*

30 *Ibid.*

In the late nineteenth century, women's input was recognised more by the art potteries connected to the Doulton and Minton factories.[31] The employment of women artists in these art potteries spurred the interest in ceramic education for women displayed by the founders of the QI and offered a model for Vodrey and other art pottery producers, indicated by the employment of Mary Ann Carr and Mary Redmond, the artist who sculpted the large medallion portrait of Frederick Vodrey (Fig. 22).[32] Redmond exhibited at the Royal Hibernian Academy in the 1880s, won public commissions at an early age[33] and was also associated with Herbert Cooper's studio.[34] Other terracotta sculptures known to have been modelled by Redmond were most likely produced at the VDP art pottery.[35] ■

31 *Ibid.*, 90–2.

32 Snoddy 2002, 552. The author writes that most of the work exhibited by Redmond at the Royal Hibernian Academy was 'portrait busts and medallions.' These included a marble bust of Edmund Dwyer Gray and a bust of W.E. Gladstone (untraced).

33 *Ibid.* The author writes: 'Redmond's crowning work was the Fr Mathew statue in O'Connell Street, Dublin'.

34 Larmour 1992, 6.

35 *Ibid.* The author writes that 'four of her (Redmond's) terracottas were bought by the Corporation of Liverpool at the Liverpool International Exhibition of 1886'.

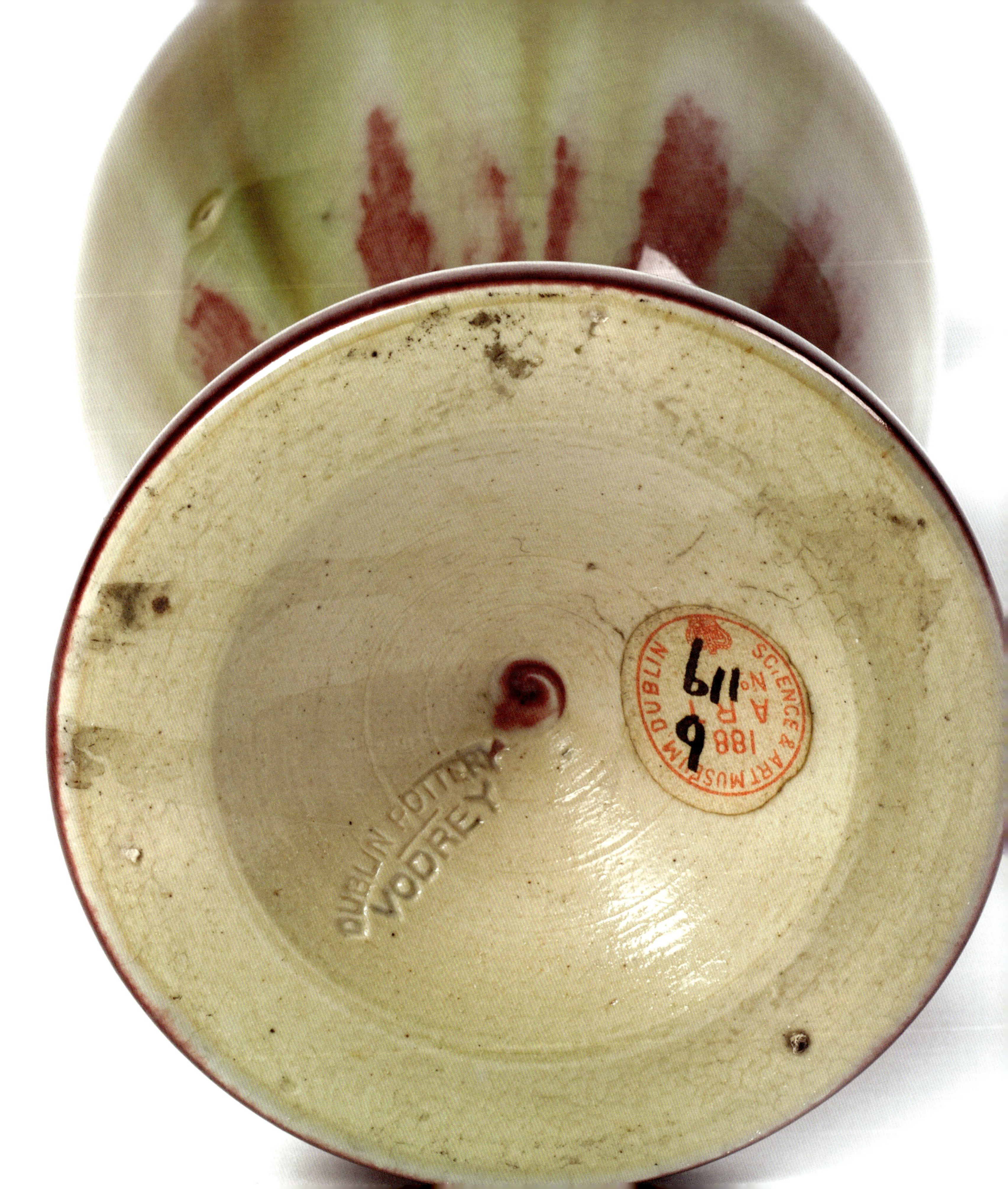
DUBLIN POTTERY
VODREY
SCIENCE & ART MUSEUM DUBLIN
A R No 188
119
9

CHAPTER 8

Frederick Vodrey (1845–97) – biography of an 'artisan entrepreneur'

Frederick Vodrey (1845-97) – biography of an 'artisan entrepreneur'

The *Pottery Gazette* welcomed the addition of 'Vodrian ware' to ceramic production in Ireland, describing it as similar to the wares of other art potteries in Scotland and England (Dunmore and Linthorpe).[1] The author praised the 'energy and enterprise' of Frederick Vodrey in his efforts 'to grope his way to discover the clays and their capabilities, to originate and adapt glazes, make his moulds, and find out the mystery of "firing"'.[2] Larmour, writing on the Irish Arts and Crafts movement, described Vodrey as a 'forerunner of the arts and crafts movement in Ireland',[3] probably because the art pottery was active before the Irish Arts and Crafts Society was established in 1894; indeed, the pottery's activity is possibly the earliest evidence of design reform ideas within the artistic community in Ireland.

Frederick Vodrey showed ambition and entrepreneurial spirit, describing himself as a 'Designer and Manufacturer'.[4] He is an interesting example of the early professional designer, a profession which emerged in the mid-nineteenth century. In her study of tableware production and consumption in the United States during the same period, Blaszczyk identified the activity of small producers who ran workshops catering for a demand for hand-painted ceramics;[5] shoppers could order their own designs or hand-paint them themselves. Vodrey's association with the Queen's Institute and the Dublin Sketching Club placed him in a similar role to Blaszczyk's 'artisan entrepreneur' in the US pottery industry; moreover, as part of a family business retailing ceramics in Dublin, he was in an ideal position to observe and respond to fashionable taste.

1 *Pottery Gazette* 8 (1 February 1883), 178.

2 *Ibid.*

3 Larmour 1992, 6.

4 *Irish Artisans' Exhibition Complete Official Catalogue*, 29. Frederick Vodrey was listed at his stand as 'F. Vodrey, Designer and Manufacturer'.

5 Blaszczyk 2000, 68–9.

Frederick was born on 2 August 1845 in Woodland Street, Tunstall, the newest town in the Potteries district of Staffordshire, England,[6] where his father, William, worked in the pottery industry;[7] his mother, Agnes (born in Scotland),[8] was from a family involved in the ceramic retail trade. The Potteries district was comprised of six adjoining towns: Tunstall, Burslem, Hanley, Stoke-on-Trent, Fenton and Longton. A christening mug dated 4 August 1845 indicates that Frederick was baptised two days after his birth (Fig. 24).

Frederick Vodrey's profile is that of someone from the artisan class who progressed from pottery worker to businessman, like others who were upwardly mobile in Stoke-on-Trent or migrated to work in the pottery industry in the United States.[9] His activity in Dublin from *c.* 1865 to 1897 illustrates the migration and upward mobility of the artisan class in Britain.[10] He was friends with Joshua Poole, who, after a brief period as manager at Belleek, moved to the United States, where he became well known for the development of a fine porcelain known as 'Lotus ware' in the East Liverpool pottery district of Ohio.[11] The social advancement of Vodrey, Poole and others in the pottery industry was due to several factors, including the benefits of education delivered by the Mechanics' Institutes,[12] which provided classes for apprentices in Stoke-on-Trent.

In 1865, when he was 20 years old, Frederick Vodrey took over the retail business started by his mother, Agnes Vodrey (née McDonald), continuing to lease a warehouse at 19 Moore Street.[13] The building was the family home and a constant base for the business, Agnes being the lease-holder from 1861 to 1865 and Frederick from 1865 to 1897.[14] The recently widowed Agnes had started the business when she moved to Dublin in 1861, at a premises called 'Staffordshire House' in No. 28 Henry Street.[15]

During the 1870s, Agnes's eldest son John was a 'china and delph dealer' in Talbot Street and George's Street; for a thirteen-year period from 1869 to 1882 (when he died young), his wife's family, by the name of Timmins, were also involved in the same business.[16] Frederick later married Annie

---

6 Molloy 1987. Frederick's birth certificate: Wolstanton and Burslem Registration District in the County of Stafford, Tunstall sub-district, 1815, no. 410.

7 The birth certificate recorded the occupation of Frederick's father as 'Potter'.

8 In the 1861 census Agnes was recorded at No. 143 Woodland Street, Tunstall, where she may have been visiting relatives. She was 46 years old, and her birthplace was recorded as Scotland.

9 Blaszczyk 2000, 2.

10 Whipp 1990.

11 Cox 1947.

12 Hudson 1851, 76. Hudson suggested that the Mechanics' Institutes were more successful than the Schools of Design in providing education for workers in the manufacturing industries.

13 In 1853/5 Griffith's Valuation records a John McDonald at 19 Moore Street with a printing office and yard. Other occupiers included Agnes Vodrey, née McDonald (F. Vodrey's mother), and Frederick Vodrey from 1871. The valuation was £40 in 1858 and remained the same in 1882–90. Rents were £60.

14 Griffith's Valuation.

15 Molloy 1987; *Thom's Street Directory of Dublin.*

16 Molloy 1987.

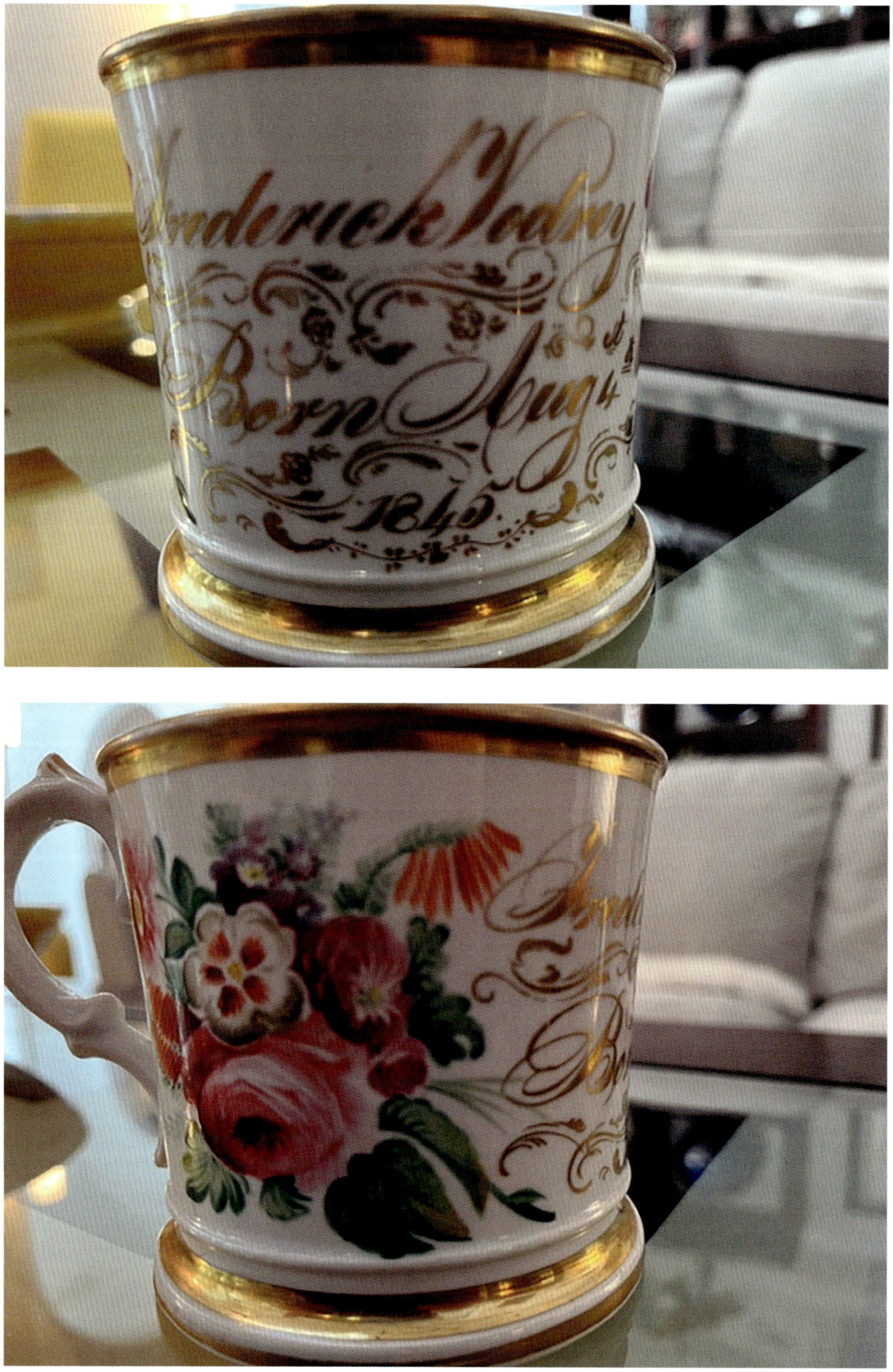

Fig. 24—Frederick Vodrey's christening mug, 1845. Inscription reads: 'Frederick Vodrey born 4th August 1845'. Hand-painted, gilt and floral decoration; Staffordshire, England. Courtesy of the Vodrey family, Canada

Cuthbert, from an established middle-class merchant family in Bray,[17] where her mother traded in ceramics, although the main family business was running coal ships between Ireland and ports in England.[18]

Whilst there is no record of where Frederick Vodrey trained in ceramic design and production, the objects produced by his art pottery reveal a knowledge of current design ideas and practice, indicating that he served an apprenticeship at one of the many potteries in Stoke-on-Trent. After he began to produce art pottery around 1873, he continued his connections with Staffordshire, making frequent trips to England, where he purchased stock for his shop;[19] he was also an agent for the Coalisland Pottery in County Tyrone. The teapot by Bailey and Co., Scotland, on display in the National Museum came from Frederick Vodrey's shop and is an indication of his diverse involvement in the ceramic retail trade.[20] The giant teapot, made for exhibition display, was most likely used by Vodrey as advertising in his shop, to excite customers' interest.

Frederick's business acumen is further indicated by his involvement in a business partnership[21] with an art pottery in Staffordshire, the Abbey Pottery in Cobridge,[22] suggesting that he may have decided to set up an alternate source of Aesthetic-style art pottery after the initial success of the Vodrey Dublin Pottery in the 1880s. It is possible that Vodrey's art pottery in Dublin was a relatively brief experiment of just twenty years, during which he employed the students at the Queen's Institute from *c.* 1872 and then potters from Staffordshire in the 1880s, when the ceramics which he advertised as 'Irish Art Pottery' won prizes in the Irish Art and Industry exhibitions. The textual sources that refer to Vodrey's art pottery are confined to a thirteen-year period. However, he held the lease at 19 Moore Street until 1897, the year of his death, after which his wife and only surviving son emigrated to Canada.[23] The lease for the shop in 37 Mary Street ended the year before Vodrey's death, which was the year his mother Agnes died,[24] indicating that there was a change in his business affairs around that time. ■

---

17 Certificate of marriage between Frederick Vodrey, merchant, of 37 Mary Street and Annie Margaret Cuthbert, solemnised in the Parish of Bray, Co. Wicklow, 9 November 1891. Registrar's District of Rathdown. The marriage took place 'at 26 Eglinton Road, Bray according to the Form and Discipline of the Presbyterian Church'.

18 Ships Records, the National Archives, Dublin. Richard Cuthbert owned the *William and Margaret* (reg. no. 1898) from *c.* 1868 to 1901; William Cuthbert owned the *Susanna* (reg. no. 9311) from *c.* 1875 to 1889. Both ships sailed between Bray, Co. Wicklow, and Whitehaven in England.

19 *Pottery Gazette*, July 1897, p. 895. Frederick Vodrey was described as 'one of the principal buyers in the glass and china trade' in Dublin.

20 NMI records, NMI registration no. 1949.34. The 'large advertising teapot made by Bailey & Co., Scotland', was 'one of three held by Vodrey' and was 'presented by Miss Nellie Byrne whose father worked with Vodrey'.

21 Bergesen and Godden 1991, 250. The partnership existed from 1887 to 1891.

22 *The Postal Directory for the Potteries with Newcastle and District* (1888), 157: 'Sant Vodrey, earthenware manufacturers, Abbey Pottery, Cobridge'.

23 Death certificate for Frederick Vodrey, 19 October 1897, at 29 Lower Abbey Street. Registrar's District No. 2, North City. Frederick Vodrey was 52 years of age; the cause of death that was registered by his widow, Annie M. Vodrey, was 'Enteritis Astheria', a common illness in cities during the nineteenth century, owing to poor sanitation.

24 Registration of death for Agnes Vodrey, 24 January 1896, 'widow of pottery vane'. Registrar's District of North Dublin.

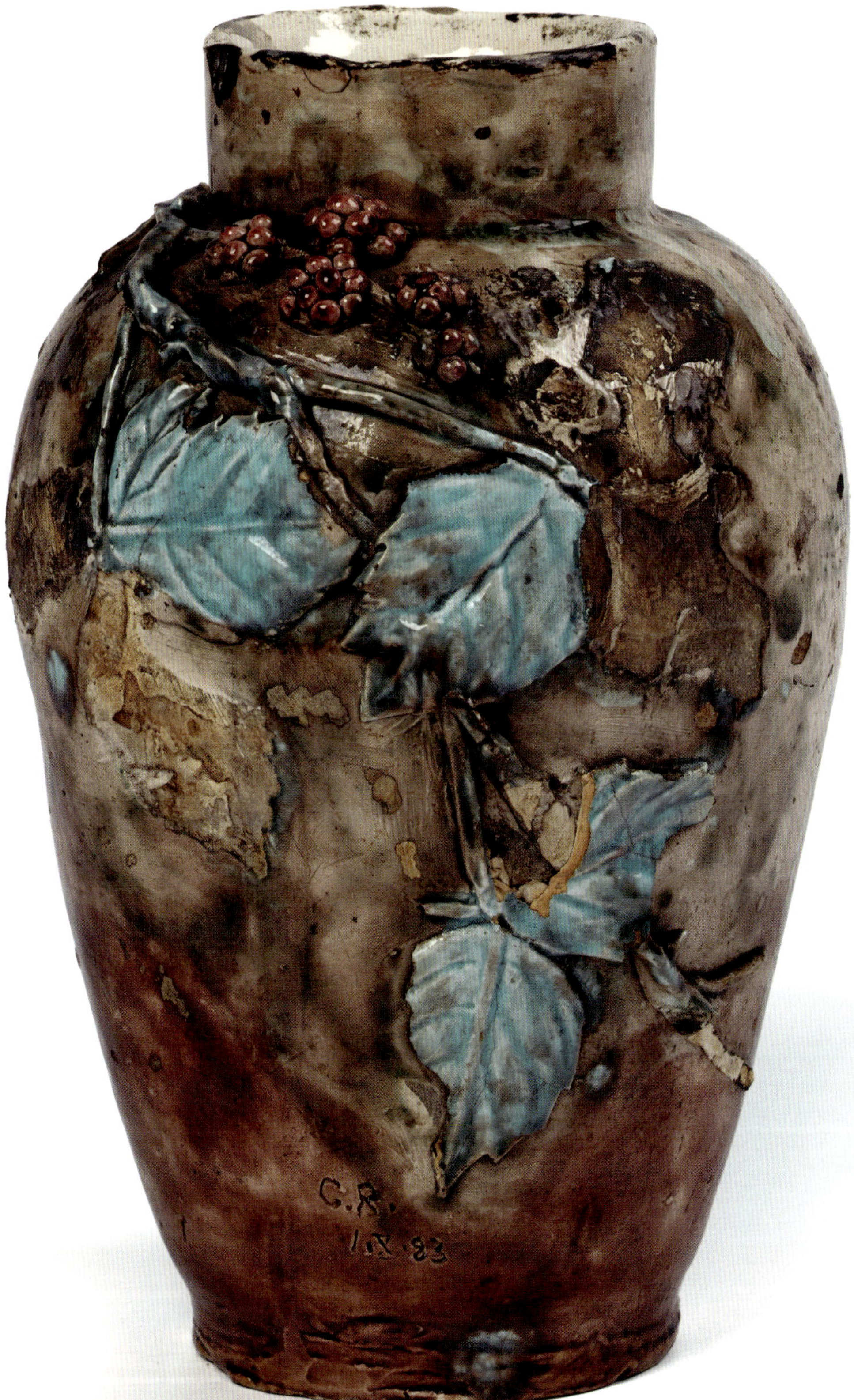
C.R.
1.X.83

CHAPTER 9

Dublin Sketching Club exhibits 'Artistic Pottery'

Dublin Sketching Club exhibits 'Artistic Pottery'

In *The Aesthetic Movement—prelude to Art Nouveau*, Elisabeth Aslin equates the use of the term 'artistic' with the popularisation of arts and crafts ideals, the demand for which was met by producers of art industries such as Frederick Vodrey's art pottery.[1] Vodrey's association with the Dublin Sketching Club is evidence that he and the DSC members were interested in the pursuit of the 'artistic' in ceramic production, becoming involved in a collaboration which was both creative and a response to the current trend for art manufactures (Fig. 25). During the 1880s some members of the DSC produced art pottery for a relatively short period,[2] advertising 'Artistic Irish Pottery' in the newspapers.[3]

Over a period of five years, from *c.* 1879 to 1886, the ceramics made or decorated by members of the DSC, both china plaques and hand-modelled earthenware art pottery, were exhibited and listed in the annual catalogue under various titles, including 'Porcelain', 'Pottery' and 'Artistic Pottery'.[4] Some of the group visited Vodrey's art pottery to learn and use the facilities; in spite of initial enthusiasm, however, numbers dropped off, possibly owing to the location of the workshop on the north side of the city.[5]

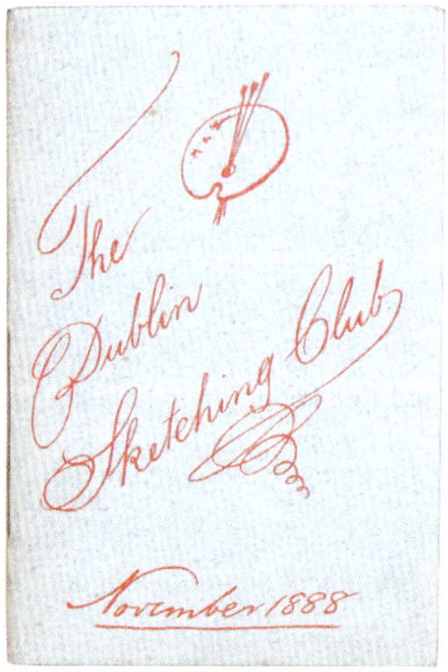

Fig. 25—Booklet cover for 'The Dublin Sketching Club November 1888'. Courtesy of the National Library of Ireland, MS Acc. 4786, Box 1.

1 Aslin 1981, 128.

2 *Catalogue of the Dublin Sketching Club 1880.* The exhibition, held in Leinster Hall, had a long list of pottery exhibits under the title 'Artistic Pottery', pp 18–21.

3 'Notices', *Freeman's Journal*, 5 December 1883, 1.

4 National Gallery of Ireland archives, facsimile copies of exhibition catalogues of the Dublin Sketching Club.

5 Minute Books of the Dublin Sketching Club, National Library of Ireland, MS Acc. 4786, Boxes 1–3. Minute Book 1881–5, 79, 94.

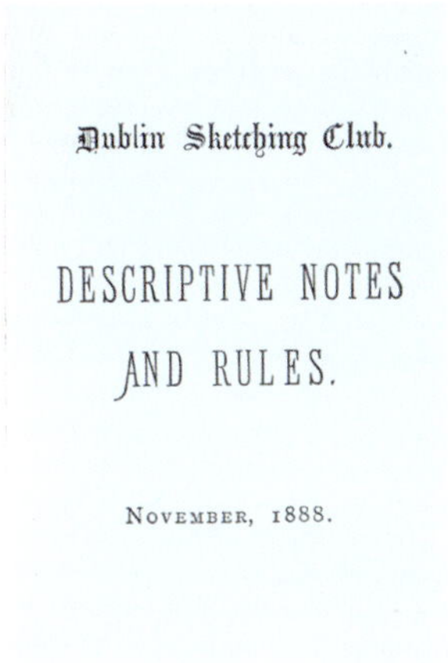

Fig. 26—From a booklet titled 'Dublin Sketching Club 1888'. Inside cover page, 'Descriptive notes and rules'. Courtesy of the National Library of Ireland, MS Acc. 4786, Box 1.

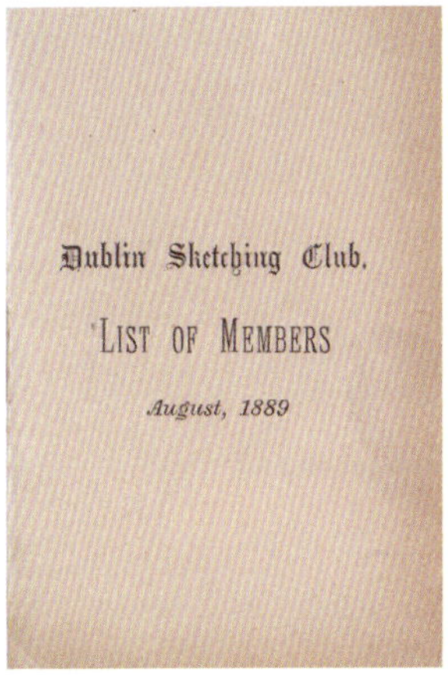

Fig. 27—Cover of booklet titled 'Dublin Sketching Club. List of Members August 1889'. Courtesy of the National Library of Ireland, MS Acc. 4786, Box 1.

The Dublin Sketching Club, founded on 20 October 1874,[6] held its first exhibition in 1876[7] and had annual exhibitions every December thereafter.[8] It is still active today and is known as the Dublin Sketching and Painting Club. The Minute Books from the 1880s and 1890s reveal an evolving organisation that developed into a social club, with a premises in No. 5 Leinster Street and a clearly defined set of rules (Figs 26 and 27).[9] The members of the DSC included both professional and amateur artists, featuring well-known names like John Butler Yeats, Walter Frederick Osborne and William Orpen.[10] The names of other prominent artists, such as Richard T. Moynan, J.M. Kavanagh, S. Catterson Smith and R.A. Hayes, all of whom played a role in Irish art during the nineteenth century, appear in the Minute Books.[11] When women became associate members in the late 1880s, their names were listed in the annual exhibition catalogues; by the 1920s they were almost equal in number to the men.

6 Dublin Sketching Club website, https://dublinpaintingandsketchingclub.ie. The Club was founded in the home of Dr Booth Pearsall HRHA, with Alfred Grey as its first president and Alexander Williams RHA as treasurer.

7 Armstrong-Duffy 1987, 13.

8 'The Dublin Sketching Club', *Freeman's Journal*, 26 December 1882. The annual exhibitions were first held at Cranfield's Gallery in Grafton Street. This venue was changed to Leinster Hall in Molesworth Street in 1884.

9 Minute Books of the Dublin Sketching Club, National Library of Ireland, MS Acc. 4786, Boxes 1–3. In the Minute Book 1885–91, 229–30, there is an announcement that 'the meeting of the Club has been held at the New Rooms 5 Leinster Street', and the schedule of opening times was given as follows: 'Working Members and Associates 9 am to 6 pm and on Wednesdays to 11 pm'. The Club was open 'to Lady members, Mondays 10 am to 4 pm'.

10 Dublin Sketching Club website, https://dublinpaintingandsketchingclub.ie.

11 Minute Books of the Dublin Sketching Club, National Library of Ireland, MS Acc. 4786, Boxes 1–3.

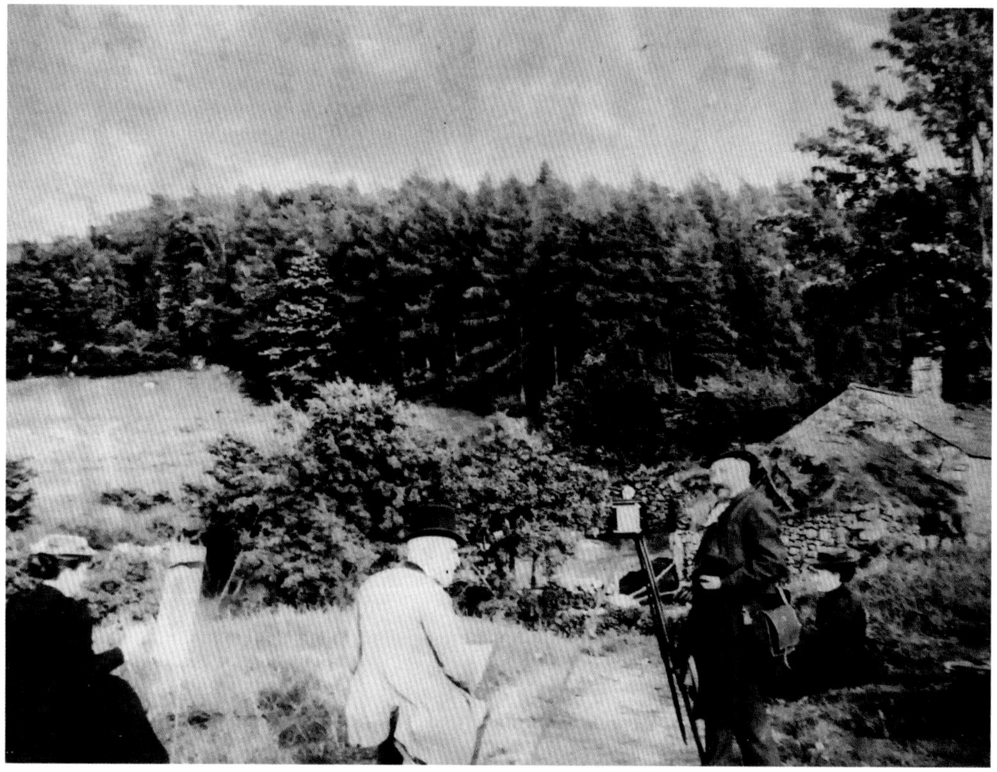

Fig. 28—Painting excursion to the Dublin Mountains. Members of the Dublin Sketching Club painting outdoors at Glen Duagh, Rockbrook, 1895. Courtesy of the National Library of Ireland.

The group was so successful that 'most of the active members of the RHA became members'.[12] Activities included weekly two-hour sketching sessions and 'fortnightly summer sketching expeditions'.[13] Some members experimented with early photography after the DSC amalgamated with the Dublin Amateur Photographic Club in 1883 (Fig. 28).[14]

In 1885 the Club became the focus of controversy when it invited artists from outside Ireland to exhibit and James MacNeill Whistler, an American artist living in London, showed paintings, including 'Portrait of my Mother'.[15] Whistler's work drew criticism, being considered 'modern'; a critique in the *Irish Times* referred to his new style of minimalist abstract paintings as 'mere daubs', indicating the conservative attitudes held by some in the Dublin art scene at the time.[16]

The DSC was preceded by several earlier sketching groups such as the Dublin Amateur and Artists' Society, founded by women, who were 'the instigators' of much of the sketching activity in nineteenth-

12 Armstrong-Duffy 1987, 13.

13 *Ibid.* There is a leaflet in the DSC Minute Book 1885–91, 54, 'Subjects for May 1887', announcing the 'First Excursion, 14th May 1887. Starting from 9 Merrion Row, at 11.15 a.m. by car to Glendouagh, via Rockbrook, returning by Glencullen and Stepaside. Luncheon at 3 p.m. in Glendouagh'. Other excursions that year included trips to the Dargle, Lucan Demesne, Killiney Hill and Howth Demesne.

14 Minute Book of the Dublin Sketching Club 1882–4, 40–1.

15 Dublin Sketching Club website, https://dublinpaintingandsketchingclub.ie.

16 *Ibid.*

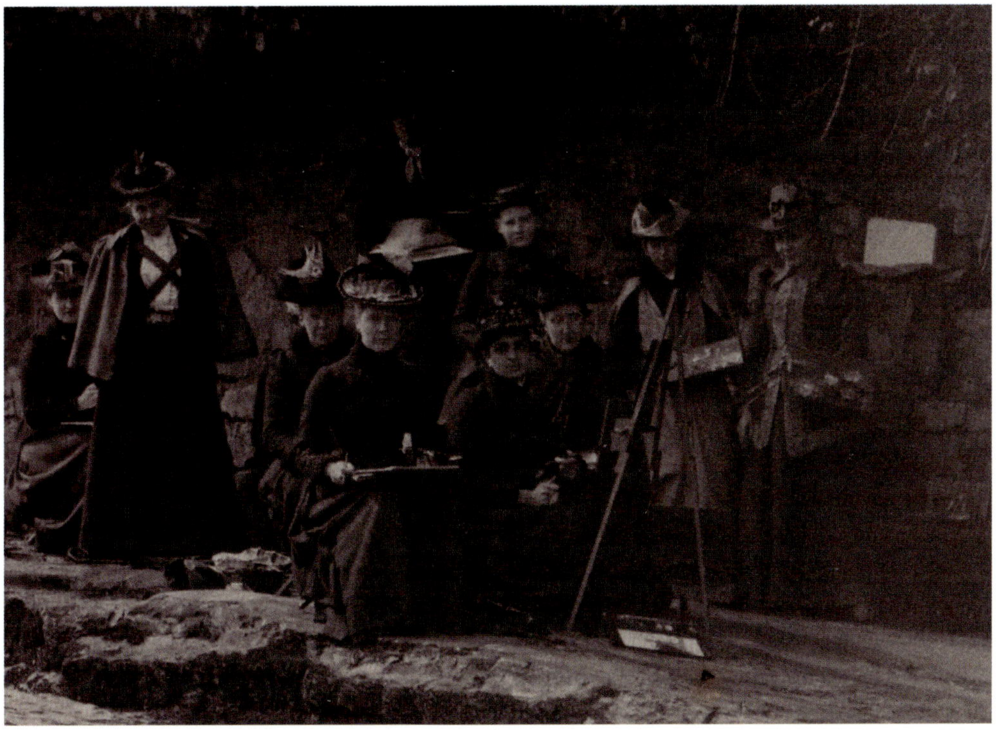

Fig. 29—Women sketching outdoors (detail), coastal location. From *Photographs of Irish scenery* by T.F. Geoghegan, c. 1890. Courtesy of the National Library of Ireland. The photograph portrays women's active interest in art education. The fashion for hats with birds, displayed here, was challenged by the campaigning of animal rights activists like Florence Bailey, a pioneering naturalist in the United States.

century Ireland; it amalgamated with the DSC in 1888 (Fig. 29).[17] Included in the minutes for the DSC is an advertisement for art classes 'for ladies' given by the artist Richard T. Moynan (1856–1906),[18] known for promoting the role of the artist in society.[19] According to Armstrong-Duffy's research, the women's sketching groups in Waterford, Dublin and Belfast were highly organised, ambitious and competitive. They held annual exhibitions with prizes, and invited members of the RHA to 'select and judge'.[20]

In contrast, accounts of the DSC's activities describe a group with the character of a gentlemen's club. Annual exhibitions were opened by the lord lieutenant and accompanied by musical entertainment. Women were involved from the start but only formally included as 'corresponding members' in 1885.[21] The DSC was based at various premises and was a social success for twenty years, although a split in 1888 led to the

17 Armstrong-Duffy 1987. The author writes that the Dublin Amateur and Artists' Society was founded by Miss Deane and run by Miss Benson from 1874. The first sketching club was the Irish Amateur Drawing Society, based in Lismore; it held annual exhibitions from 1877.

18 Minute Book of the Dublin Sketching Club 1892–5, 60.

19 *Dictionary of Irish Biography*, entry by Dr Maeve O'Regan. There are two paintings by Moynan in the National Gallery of Ireland that explore this theme: 'The Artist in his studio: we hope we don't intrude' (NGI 4488) and 'Taking Measurements: The Artist copying a Cast in the Hall of the National Gallery of Ireland' (NGI 4562).

20 Armstrong-Duffy 1987, 12.

21 *Ibid.*, 13.

formation of a splinter group called the Dublin Art Club, after which artists exhibited with both groups.[22]

The DSC was associated at different times with the porcelain-painter Herbert Cooper and the art pottery 'Designer and Manufacturer' Frederick Vodrey. Members attended classes with Cooper and the sculptor Henry Emery,[23] when 'modelling in clay was carried on in the Modelling room',[24] and they fired and glazed their pottery work with Vodrey.[25] The Minute Book for 1883 records that some members visited Vodrey's premises, where 'Mr Vodrey of Moore St. met the members in a most spirited manner offering a room for their use on his premises where the members or their friends might work or look on'. Subsequently 'some meetings took place and work commenced'; however, 'perhaps owing to the locality of the work room and the fact of its being on the north side of the city the attendance of members gradually dropped off and the enthusiastic Hon Treasurer was allowed to sip his cup of social beverage in solitude'.[26] Nevertheless, although interest in visiting Vodrey's workshop waned amongst members, it is evident that some, including Russell, continued and 'met at Mr Vodrey's Pottery at 7.30 pm for Work, Mrs Vodrey being present for a short time', and 'Good work was done by Mr Russell and Middleton and Mr Oldham encouraged them'.[27]

At first the ceramic exhibits shown at the annual DSC exhibitions consisted of porcelain or china plaques painted mainly by Herbert Cooper, who was on the committee,[28] and Alexander Williams (1846–1930),[29] who was the club's honorary secretary, a painter, and a member of the RHA. In 1881 Williams exhibited nine china plaques painted with original scenes,[30] and Thomas Longfield also exhibited hand-painted ceramics that year.[31]

---

22 Armstrong-Duffy 1987, 13. The DSC was based first at 212 Brunswick Street (now Pearse Street), then at the Institute of Porcelain and Painting, 27 Molesworth Street, for two years from 1883, and then at Leinster Street.

23 *Ibid.*, 13. The author refers to the minutes of the DSC's AGM in 1885: 'In 1883 the Club offered members classes in the Art of Modelling in Clay at the Institute of Porcelain and Painting in no. 27 Molesworth Street. Two years later, when they moved premises in Merrion Row, they introduced sessions with a "Draped Model". It was at this time that Corresponding Members "who may be LADY ARTISTS" were introduced.'

24 Minute Book of the Dublin Sketching Club 1883, 13. The minutes indicate that the 'Modelling room' was probably at 27 Molesworth Street.

25 Minute Book of the Dublin Sketching Club 1885, 94. There is a letter of agreement between Mr Vodrey and the Dublin Sketching Club dated 19 March 1885. The Club could use the facilities at the pottery workshop. Vodrey offered to sell the members clay at 3d. per lb. or the pot in the 'green' state at 6d. per lb. He also agreed to fire and glaze the pots made by the members. Firing would be priced by cubic space in the kiln. It cost over a shilling to 'fire, colour and glaze it in majolica colours'. Members were also invited by Vodrey to exhibit their work on his stand at the forthcoming Artisans' Exhibition. I am grateful to Dairine Coffey and the late Shirley Armstrong-Duffy who shared this information with me.

26 Minute Book of the Dublin Sketching Club 1885, 94.

27 *Ibid.*, 79.

28 *Catalogue of the Dublin Sketching Club, Seventh Season* (1879–80), 11. Herbert Cooper, listed as a committee member, exhibited seven sketches and studies. In a section entitled 'Pottery', prices for paintings on porcelain exhibited by him ranged from 5s. for a 'Vase with ivory ground and roses' to £1 15s. for a 'China Plaque with Black Ground and Sunflower'.

29 Snoddy 2002, 711–13. Alexander Williams RHA is described as a 'landscape and marine painter' who won an Art Union of Ireland prize three times; he was also a keen naturalist and wrote articles on the subject for the *Irish Naturalist* (1908–10). He was an active member of the RHA and the Dublin Sketching Club from the 1870s to the early twentieth century; he travelled extensively and exhibited in England, Canada, South Africa and Australia. In 'Fifty years of Irish painting', *Capuchin Annual* (1949), Thomas McGreevy (director of the National Gallery of Ireland) described him as 'popular' and as a painter of the *pittoresque* in nature with a 'genuine lyrical quality'.

30 *Catalogue of the Dublin Sketching Club, Eighth Season* (1881–2), 10, entries 142–50. These included a china plaque entitled 'Fresh Breeze' and another showing 'Waterfall, Owenriffe, Oughterard, and Galway'. In the following year, 1883, Williams again exhibited hand-painted ceramics.

31 *Ibid.*, 11. Longfield exhibited two China plaques, one with fruit and the other with a head of Raphael and border from an Italian design.

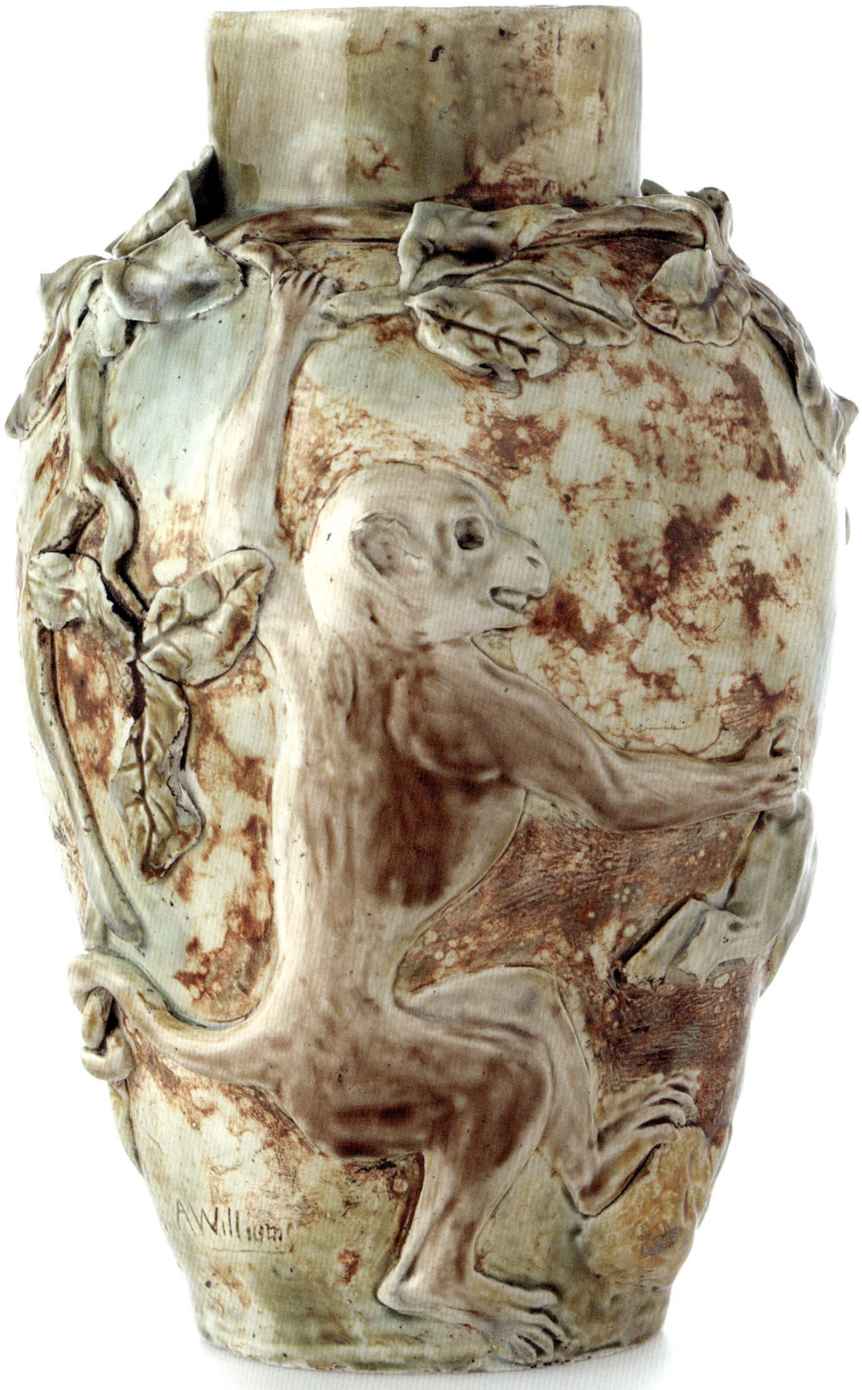

Fig. 30—Vase, 'Monkey and Rabbit', by Alexander Williams RHA. Signed 'A. Williams' on the side, 'DSC' underneath; c. 1883; 21cm x 13 cm. NMI 1913.13. Cat. no. 57.

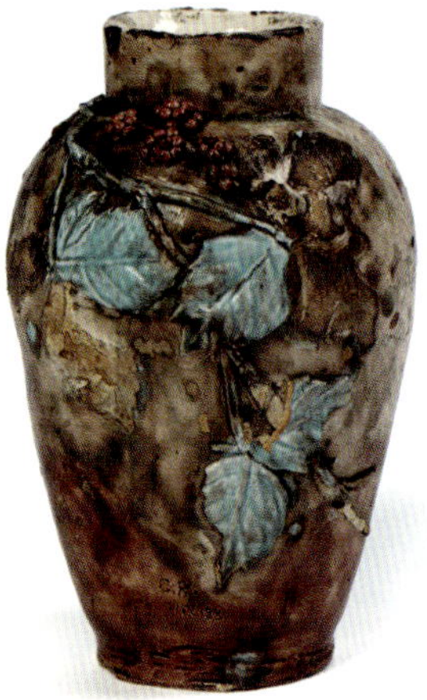

Fig. 31—'Blackberry vase' by Charles Russell. Inscribed 'DSC 1883' under base and 'C.R. IX 83' at the bottom, to the left of the bramble branch; 1883; 20cm × 13.5cm. NMI 1980.13. Cat. no. 51.

The exhibition of ceramics by the DSC shows the members' interest in craft and the elevation of ceramic work to an art form equal to painting. Evidently artists were using ceramics as a new medium for their painting and artistic expression, which probably attracted buyers to their work. In a section entitled 'Artistic Pottery' in the 1883 annual exhibition, the group exhibited an extensive list of earthenware as well as china plaques, including a vase by Williams[32] entitled 'Monkey and Rabbit' for 10s. 6d., which may be the vase in the National Museum collection signed 'A. Williams' (Fig. 30; cat. no. 57).

There is another vase in the Museum collection, of the same shape but with different decoration. This was made by Charles Russell, and the similarity in shape indicates that the two could have been made during workshops held by the DSC (Fig. 31; cat. no. 51). The 1883 exhibition was held at the Institute of Porcelain, 27 Molesworth Street, and the earthenware pieces, priced considerably lower than the china plaques, were produced during the classes in Cooper's studio.

Studies on class in Britain during the nineteenth century reveal that social activities amongst 'subcultures' (other than church-related activities) played a role in the development of the middle classes.[33] Despite the strong influence of religion on class identity in Irish society, the activity of the Dublin Sketching Club reveals a degree of pluralism amongst the upper and middle classes. The DSC was a meeting ground for people from diverse backgrounds, leading to the artistic association between Vodrey, an artisan from the Staffordshire Potteries, Russell, a Scottish portrait-painter with 'Jacobite sympathies married into an upper-class Catholic family',[34] and Thomas Longfield, the museum official from the Anglo-Irish ruling class. The Club held popular social events, providing a forum for artists and intellectuals during the 1880s, in line with ideals expressed by the nationalist writer Thomas Davis, who had called for the establishment of a National Gallery which could be a non-partisan and non-sectarian meeting ground in Irish society.[35]

The initiative for the Dublin Sketching Club's venture into art pottery came from one of its founders, Mr Booth Pearsall, an amateur member of the group, who held the inaugural meeting of the DSC at his home. A lecture given by Pearsall, entitled 'Sketching from nature', revealed the Club's intention to embrace current ideas from abroad and develop a freer approach to painting whereby the 'artist is an interpreter of nature'.[36] The group's excursions to sketch outdoors in the countryside indicate the influence of the *plein air* painting prevalent in Europe at the time, evident in Pearsall's detailed instructions on the way to observe light and shade and 'to always draw with loving care the shape and

32 *Catalogue of the Dublin Sketching Club* (1883–4), exhibit no. 436.

33 R.Q. Gray, in Grossick 1977, 147.

34 Conversation with Peter Healy (grandson), 18 December 2003. The family of Russell's wife were wigmakers on Sackville Street (O'Connell Street). According to Healy, whilst Charles Russell was 'apolitical' and not very sympathetic to the nationalist cause, he was married into 'die-hard Fenians', although 'his mother-in-law was more "county" from Malahide'.

35 Thomas Davis, 'National Art', in Rolleston 1889, 151–2.

36 Pearsall 1886.

character of the cast shadows'.[37] There was an emphasis on spontaneity when sketching 'rapidly moving skies, and sea waves', so that 'for open air sketching you must cultivate swiftness of eye, hand and brain'.[38]

The catalogue of the 1883 annual exhibition announced that the show included 'A Collection of Art Pottery made, fired, and decorated by members of the Club, and on the Club premises, Mr H. Cooper's studio, 27 Molesworth Street'.[39] The announcement reveals enthusiasm for the 'artistic' and a strong awareness of Arts and Crafts ideals:

> '... the members have succeeded in perfecting several specimens of this delightful Art and proved the possibility of producing really fine work of this kind in Dublin. Working only one evening in the week, the members produced results which should encourage practical men; and if such can be obtained by Artists, Amateurs, and Gentlemen during a social evening of a few hours' duration, what work could not be produced by a constant application to this beautiful and useful branch of Art Industry ...'[40]

The group's interest in participating in 'Art Industry', china-painting and the making of pottery could have come from a mix of artistic and fiscal motives. On the one hand, artists such as Russell and Williams probably regarded ceramics as an opportunity for extra income; on the other hand, the above statement shows an awareness of craft skills as an integral part of the artistic process. In a previous DSC exhibition another member, Thomas Longfield, curator of ceramics at the National Museum, exhibited a sketch entitled 'Ceramic Study in the Japanese Style, old Japanese and Dresden',[41] which is evidence of the Museum curator's involvement in the artistic circle and the position of ceramics in the group's artistic endeavours.

In 1885, when Booth Pearsall was president of the Club and Charles Russell[42] was vice-president, Russell exhibited 22 items of hand-painted pottery. These were jardinières in Celtic and Moorish styles and 'Ginger jars, Blue and White, Keltic, Under Glazed' for 'seven shillings and sixpence', prices for this art pottery ranging from 5s. to £1.[43] At the same time Frederick Vodrey, who was firing Russell's hand-painted ceramics, collaborated with Russell in designing and producing ceramics moulded with Celtic patterns and stamped with the impressed mark of the Vodrey Dublin Pottery. Whilst Russell worked mostly as a portrait-painter, he also painted landscapes and religious murals.[44] ■

---

37 *Ibid.*

38 *Ibid.*

39 *Dublin Sketching Club Catalogue, Tenth Season* (1883–4), 3.

40 *Ibid.*

41 Stewart 1997, 425. T.H. Longfield is listed as exhibiting this painting with the DSC in 1880, exhibit number 131.

42 Snoddy 2002, 575–6. Charles Russell (1852–1910), originally from Scotland, came to Dublin in 1874 and was employed by the photographer Chancellor at 55 Lower Sackville Street (O'Connell Street), painting portraits from photographs. He also painted and exhibited landscapes. He was elected an associate of the RHA in 1891 and a member in 1893.

43 *Catalogue of the Dublin Sketching Club, Twelfth Season* (1885–6), 21–2. 'Pottery by Charles Russell', no. 356–78. Other exhibitors of ceramics were E. Eagle, E. Oldham, and T.B. Middleton.

44 Conversation with Peter Healy (grandson), 18 December 2003. The Baxter family in Scotland has a collection of Russell's paintings. An example of Russell's religious murals can be seen at St Michael's Church in Enniskillen, and his 'The Life of Saint Ignatius' at St Francis Xavier's Church in Gardiner Street, Dublin. Russell also painted the portrait of a singer from Liverpool, Zella de Luce, who played the title role in *Carmen*, possibly the first time it was produced in Dublin.

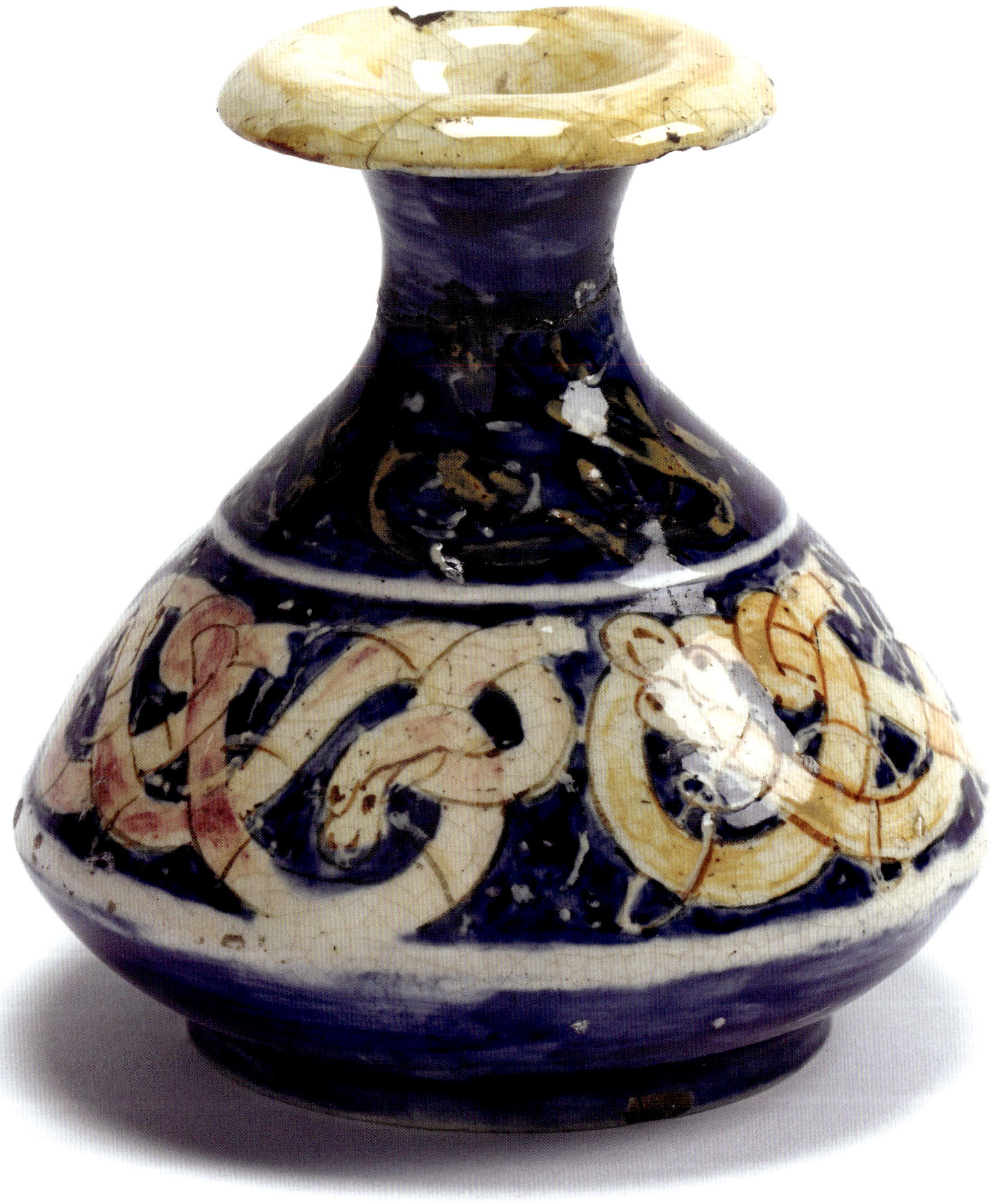

CHAPTER 10

Charles Russell's sketch-book as evidence of collaboration

Charles Russell's sketch-book as evidence of collaboration

Charles Russell's sketch-book reveals valuable information about the design process which created the Celtic designs for the Vodrey Dublin Pottery.[1] It includes sketches of zoomorphic creatures from the Book of Kells, notes indicating collaboration between Vodrey and Russell, and evidence that they discussed Ogden Rood's colour theory, known to designers at the time (Fig. 32).

This is also indicated by the use of primary colours on two vases hand-painted by Russell with the impressed mark of the Vodrey Dublin Pottery. These two vases were presented to the National Museum by his descendants. One bears the words *Blian sona nua agat* ('Happy New Year') in old Irish script, which suggests that it was made to be sold at the annual exhibition held by the Dublin Sketching Club just before Christmas (Fig. 33; cat. no. 53). The Gaelic words on this piece of art pottery produced by Vodrey are a strong statement of national identity and 'ethnic nationalism' and show how the Irish-language revival and the establishment of the Gaelic League (1893) influenced Irish material culture.[2]

The sketch-book contains evidence of discussion and collaboration between Russell, Vodrey and possibly others involved in the design process. The portrait of an unidentified man (Fig. 34) suggests that a third person was involved in discussions. According to ceramic design historian Gordon Elliott, owing to the nature of the ceramic design process the development of ideas was frequently

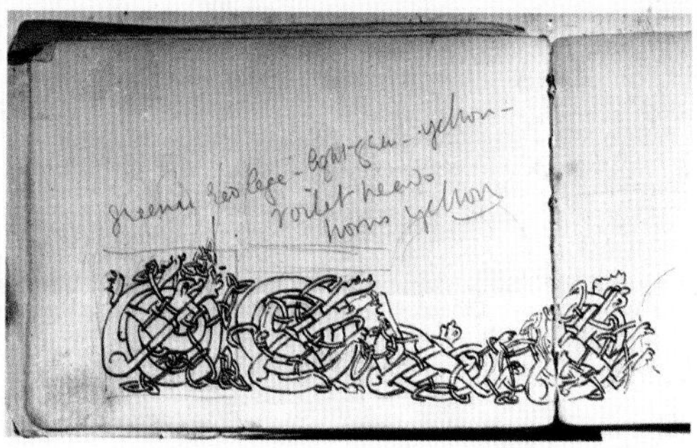

Fig. 32—Drawing of Celtic interlace pattern from Charles Russell's sketch-book, facsimile copy. NMI AI/154/003.

1 Charles Russell's sketch-book, facsimile copy. NMI reg. no. AI/154/003.

2 Moody and Martin 2001, 246–8. The Gaelic League was by Douglas Hyde (later first president of Ireland) and Eoin Mac Neill. Charles Russell's son, Seán Russell, was a member of the organisation (Peter Healy, pers. comm., 18 December 2003).

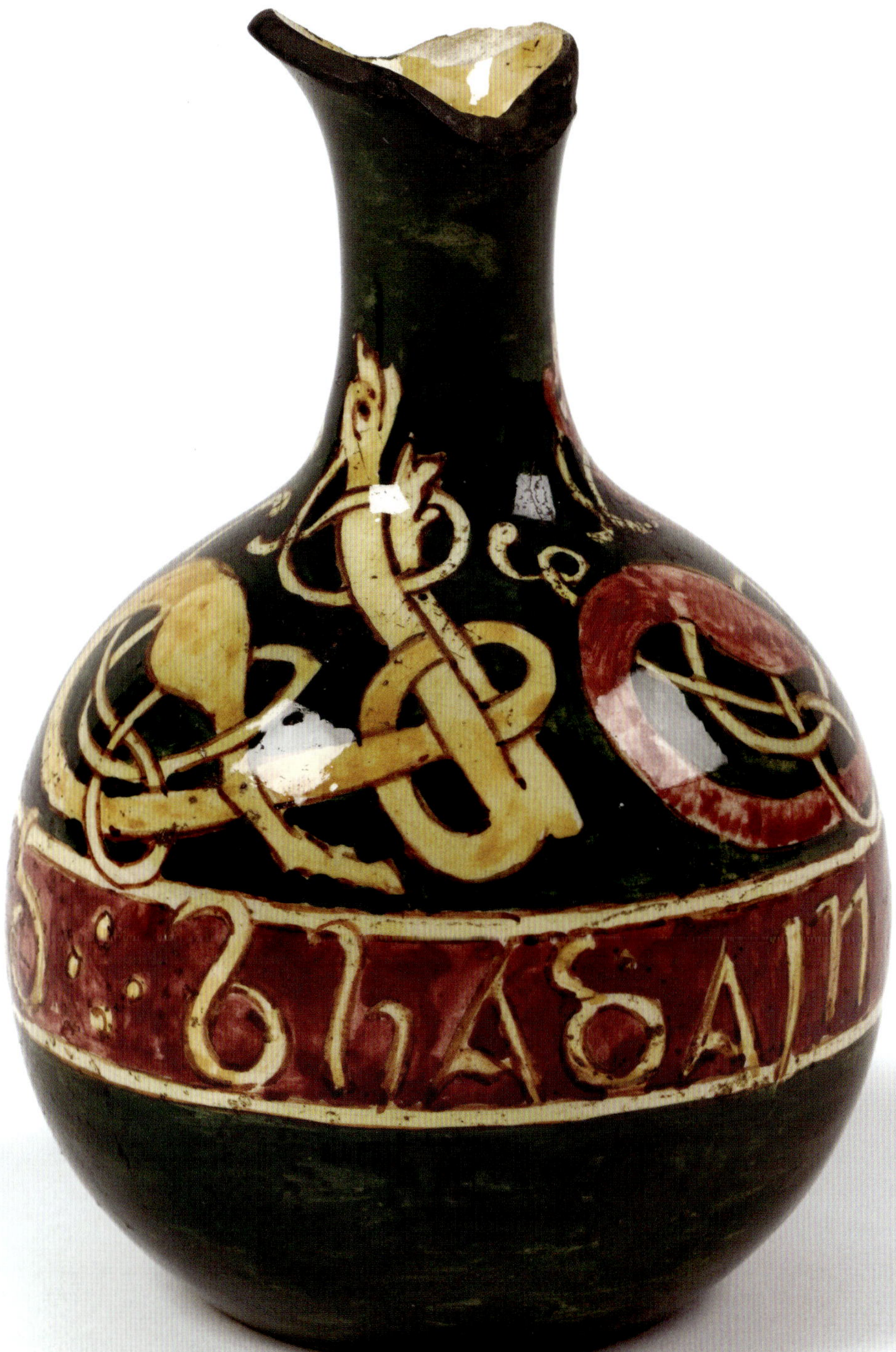

Fig. 33—Vase; Celtic interlace and zoomorphic designs hand-painted in green, yellow and burgundy, and the words 'Bliain sona nua agat'. 'C. Russell pinxii 6.11.85' inscribed underneath; 13cm x 8cm. NMI 1980.15. Cat. no. 53.

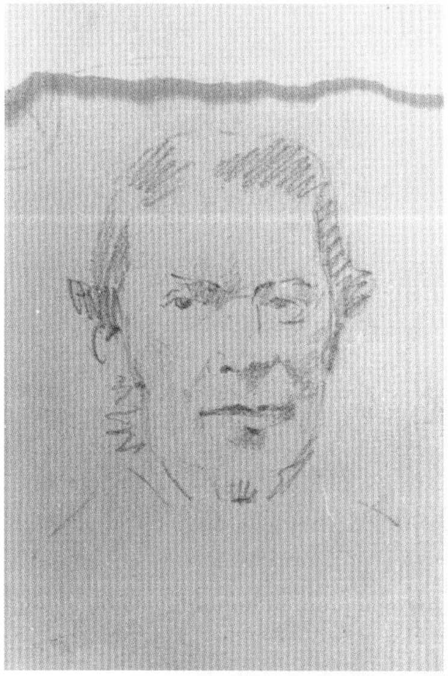

Fig. 34—Drawing/portrait of an unidentified man from Charles Russell's sketch-book. NMI AI/154/003.

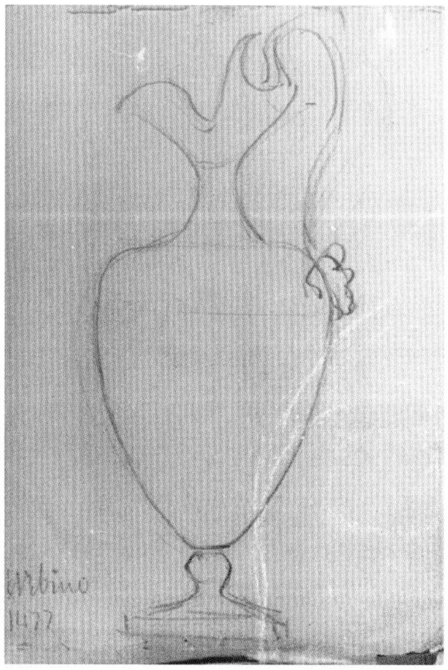

Fig. 35—Drawing of a Classical ewer from Charles Russell's sketch-book. NMI AI/154/003.

practice-based and involved several people.[3] Given that the large Celtic jardinières were moulded, there were others at the Vodrey Dublin Pottery besides Frederick Vodrey and Russell who were involved in design and production. These were Patrick Slevin, 'Presser and Mould-maker', and Thomas Vodrey, 'Pressing and Casting', who were listed in the catalogue of the Irish Artisans' Exhibition (1885).[4]

The drawing of a Classical-style ewer in Russell's sketch-book (Fig. 35), one of the many ornamental designs produced by the pottery, indicates that this may have been a form considered for use in the production of Celtic designs, although there are no known examples of this shape with Celtic decoration. The similarity between this drawing by Russell and the ewer produced by the Vodrey Dublin Pottery (Fig. 47; cat. no. 31) confirms the association between Vodrey and Russell and gives a glimpse of their collaboration.

Vodrey and Russell's interest in copying the designs from the Book of Kells was prompted by the attention given to Irish antiquities. Celtic-style brooches had been produced by the jewellers Waterhouse and Co. since the 1850s, and the Waterhouse brochure drew connections between the designs on the Tara Brooch and those in the Book of Kells. The manuscript in Trinity College Library had aroused public interest during the visit of Queen Victoria and Prince Albert to Dublin in 1849.[5] The association of Queen Victoria with the Book of Kells and the fact that Owen Jones had included the Celtic style in *The grammar of ornament* as one from the British Isles reveal a different context for the revival of Celtic

3 Elliott 2000, 12.

4 *Irish Artisans' Exhibition Complete Official Catalogue*, 29.

5 George Petrie in *Saunders's News-Letter*, 9 December 1850. From Waterhouse and Co., *Ornamental Irish antiquities* (Dublin, 1853), 13.

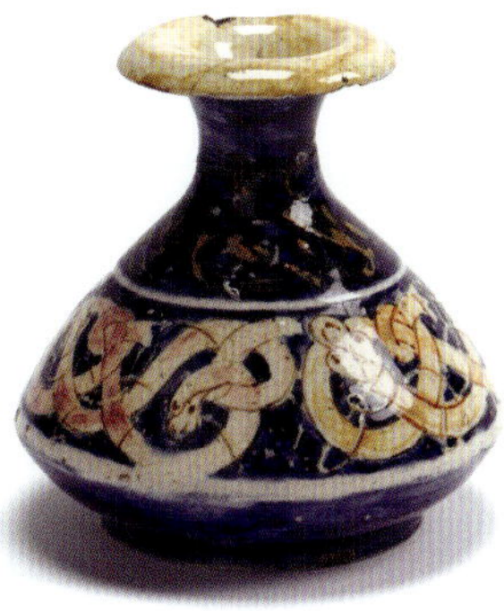

Fig. 36—Vase decorated with hand-painted Celtic interlace and zoomorphic designs, yellow on a blue ground; 8cm × 8cm. 'C Russell 31.10.85' inscribed underneath. NMI 1980.6. Cat. no. 50.

ornament in Dublin other than associations with Irish national identity.[6] It was acknowledged by Petrie that the Tara Brooch probably originated in Scotland, confirming that there was a perception in the nineteenth century of Celtic style as an aspect of British and imperial identity.

The second vase hand-painted by Charles Russell was also influenced by his drawings of zoomorphic and spiral forms in the Book of Kells and evident in his sketch-book (Figs 36 and 37).

Whilst both Russell and Vodrey were probably aware of Owen Jones's *Grammar of ornament*, there is little evidence that it had a direct influence on the designs for the pottery. Russell's notes refer instead to Ogden Rood's colour theory (1848) rather than those of Chevreul or Field quoted by Owen Jones, although interest in the physiological effects of colours was common to all of these theorists. The design of the Celtic-style objects produced by Vodrey was influenced by a blend of sources, including images from the Book of Kells in Trinity College Library and the colour theories of Ogden Rood. ■

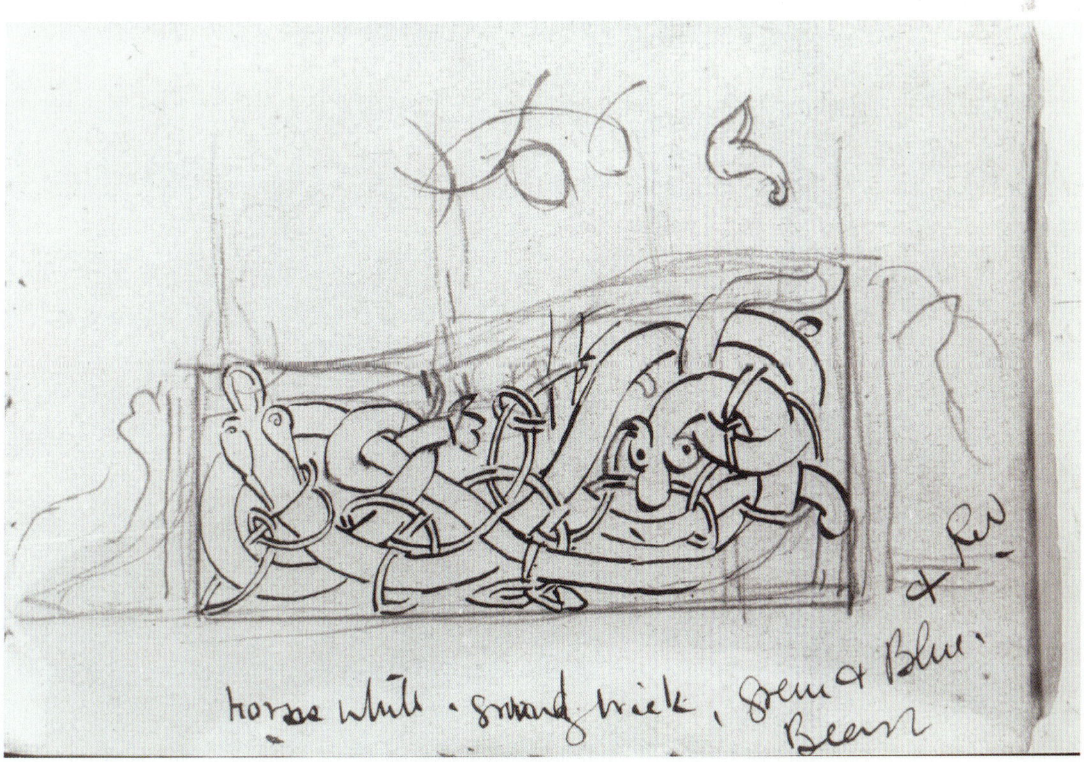

Fig. 37—Drawing of Celtic interlace pattern from Charles Russell's sketch-book. NMI AI/154/003.

6 Jones 1856.

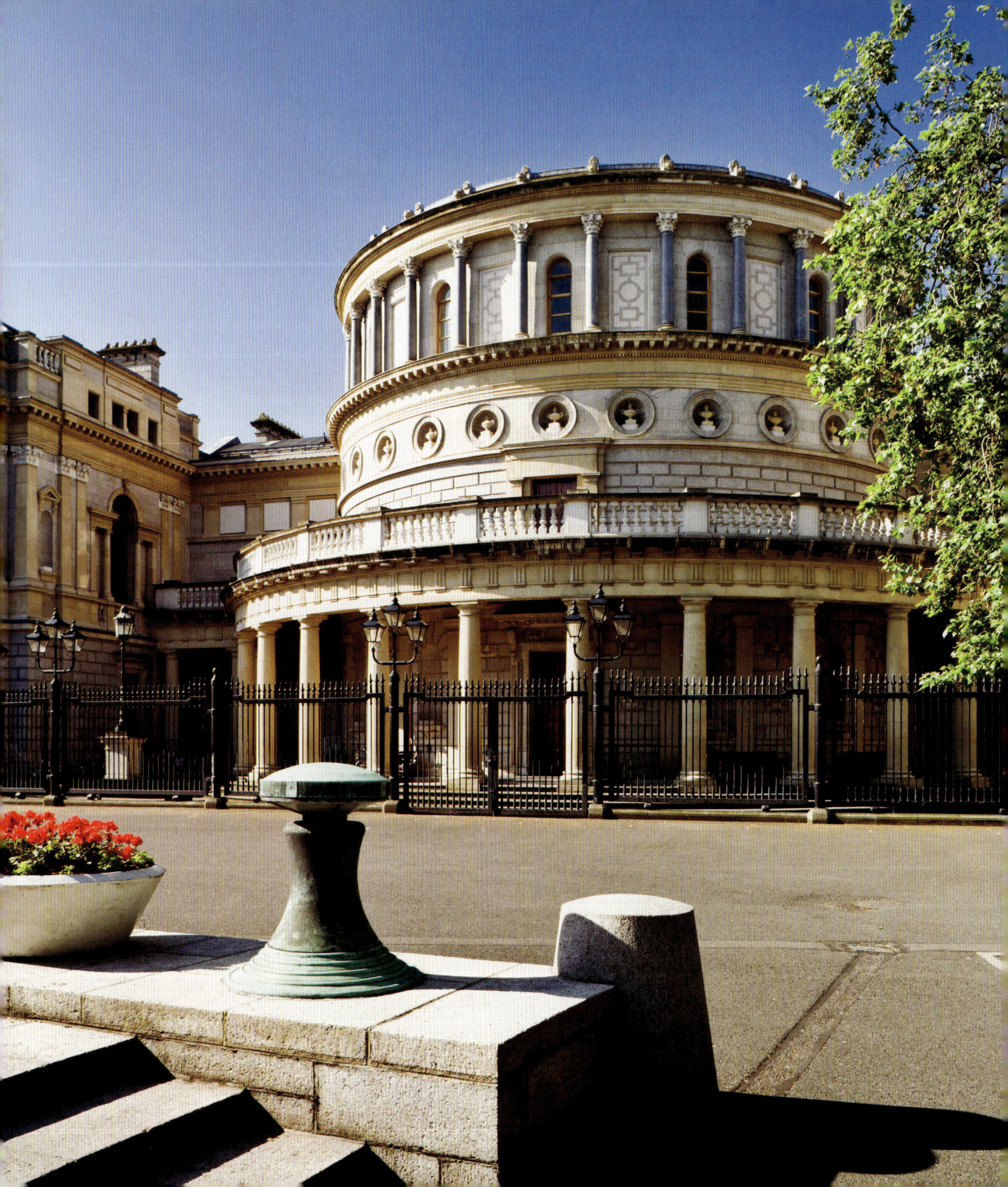

CHAPTER 11

The National Museum and education for design

Fig. 38. Exterior of National Museum of Ireland, Kildare St, Dublin. Courtesy of the National Museum of Ireland.

The National Museum and education for design

The ceramic collection at the National Museum of Ireland was begun in the 1850s by Sir Robert Kane, Director of the Museum of Industry in Dublin (this institution pre-dated the National Museum of Science and Art established in 1877).[1] In the 1870s the ceramic collection begun by Kane was further developed by Thomas Longfield, Assistant Keeper of Art and Industry from 1879, and then Keeper from 1890 until his retirement in 1906.[2] Longfield was an architect with a knowledge of the language of style.[3] His article 'On ornamental design', published in two parts in the *Irish Builder*, gives us insight into the meaning and language of styles fundamental to the design process in the nineteenth century.[4] The continuing development of the ceramic collection for educational purposes and the promotion of design for industry was the policy of the Department of Science and Art in London, of which the Dublin Museum was a branch.

George Coffey, an antiquarian scholar, was the other key writer on ornament in Ireland.[5] McBrinn has noted that Irish antiquarians recognised the common 'universal principles' in all forms of design, from architecture to objects.[6] As Keeper of Antiquities at the National Museum, Coffey wrote the *Guide to the Celtic antiquities of the Christian period*.[7] His antiquarian scholarship extended to an interest in arts and crafts and the

---

1 White 1911, 30.

2 *Ibid*., 31.

3 Association of Architects of Ireland (AAI) archives. Thomas Henry Longfield was one of the founder members of the AAI in 1872. He was secretary in 1873–4, treasurer in 1875 and vice-president in 1876–7. He was also an elected associate of the RIAI from 1874 and a member by 1896. According to the archives, however, 'There is no record of any building having been erected to his designs, and his exhibited and published drawings suggest that his real interest always lay in the decorative arts. He gave up architecture as a profession after being appointed Art and Industry Assistant at the Science and Art Museum on 25 August 1879.'

4 *Ibid*. T.H. Longfield read two papers 'On ornamental design' to the association: on 22 January 1874, published in the *Irish Builder*, 1 February 1874, 44–6, and on 25 February 1875, published in *The Builder*, 13 March 1875, 237–9.

5 A commemorative plaque in the National Museum of Ireland (Kildare Street) states that 'George Coffey (1857–1916) was Keeper of Antiquities at the National Museum (1897–1914)'.

6 McBrinn 2009, 213.

7 Coffey 1909.

education of artisans; he was on the committee of the Arts and Crafts Society of Ireland[8] and a member of the Council of the City of Dublin Technical Schools.[9]

Longfield ended the first of his two lectures with praise for Owen Jones and the Moorish style, which he promised to discuss further in his next lecture: 'The beautiful geometric forms of the Moresque wall decoration and system of pendentive arching cannot fail to delight anyone who has had the pleasure of seeing Mr Owen Jones' beautiful decoration of the Alhambra Court in the Crystal Palace'.[10] These remarks indicate that Longfield, like Vodrey, was engaged with the current design taste and ideas represented by Owen Jones's influential book *The grammar of ornament*.[11] He also discussed and illustrated the styles of ancient Egyptian and Greek art and architecture.[12]

Longfield's second lecture on the subject revealed a close understanding of the use of ornament and the creative process in design. He stressed that the purpose of the study of ornament is not to 'copy' but to 'engraft our originality of conception'.[13] By this he indicated that design ought to be based on the assimilation and interpretation of existing forms rather than imitation. According to Longfield, ornament from different historical periods could inform the creative process in design. His views reflected the current ideas on design methods in London, and echoed writers on design education whose teachings formed the education of design students in the nineteenth century.

When Longfield began his role as Assistant Keeper of Art and Industry in 1878, the Museum was still in temporary accommodation; in 1884, in his Director's report, Professor Ball praised his work in setting up the displays of the temporary 'Art Museum'.[14] Photographs of the ceramic display were accompanied by Longfield's portrait in a later *Museum Bulletin*.[15] In his dual role as writer on ornament and Keeper at the Museum, Longfield became a catalyst for the interaction of design theory and ceramic production. He was instrumental in creating an environment conducive to Vodrey's production of art pottery in a variety of styles. As a collector of ceramics, he had a special interest in the ceramic collection and later bequeathed his own private collection to the Museum.[16]

During Longfield's time as Keeper, the ceramic collection at the National Museum included 'English,

---

8 Larmour 1992, 7–8.

9 George Coffey, 'The proposed Technical Instruction Bill, and the Science and Art Department', in *Report of the Royal Commission on Technical Instruction* (1889), 403–29. Coffey expressed strong and sometimes critical views on the Department of Science and Art's provision of education for artisans. He considered that the decentralised system in European countries such as Germany was preferable to the centralised system which operated from the Department of Science and Art in London.

10 Longfield 1874.

11 Jones 1856. Owen Jones was known for his design of the colour scheme in the Crystal Palace. He was the author of two influential books with chromolithographic illustrations: *Plans, details, and sections of the Alhambra* (London, 1842–5) *with French* architect Jules Goury *and Grammar of ornament* (London, 1856).

12 Longfield 1874, 44.

13 Longfield 1875.

14 *Department of Science and Art (31st Report)* (1884), 309–11. Report of Director (Dublin), Appendix H. Professor Ball, the Director of the Dublin Museum, referred to the 'temporary Art Museum' adjoining the Shelbourne Hotel. He praised Longfield's 'skill and good taste' in setting up the exhibits.

15 *Museum Bulletin: National Museum of Science and Art, Dublin* (1912): pl. vii, photo of Thomas H. Longfield; pl. xi, ceramic display (1883).

16 The National Museum of Ireland Archive: Box 218, 1908. Papers of the loan and purchase of T.H. Longfield's collection of porcelain. The Museum noted that: 'The collection is a particularly valuable one having been formed by Mr Longfield and his father both of whom were connoisseurs and collectors'. The collection was valued at £1,014 by a Mr Caddie, who was described as 'an expert especially on English pottery and porcelain'.

Continental, Oriental pottery, and porcelain' and a new acquisition of German stoneware.[17] Donations of Staffordshire ceramics were received from Booth Pearsall, a prominent member of the Dublin Sketching Club, and Frederick Vodrey. Vodrey's first donations to the Museum collection, in 1884, included items made in English factories as well as some pieces of his own pottery made in Dublin,[18] indicating that he was already keen to contribute to the teaching and instruction value of the collection. As a retailer of ceramic wares produced in the Stoke-on-Trent industry, he was able to donate objects that could demonstrate different techniques and methods of production.

In 1886, following the success of the Vodrey Dublin Pottery at the Art and Industry exhibitions, the Museum acquired more art pottery from Frederick Vodrey.[19] Longfield's annual report noted that Vodrey had donated '47 specimens of glazed pottery'.[20] This second donation was a group of art ceramics with the Vodrey Dublin Pottery mark. Thus Vodrey had moved from being a retailer of imported ceramic wares to being a producer of ceramics made with Irish clays. Although the Museum was in temporary accommodation waiting for the building of a new Museum of Science and Art, there was a concerted effort on Longfield's part to develop the ceramic collection, which included examples of the developing ceramic industry in Ireland.

When the Department of Science and Art took over the running of the Museum in the 1870s, the contents of the Museum of Industry and the antiquities collection of the Royal Irish Academy were eventually transferred to a new, purpose-built building, the National Museum in Kildare Street. Longfield was the 'first who held the appointment of Keeper to the art collection when it was transferred from the Royal Dublin Society'.[21] According to his obituary in the *Irish Times*, Longfield oversaw 'the entire arrangement of the art exhibition in the new building in Kildare Street', and his 'energy and enthusiasm' were responsible for many 'valuable acquisitions'.[22]

Scholarship has shown that there was much resistance to the establishment of the new Museum, particularly from the Royal Dublin Society (RDS), which regarded itself as already carrying out similar functions of education and development in science and the arts, including lectures and competitions.[23] In 1868 a commission was set up to report on the establishment of a branch of the Department of Science and Art in Dublin. Following negotiations with the Royal Dublin Society and the introduction of the Museums Act (1877), the registrar of the RDS became Director of the new branch of the Department of Science and Art in Dublin.[24]

17 *Department of Science and Art (31st. Report)* (1883). Longfield's Report, Appendix C, 316–17.

18 *Department of Science and Art (32nd Report)* (1884). Report of the Director of the Science and Art Museum, Dublin. Appendix II, 'appendix B to Professor Ball's Report', 284. Vodrey's donation was listed as follows: 'Mug, early, printed Worcester; Mug, Herculaneum pottery, Liverpool; Mug, Staffordshire'.

19 Register of Objects, National Museum of Ireland (1886:19): 'Forty-seven specimens of glazed pottery. Modern Irish (Vodrey Dublin).' These were presented by 'F. Vodrey Esq. on 29th March 1886'. Vodrey also presented the trade card which he displayed at the Artisans' Exhibition in 1885.

20 *Department of Science and Art (34th Report)* (1887), 309.

21 *Irish Times*, 18 July 1906.

22 *Ibid.*

23 Turpin 1983, 42.

24 White 1911, 30. William Edward Steele was Director of the Museum from 1877 to 1883. The first board meeting of the Science and Art Museum and Botanic Gardens was held on 4 March 1881.

There was a delay between the first plan for the Museum under the Department of Science and Art and the laying of the foundation stone for the new building in Kildare Street in 1885,[25] and the new Museum was officially opened in 1890. The opening ceremony was a colourful event presided over by the prince of Wales, with a fanfare of trumpets and attended by members of the Royal Dublin Society and the Royal Irish Academy. The lord lieutenant's speech indicated that 'the museum's purpose during the early Celtic Revival of the 1890s was industrial education for Irish students (modelled on the South Kensington Museum)'.[26] The establishment of this new Museum of Science and Art gave students and the general public access to the collections for the purposes of enjoyment and study.[27]

The ceramics acquired by the National Museum from the Vodrey Dublin Pottery in the 1880s demonstrate the vocabulary of designers in the nineteenth century and suggest an exchange of ideas between Frederick Vodrey and curators at the National Museum. The writings of Thomas Longfield and George Coffey represent the intellectual and artistic environment within which Vodrey's art pottery designs were produced, revealing a convergence of Irish antiquarianism and design theory during the 1880s and 1890s.[28] Both curators were active in Dublin's artistic community, Longfield as a member of the Dublin Sketching Club who entered exhibits in the annual exhibitions, and George Coffey in his provision of a lecture on Celtic ornament to the Club. The influence of ideas from these two men is an important context for Vodrey's designs and the development of the Museum's ceramic collection. ■

25 Museum of Science and Art, Dublin: 'Ceremonial at the Laying of the First Stone of the Museum of Science and Art, and of the National Library, Ireland. Pamphlet of directions for the ceremonial proceedings to be held on Friday, 10th April 1885' (NLI, ILB D4 P1).

26 Bourke 2011, 195.

27 *Ibid.*, 180.

28 Molloy 2020.

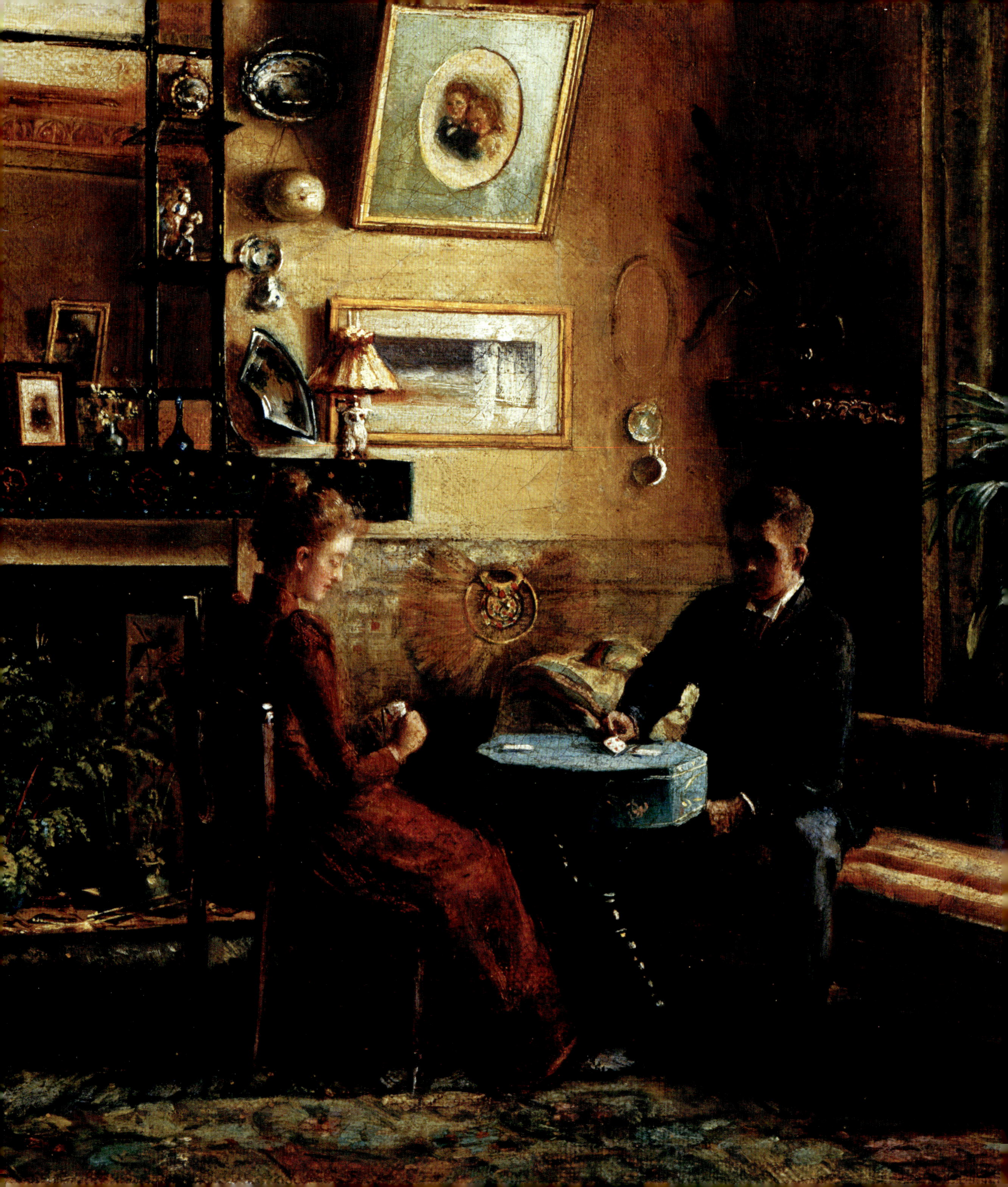

CHAPTER 12

Art decoration in the Aesthetic interior

Art decoration in the Aesthetic interior

The art ceramics in the National Museum open a window onto a long-since-disappeared world of design and taste in Dublin, inspired by the values of the Arts and Crafts reformers and developed by a second generation, followers of the Aesthetic taste made popular by the most famous 'Aesthete', the playwright Oscar Wilde.[1] The varied styles and bright glazes of these objects by the Vodrey Dublin Pottery and the Queen's Institute exemplify the Aesthetic taste, of which there had been little previous evidence in Dublin[2] other than the exhibition by the artist John McNeill Whistler of 25 paintings at the Dublin Sketching Club in 1885.[3]

The Aesthetic taste is best understood within the context of the Queen Anne movement in architecture, also known as the 'Domestic Revival'.[4] The latter combined the earlier nineteenth-century interest in Gothic Revival with a renewed interest in Classical English architecture from the eighteenth century.[5] It was characterised by details of classical design and red brick.[6] There was a rejection of the 'puritan values of older Victorian parents', support for equal rights for women and workers, and improvement of working and living conditions for the poorer classes.[7]

In terms of art and design, the 'Aesthete' promoted the 'cultivation of artistic sensibilities and a beautiful environment'.[8] A well-known example of the new style of architecture was a development

---

1 Naylor 1971, 115. The author noted that the popularity of the Aesthetic taste spread through Oscar Wilde's 1882 lecture tour of the United States.

2 S. Solicari, in Calloway and Federle Orr 2011, 148–51.

3 Dublin Sketching Club website, https://dublinpaintingandsketchingclub.ie. The paintings caused great controversy and were criticised in the *Irish Times*.

4 Pevsner 2008 [1936], 59–62.

5 Girouard 1977, 19.

6 Pevsner 2008 [1936], 58–9.

7 Girouard 1977, 4–5.

8 *Ibid*.

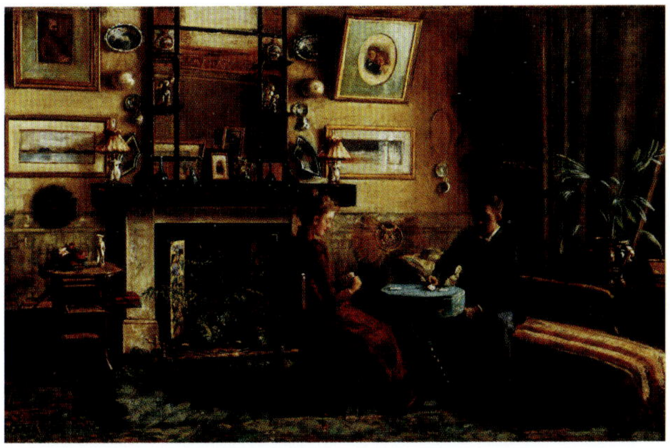

Fig. 39—'A Game of Cards' by Nancy A. Sabine Pasley, oil on canvas, *c.* 1890; Museum of the Home (formerly the Geffrye Museum), London, 81/1996. The use of furniture for display of ceramic ornaments or bric-à-brac was a feature of the nineteenth-century home interior; the display of art pottery can be seen on the overmantel.

in West London called Bedford Park, the first 'garden suburb', described as 'an aesthetic Eden'.[9] The architect for the initial phase was Edward W. Godwin, whose work in both architecture and furniture became the best-known statements of the Aesthetic style.[10] In Ireland it was a model for other suburban architecture and design.[11]

The use of furniture for display[12] shown in paintings such as 'A Game of Cards' by the English artist Sabine Pasley (Fig. 39) is confirmed by a popular writer on interior decoration, Mrs Haweis, in her book *Beautiful houses* (1882): 'The mantelpiece, very prettily designed to enclose in its crannies innumerable cups and vases, is painted in two yellows, like the primrose'.[13] Advice on interior decoration in the later nineteenth century emphasised the use of lighter, softer colours such as yellow and green. Artistic furniture also included the 'whatnot' for display of miniature ceramic objects, such as the example made by the Arts and Crafts decorators Morris and Co. and illustrated in the *Cabinet Maker and Art Furnisher* (Fig. 40).[14]

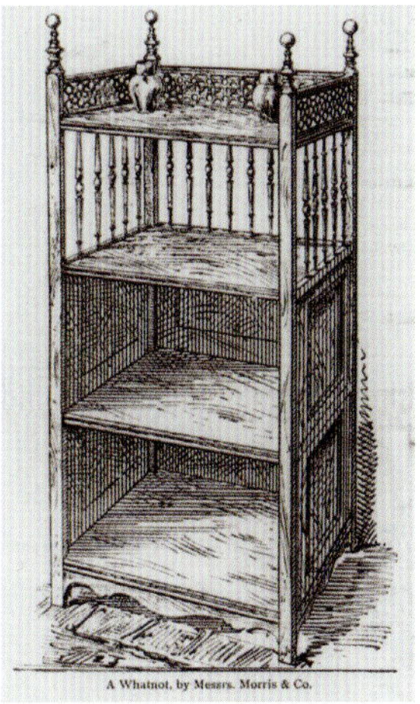

Fig. 40—'A Whatnot, by Messrs. Morris & Co.', as illustrated in the *Cabinet Maker and Art Furnisher*, 1 February 1884.

Research into the domestic life of Irish middle-class households in the new suburbs reveals evidence that the middle classes were following this taste, as in London and other cities in Britain and the United States.[15] There is photographic evidence showing that the overmantel and whatnot were in Dublin homes,[16] and artistic furniture was produced in Dublin by T.R. Scott,[17] who was active in the development of art industry and who reported to the Royal Commission on Technical Instruction.[18]

Some elements of late nineteenth-century interior decoration in Dublin

9 Cooper 1987 [1998], 7.

10 *Ibid.*, 115–17.

11 Williams 1994, 392. The Burnaby estate in County Wicklow, planned and built *c.* 1890–1910, is a prominent example.

12 Girouard 1977, 132

13 *Ibid.*, 131. Mrs H.R. Haweis wrote several books on home decoration: *The art of beauty* (1878), *The art of decoration* (1881) and *Beautiful houses* (1882).

14 'A Whatnot by Messrs. Morris & Co.', *The Cabinet Maker and Art Furnisher*, 1 February 1884, 141.

15 Hearn 1998, 62–4.

16 *Ibid.*, 78, 80–1.

17 *Dublin University Review* 2 (April 1886), 285: advertisement for 'T.R. Scott & Co. Artistic Cabinet Manufacturer'.

18 Royal Commission on Technical Instruction 1884, 77–85.

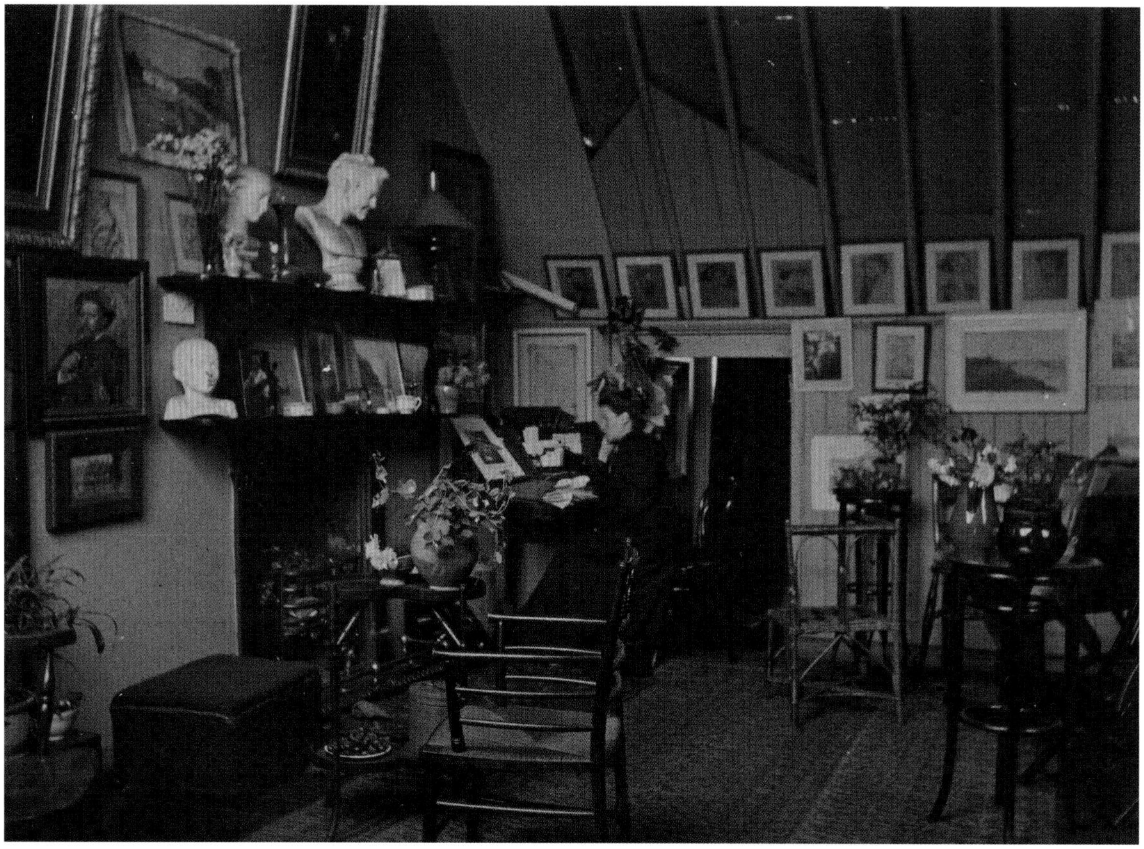

Fig. 41—Woman (unidentified) in an interior/artist's studio, Dublin, c. 1890, by Thomas Geoghegan. Courtesy of the National Library of Ireland. While the ceramics in the room cannot be identified for certain as Vodrey Dublin Pottery, some objects, particularly the two (vase and jardinière) on the table in the right foreground, are similar to the art pottery produced by Frederick Vodrey.

can be seen in a photograph taken by Thomas Geoghegan (Fig. 41).[19] The chestnuts and chrysanthemums indicate autumn, and the casual, spontaneous display of ceramics and paintings suggests the home of an artist, yet the woman's pose and the placing of the furniture appear rather studied and to have been calculated by the photographer.

According to writers at the time, the ideal Aesthetic interior included the display of edifying books alongside ceramics and paintings, as illustrated in Fig. 42, and was to be less cluttered than the mid-Victorian home. There was an emphasis on 'art for art's sake', a ceramic object having a value equivalent to that of a painting as a mode of self-expression.[20]

Interest in ceramics amongst followers of the Aesthetic taste originated in the collecting of Oriental blue and white ceramics, as well as examples from Delft and early English factories.[21] The early follower of Aesthetic taste, or 'Aesthete', was a 'connoisseur who collected antiques' and thus by definition from

19 NLI ALB 8:40. Thomas Geoghegan, photographer, was recorded at two addresses: 8 Lower Sackville Street (O'Connell Street) and 2 Essex Quay.

20 Aslin 1981, 111.

21 Anderson 2009, 109–10.

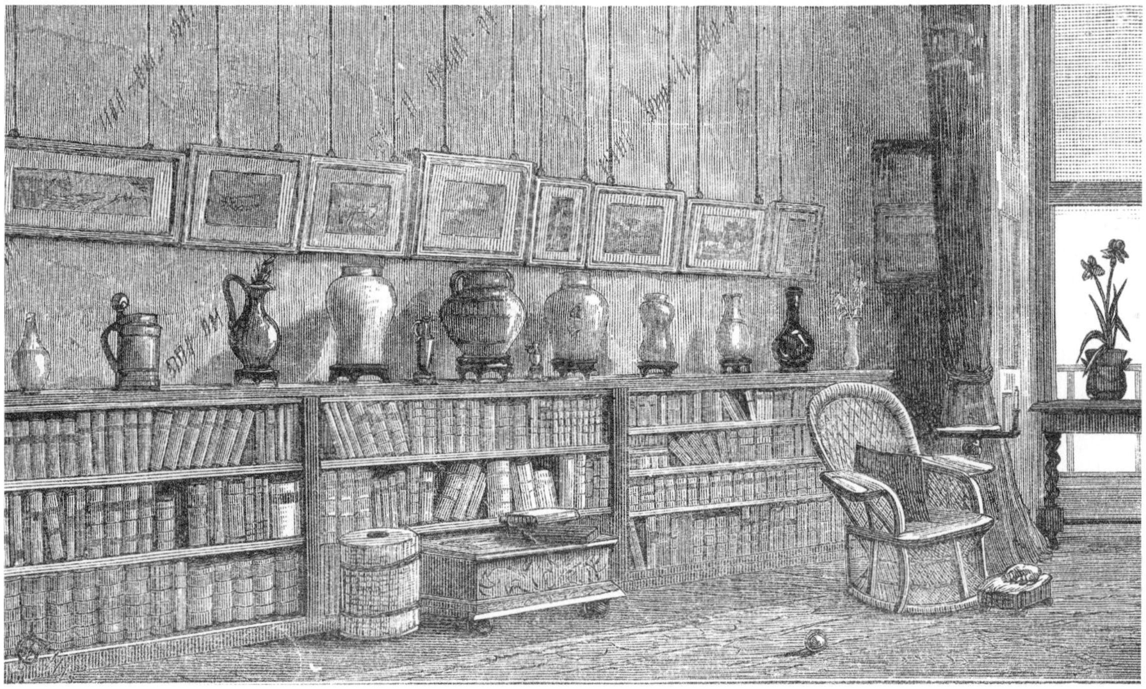

Fig. 42—Illustration from *A plea for art in the house* by Revd W.J. Loftie (1876). Courtesy of the National Library of Ireland.

the 'privileged and monied classes'.[22] This upper-class taste spread to the middle classes, and by the 1880s the Aesthetic style had become popular and was transmitted through several advice manuals for furniture-makers and the householder.[23]

These journals and advice manuals were directed largely at a female readership.[24] In Ireland, *Findlater's Ladies Housekeeping Book*, a popular guide to home management, included advertisements for house furnishing.[25] Some writers promoted the values of a comfortable and moral family home.[26] Details of interior spaces described by the novelist Elizabeth Bowen also provide some insight into the Dublin home, albeit a generation later, when she reflects on the environment of a late Victorian childhood.[27] A reduction in the use of carpets and heavy curtains in favour of light, airy interiors and dust-free spaces was considered healthier and promoted by the health reform movement.[28] This is demonstrated by Bowen's description of her bedroom, where 'Victorian taste was already giving way to the simpler styles favoured by

22 *Ibid.*, 117.

23 Aslin 1981, 4. 'By the 1880s what had been an art movement had become a fashionable mania and every household from the highest to the most humble contained the required Japanese paper fan or parasol or Wedgwood plate with Japanese based decoration.'

24 Gere and Hoskins 2000, 77–81. The authors list C.L. Eastlake's *Hints on household taste in furniture, upholstery, and other details* (1868) and Mrs Haweis's *The art of beauty* (1878) and *The art of decoration* (1881).

25 Hearn 1998, 70.

26 Gere and Hoskins 2000, 77–81. The authors name *A plea for art in the house* by Revd W.J. Loftie.

27 Customs and manners are also described in James Joyce's *Dubliners* and *Portrait of the artist as a young man.*

28 Forty 1986 [1987], 159–62.

the Edwardians',[29] as signified by the 'light green moire wallpaper' and the 'white muslin inner curtains'.[30]

One of the most significant furniture designers in the Aesthetic style was the architect Edward W. Godwin, whose designs were in a distinctively 'Anglo-Japanese style'.[31] He undertook private commissions and also produced designs for commercial manufacturers of furniture, textiles and wallpaper that exerted a wide-ranging influence.[32] He designed the only known Aesthetic interior in Ireland, for an aristocratic client at Dromore Castle, Co. Limerick.[33] Godwin, James McNeill Whistler and Oscar Wilde were regarded as 'the leaders of the Art or Aesthetic Movement'.[34]

Godwin's designs for the interior of Dromore Castle showed early signs of 'several of the trade-marks of the Aesthetic Movement'.[35] He subsequently designed 'a number of interiors in London, both for himself and various friends', including Whistler and Wilde.[36] The Aesthetic taste was promoted in London society by Whistler and Wilde.[37] When Wilde gave a lecture in Dublin, he was referred to as the 'founder of aestheticism'.[38] His 1882 lecture tour in the United States, where he spoke about taste and design for the interior and for dress, was widely publicised.[39] In spite of a romanticised view, Wilde's Aesthetic ideals included 'a clean unpolluted environment and improved social conditions',[40] moral values which were developed by later generations.

Designers such as Godwin introduced the simplicity and functionality of Japanese design to an élite clientele in the 1860s. Eastlake's *Hints on household taste* (1868) conveyed these new principles of design to a wider audience.[41] He coined the term 'art furniture' and promoted 'a move away from high Victorian taste to individually designed pieces made by rural craftsmen'.[42] Eastlake criticised the ugliness of mass production and the resulting loss of craftsmanship.[43] He maintained that 'good design' and 'good taste' needed to be guided by knowledge and education rather than by fashion.[44] These ideas would have influenced Irish consumers and prompted them to support the crafts produced by the home industries, including Vodrey's art pottery.

---

29 Hearn 1998, 82.

30 *Ibid.*

31 Cooper 1987 [1998], 120–1.

32 *Ibid.* These included commissions for James McNeill Whistler and Oscar Wilde.

33 Aslin 1986, 6. Godwin made several trips to Ireland, where his brother was working as an engineer. Dromore Castle was designed for the earl of Limerick, the exterior being in medieval or Gothic Revival style.

34 *Ibid.*, 9.

35 *Ibid.*

36 Cooper 1987 [1998], 120–1.

37 Gere and Hoskins 2000, 20–4.

38 *Dublin University Review* 1 (1) (February 1885), 15.

39 Aslin 1981, 110. Wilde's lecture was entitled 'The Practical Application of the Principles of the Aesthetic Theory to Exterior, Interior House Decoration with Observations Upon Dress and Personal Ornaments' (May 1882).

40 *Ibid.*, 110.

41 *Ibid.*, 60–2.

42 *Ibid.*, 62.

43 Eastlake 1868.

44 *Ibid.*, 13–14, 94–5.

A reported feature of the Irish Aesthetic interior was the use of Celtic motifs,[45] of which significant evidence is yet to be uncovered. A prominent early example was Godwin's design for Dromore Castle, in which there was a ceiling 'decorated with Celtic scrolls' and 'Chinese imperial yellow silk upholstery'.[46] The Celtic style was part of the late Victorian Aesthetic taste in Dublin and further afield, evolving into the Art Nouveau designs by Rennie Mackintosh in Glasgow and the silverware designed by Archibald Knox for the London store Liberty's. Scholarship has demonstrated the links between the Arts and Crafts movements in Ireland and Scotland.[47] In this regard, there is a direct connection between the sinuous organic forms of the Art Nouveau style and naturalistic forms in Celtic interlace designs.

Earlier in the nineteenth century, and before the emergence of the Art Nouveau style, Celtic Revival jewellery produced in Dublin was praised by Eastlake, thereby indicating that the style was part of fashionable taste in Britain.[48] The collectors of Celtic jewellery have been described as 'young Aesthetes' whose ideas of 'romanticised beauty' later met 'an era of revolutionary terror'.[49] The Celtic style was one of many styles included in Owen Jones's *The grammar of ornament*, an illustrated manual for architects and designers.[50] It has been noted that the association of the ruling class with the Gaelic native culture of the island could be interpreted as a means of asserting dominance and power.[51] It preceded the shift towards a more single-minded nationalism, which elevated Celtic style to the level of a national style, distinctly representative of Irish identity. ■

45 Hearn 1998, 79.

46 Cooper 1987 [1998], 120. The author writes that work for Dromore Castle was significant in Godwin's early career development.

47 Gordon Bowe and Cumming 1998.

48 Eastlake 1868, 229: 'The very successful copies of ancient Irish brooches, executed by two Dublin firms, Messrs. West and Messrs. Waterhouse are well worth notice'.

49 McBrinn 2009, 209.

50 Jones 1856.

51 Crooke 2000, 69, 96.

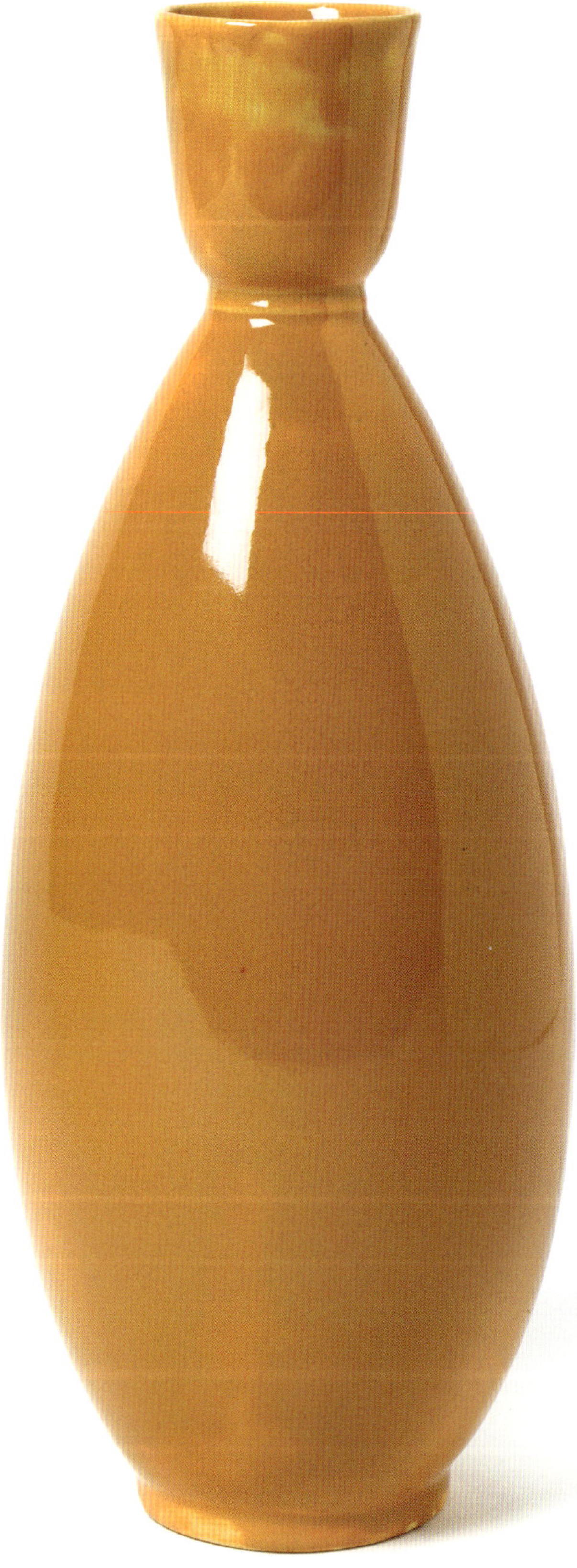

CHAPTER 13

The Aesthetic object

The Aesthetic object

Whilst the Aesthetic taste promoted by Wilde and others in the 'Art Movement' was criticised for degenerating into 'a mania for sunflowers, strange colours and terracotta ornaments', it had an enduring influence on ceramic design.[1] In the 1870s, pottery manufacturers 'began to produce, alongside their commercial ranges, "Art Pottery"' that 'appealed to more refined tastes'.[2] The move away from industrialisation and towards small-scale craft production influenced the larger manufacturers and also laid the foundation for studio pottery in the twentieth century.[3]

The flower-form vase in the Museum's collection (Fig. 43; cat. no. 30) is an early example of the Art Nouveau style, comparable to Charles Ashbee's design for a glass decanter with silver mounts.[4] The shape of the vase is based on a natural form, and the expression of nature's energy is similar to designs by Christopher Dresser produced by the Linthorpe Pottery.[5]

In the nineteenth century there were various views on the depiction of nature in design.[6] Owen Jones thought that designers should look to architecture for their sources, while Gottfried Semper advised that craft was the source of ideas.[7] According to Semper, the crafts developed because of the human instinct for survival, and his ideas were the basis of the later Bauhaus theory of *Gesamtkunstwerk*, in which all the

---

1 Aslin 1981, 131, 144.

2 Naylor 1971, 149.

3 Aslin 1981, 131–2.

4 Victoria and Albert Museum, London: wine decanter designed by Charles Robert Ashbee (1863–1942); museum no. M.121; 1, 2-1966.

5 Interestingly, Dresser spent his early childhood in Bandon, Co. Cork, although to date there is no evidence that he had any association with Vodrey.

6 Schafter 2003, 32.

7 *Ibid.*, 36. Semper claimed that architecture itself had developed from the four original crafts or *Urformen*: pottery, weaving, carpentry and masonry.

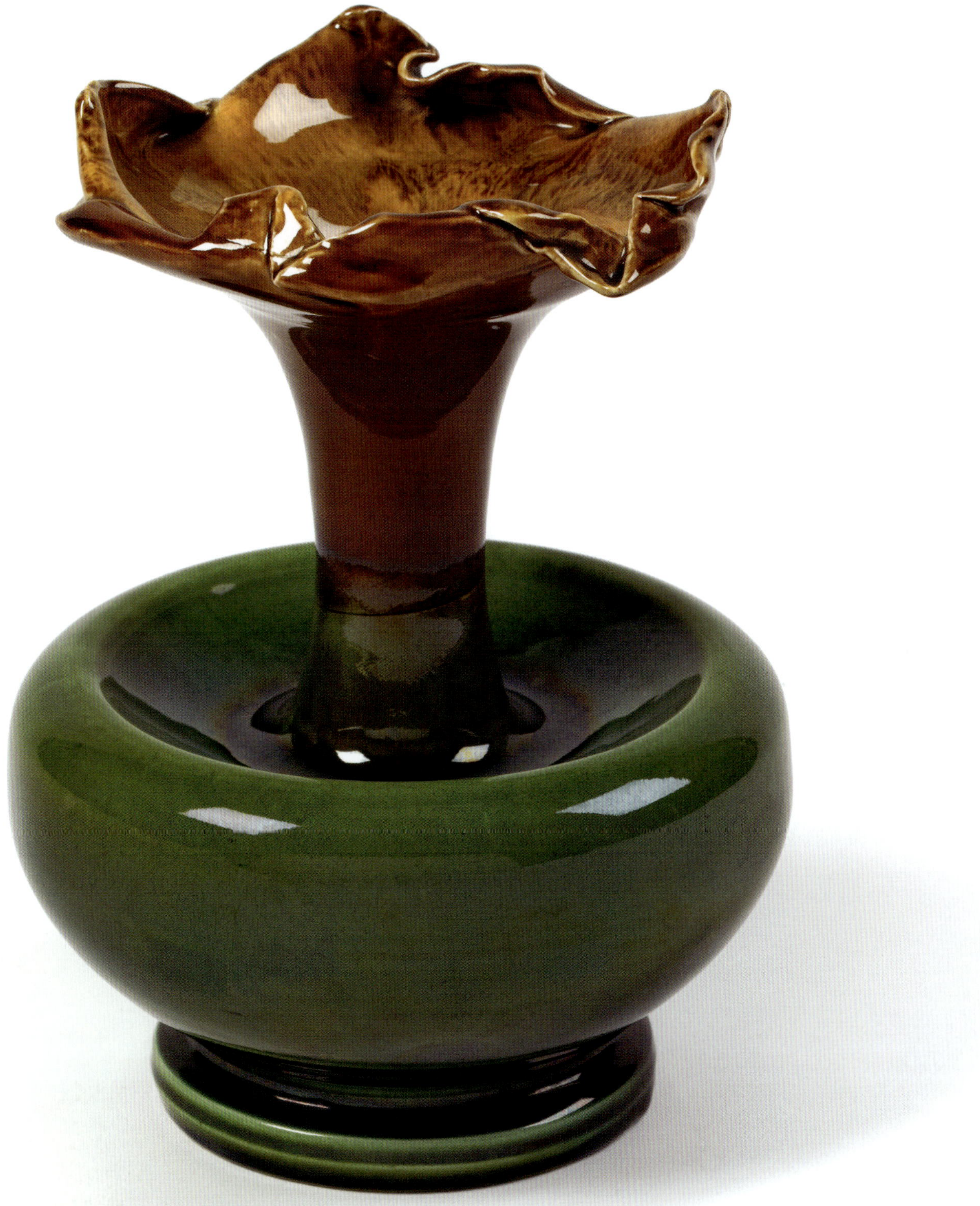

Fig. 43—Vase, flower form, Art Nouveau style, Vodrey Dublin Pottery **c.** 1886; 15cm x 10cm. NMI 1886.117. Cat. no. 30.

crafts were considered to be the foundation of architecture and an integral part of the design process.[8]

The flower-form vase is an example of the art pottery or 'Vodrian ware' produced in Dublin by Frederick Vodrey, which catered for followers of the Aesthetic taste. He advertised 'Artistic and Domestic' art pottery in a variety of styles:

> 'Pitchers, Vases, Ewers, Menu Stands, Tea Pots, Candlesticks, &c., from Celtic, Greek, Roman, Moorish, Chinese and Japanese designs, with a view to the production not only in a high degree of objects, that are attractive and useful, but also of forms that have a certain quaintness of effect'.[9]

These ceramics were produced in many bright colours:

> 'The colours obtained are Ruby (plain and in combination with Green and Brown), Olive, Orange, Canary, and a union of Orange and Brown. The richness of tint, of course, is due to the variety of tone and depth of the glaze. Some very charming marble blendings will also be noticed.'[10]

The colourful glazes on the Vodrey art pottery were similar to those advertised by art potteries in England as having 'the brilliancy of Eastern Colouring'.[11] Manufacturers responding to a demand generated by the Aesthetic taste advertised art pottery in Oriental design and bright colours.[12] Vodrey was considered to have introduced this new fashionable style in ceramics to Dublin. The earthenware ceramics produced by the Vodrey Dublin Pottery were compared favourably to art pottery from the Linthorpe Pottery in England and the Dunmore Pottery in Scotland.[13] 'Vodrian ware' was likened to ceramics produced by Wemyss, Linthorpe and the French Vallery pottery.[14]

Vodrey's designs were praised as 'regenerated domestic pottery' because they offered an alternative to what Pentland criticised as an outdated Continental taste in Dublin.[15] A witness to the Select Committee on Industries (Ireland) (1885) agreed with Pentland's criticism of consumer taste in Dublin, suggesting that there was a lack of interest in high-quality ceramic wares in Ireland[16] and that consumers in Dublin

8 Schafter 2003, 39.

9 Frederick Vodrey's trade card (1885), NMI 1886.125.

10 *Ibid.*

11 Advertisement for the Linthorpe Pottery, *The Pottery Gazette*, 1 January 1885, 95.

12 Advertisement for 'Artistic Pottery' in 'Oriental Yellow, and Turquoise bodies' by the Old Foley Pottery, *The Pottery Gazette*, 1 January 1885, 27.

13 'The China and Glass Trades in Ireland (from our correspondent)', *The Pottery Gazette*, 1 February 1884, 178.

14 Pentland 1885, 34.

15 *Ibid.*, 40.

16 Select Committee on Industries (Ireland) 1885, 111, entry 2197. In reference to the Belleek Pottery, he said: 'I saw goods to the amount of between 500L and 600L being forwarded out to Milan, Florence, Rome, Paris, Vienna, London, New York, and Philadelphia. Out of 560L which was the amount I found by examination of the invoice book, only 5L was for Ireland, so that most of the goods went abroad.'

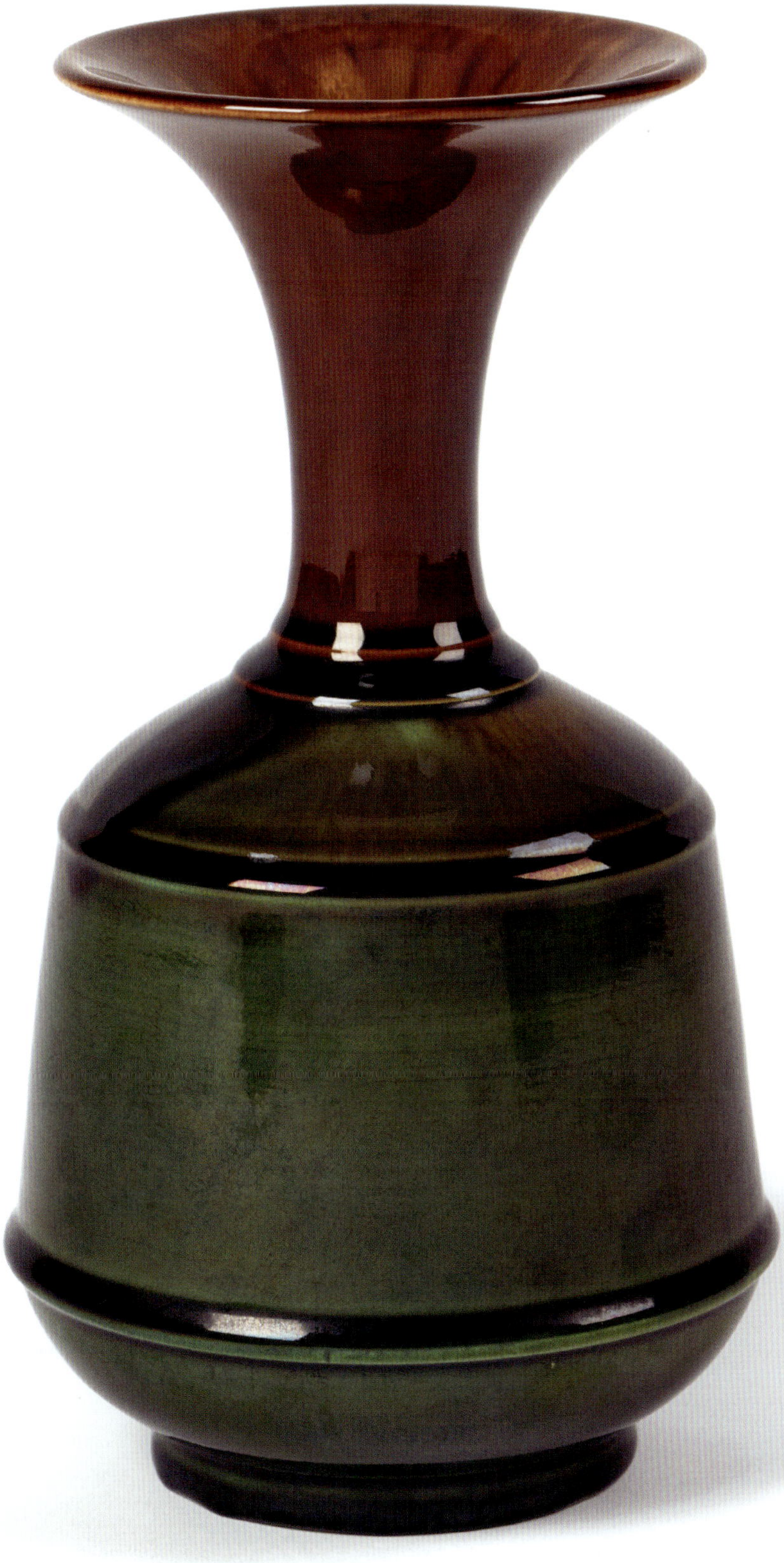

Fig. 44—Vase with flared rim, with yellow, green and brown glaze; 19cm x 4cm. NMI 1886.95. Cat. no. 19.

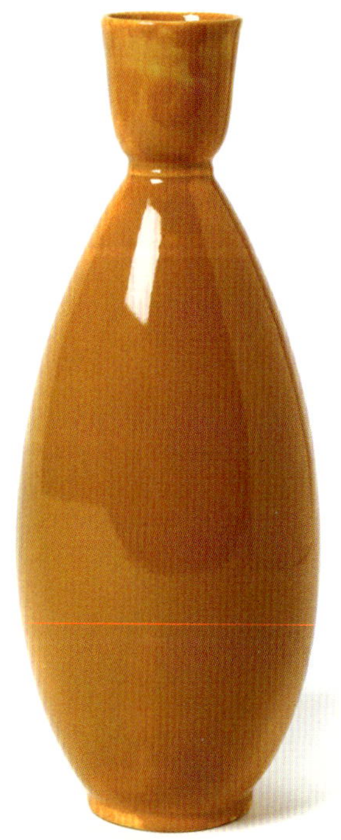

Fig. 45—Vase, saké bottle shape, yellow glaze, 30cm x 10.5cm. NMI 1886.105. Cat. no. 26.

were more inclined to buy 'cheap Glasgow pottery'[17] than luxury wares such as Belleek, which were in demand on the export market.[18] However, customers' choice of cheaper imported wares over Belleek could also have been due to the restrictions of income rather than taste, as from the outset the porcelain wares produced by the Belleek Pottery were advertised to an aristocratic, wealthy clientele.

Whilst the 'flower-form vase' illustrated in Fig. 43 has the distinctive curvilinear shape of the Art Nouveau style, other objects of a more simplified and less organic design were produced at the pottery. Comparison of the vase shown in Fig. 44 with the previous, more curvilinear Art Nouveau style of the 'flower-form vase' demonstrates the links between Art Nouveau style in the nineteenth century and the development of Modernist design as shown by architectural historian Nikolaus Pevsner.[19]

This second vase prefigures Modernism, and the simplicity of the object's form demonstrates a different approach to nature.[20] This approach is one expressed by the German theorist Riegl: that geometric forms came from the human instinct to imitate nature and that the 'contour line' was a stage of evolution towards non-representational art or abstraction.[21] Vodrey's contrasting designs, of the organic flower-form vase and the more simplified, geometric form of the long-necked vase, reveal that he understood both approaches to nature in nineteenth-century design theory.

Another object in the National Museum collection with Modernist undertones is a yellow bottle vase (Fig. 45; cat. no. 26). It may be based on a Japanese prototype, as it resembles the shape of a saké bottle, showing the influence of Japanese art and design on the new Aesthetic taste popular in Europe at the time. Although Ruskin and Morris expressed opinions that were not favourable to the new taste for Japanese design, from the 1860s it influenced work by the second-generation designers like Mackmurdo, Voysey and Mackintosh in the 'undecorated forms and construction' of their designs.[22]

The introduction of Japanese design into Europe is traced to the display of Japanese objects at the London International Exhibition (1862) and the Paris Universal Exhibition (1867).[23] This was followed by several books on Japanese ornament, such as *Art and art industries in Japan* by the collector Rutherford Alcock. The style was further popularised in *Artistic Japan* by Siegfried Bing, owner of a fashionable

17 This may refer to the Caledonian Pottery advertised in *The Pottery Gazette* on 2 February 1885, 131, and July 1891, 578: 'Murray and Co., Caledonian Pottery, Rutherglen, near Glasgow, offices, and showrooms—Dublin 61 William Street, agent Mr J.G. Macintyre'. The pottery later became better known for producing functional stoneware vessels.

18 Select Committee on Industries (Ireland) 1885, 111, entry 2197.

19 Pevsner 2008 [1936], 26–9.

20 Schafter 2003, 45. Riegl 'inverted' the views of earlier theorists Jones and Semper.

21 *Ibid.*

22 Naylor 1971, 117.

23 Durant 1986, 163–92.

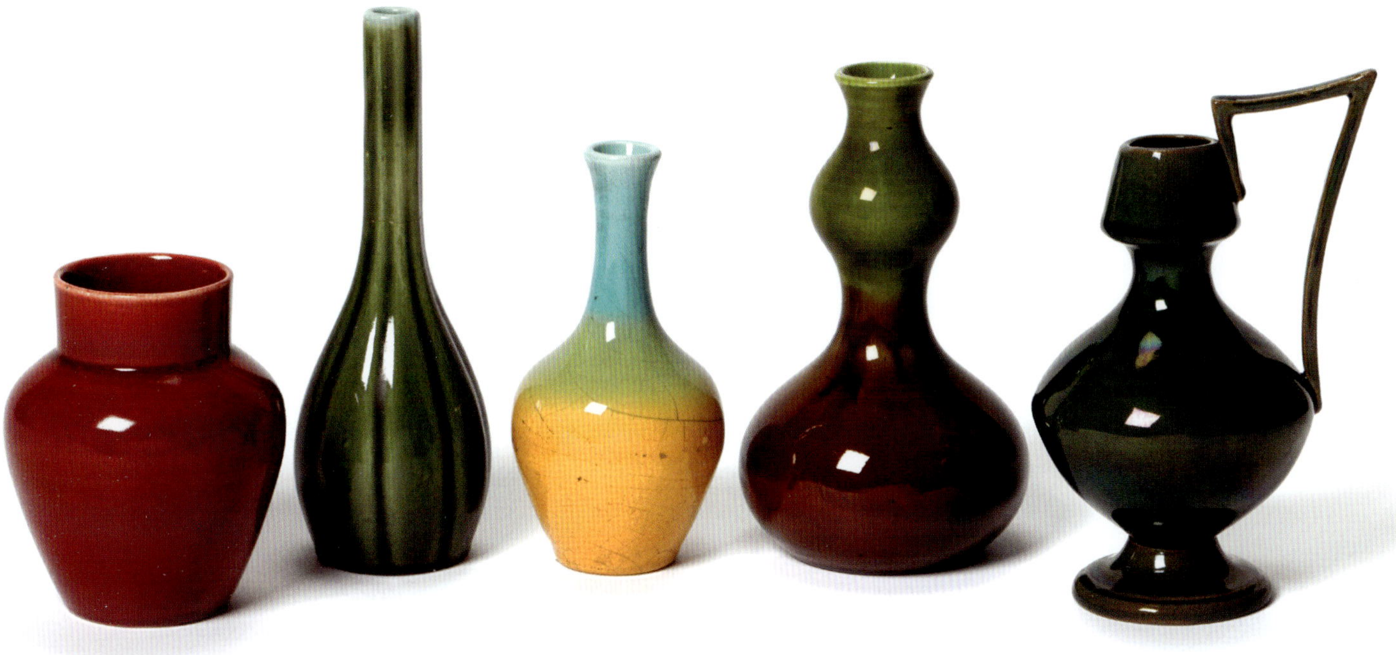

Fig. 46—Group of miniature vases designed for display on a whatnot, Vodrey Dublin Pottery, 1880s. Cat. nos 41, 42, 9, 20 and 28.

Parisian shop called L' Art Nouveau, from which the style derived its name. The shop retailed a wide range of decorative arts products and was a meeting place for 'enthusiasts of Japanese art'.[24]

The first publication to introduce Japanese ceramics to Europe, *Keramic art of Japan* (1875), emphasised patterns and forms on highly decorated porcelain such as the Imari wares, which were gaining popularity.[25] The book was illustrated with chromolithographs of objects in several private collections. Some of the plainer objects illustrated, such as a gourd-shaped bottle and a saké bottle, could have influenced Vodrey's designs. It is also likely, however, that Vodrey was influenced by Christopher Dresser's account of potteries in Japan, which noted 'a beautiful ware of soft yellow colour in Awata'.[26] Dresser's book, *Japan, its architecture, art, and manufactures*, gave extensive coverage to the pottery industry in Japan and contributed to the development of an interest in Japanese design amongst followers of the Aesthetic taste.

---

24 *Ibid.*, 170.

25 Audsley and Bowes 1875.

26 Dresser 1882.

Dresser noted that the Japanese had a 'national style of conventional ornament'.[27] He wrote that he visited 'sixty-eight potteries' and described in detail the pigments and techniques used for the decoration of ceramic wares. The monochrome glazes of Awaji wares were singled out for praise.[28] These descriptions influenced producers of art ceramics in Europe. Dresser's preference for plain coloured wares was obvious, and he was quite critical of the European taste for patterned Imari wares and 'people who pride themselves on the number of specimens and prefer mere quantity to beautiful works',[29] although he did acknowledge that this may have been because he was already familiar with these ceramics as they were collected and copied in Europe.

Dresser's comments on taste and design give us an insight into the views of a leading designer in the nineteenth century. From the 1870s there was a trend towards plainer colours and individuality of taste. According to Dresser, a house 'ought to express by its decoration, the mind, tastes and knowledge of the owner'. This view echoed those expressed by writers on home decoration throughout the later nineteenth century. In addition to describing glaze colours and decoration on ceramics in the Japanese potteries, Dresser also discussed the form of objects. He was interested in the Japanese use of nature as seen in branch-like handles or gourd-shaped vases[30] like those produced by the Vodrey Dublin Pottery, examples of which can be seen in a group of miniature vases from the National Museum collection (Fig. 46; cat. nos 41, 42, 9, 20 and 28). These small objects were made to be placed on the whatnot or overmantel in the Aesthetic home.

Dresser also praised the humorous element in Japanese ceramics, and another of his influences can be seen in Vodrey's use of animal forms for functional wares, such as the use of the frog, symbol of fertility in Japanese culture, as a paperweight or match-holder. There are examples in the National Museum (Fig. 47; cat. nos 6, 7 and 45) and the Ulster Museum.

In addition to the Japanese influence, many designs produced by the Vodrey Dublin Pottery were based on the Classical shapes and proportions of ancient Greek and Roman ceramics, such as the Classical ewer shape in the NMI collection (Fig. 48; cat. no. 31). Dresser compared Japanese ceramics with those of ancient Greece, asserting that Japanese manufacture was superior in the production of porcelain and its decoration. Nevertheless, he wrote, 'As regards the beauty of form, it must be admitted that the Japanese are far behind the ancient Greeks and Japanese shapes certainly often display quaintness rather than grace'.[31]

The two-tone glaze in green and red applied to the Classical shape demonstrates Frederick Vodrey's ability to combine two influences from Dresser's writings—the Classical form with the Japanese-inspired colours. The design of this ewer also bears some resemblance to an earlier terracotta ewer produced at the Florence Court Tile Works in County Fermanagh. This was shown at the 1853 Exhibition and 'subsequently as an exhibit in the Industrial Museum of Ireland'[32] to demonstrate the use of Irish clays for ceramic production.

27 Dresser 1882, Preface.

28 *Ibid.*, 391.

29 *Ibid.*, 393.

30 *Ibid.*, 402–3.

31 Dresser 1882, 402–3.

32 Dunlevy 1988, 26. The ewer by the Florence Court Tile Works, of which Vodrey was probably aware, is illustrated on the cover of the book.

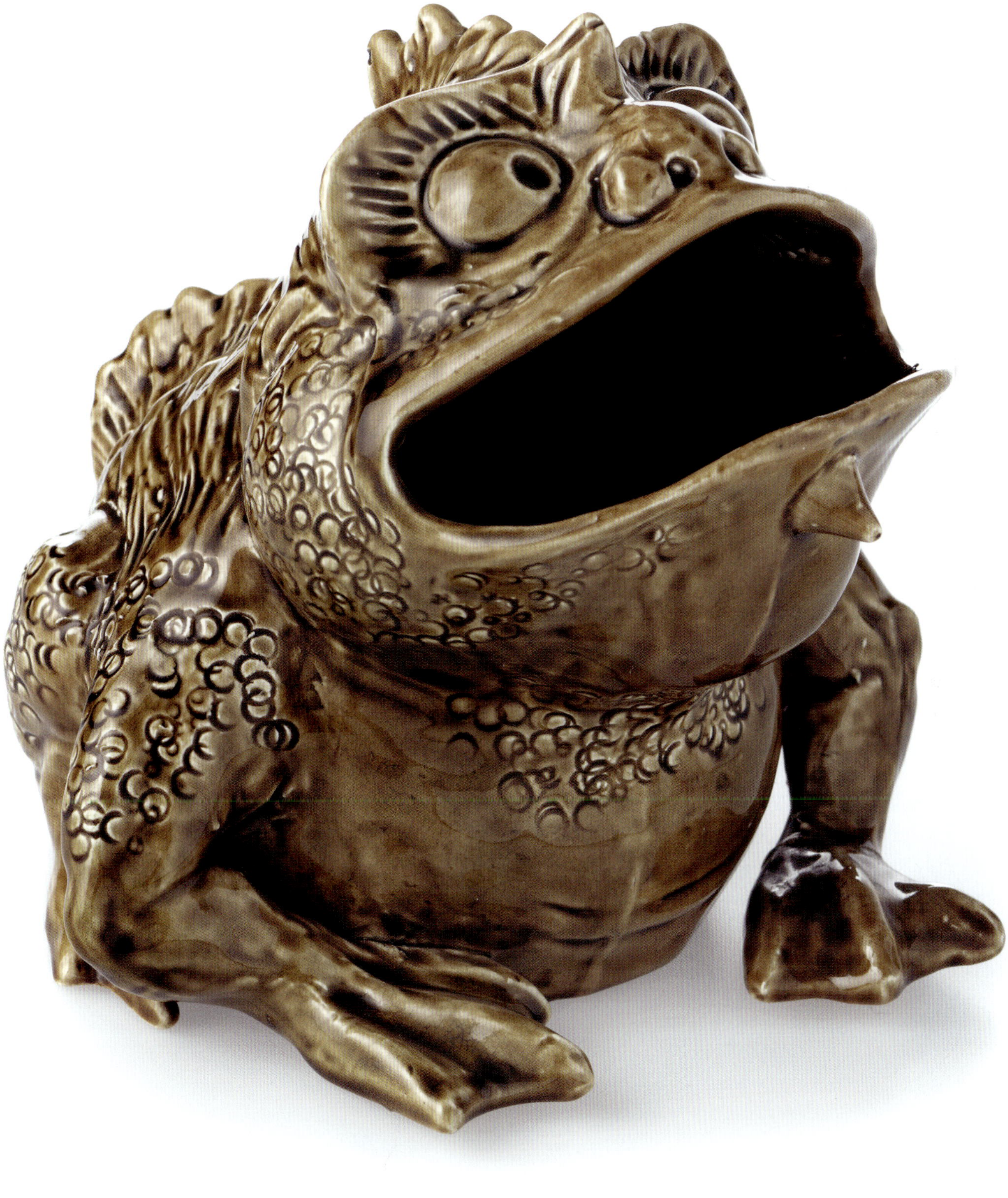

Fig. 47—Frog, seated, with open mouth; green glaze; 17cm x 15cm; 'Vodrey Dublin Pottery' (handwritten style), c. 1886. National Museum of Ireland, NMI 1886.83. Cat. no. 7.

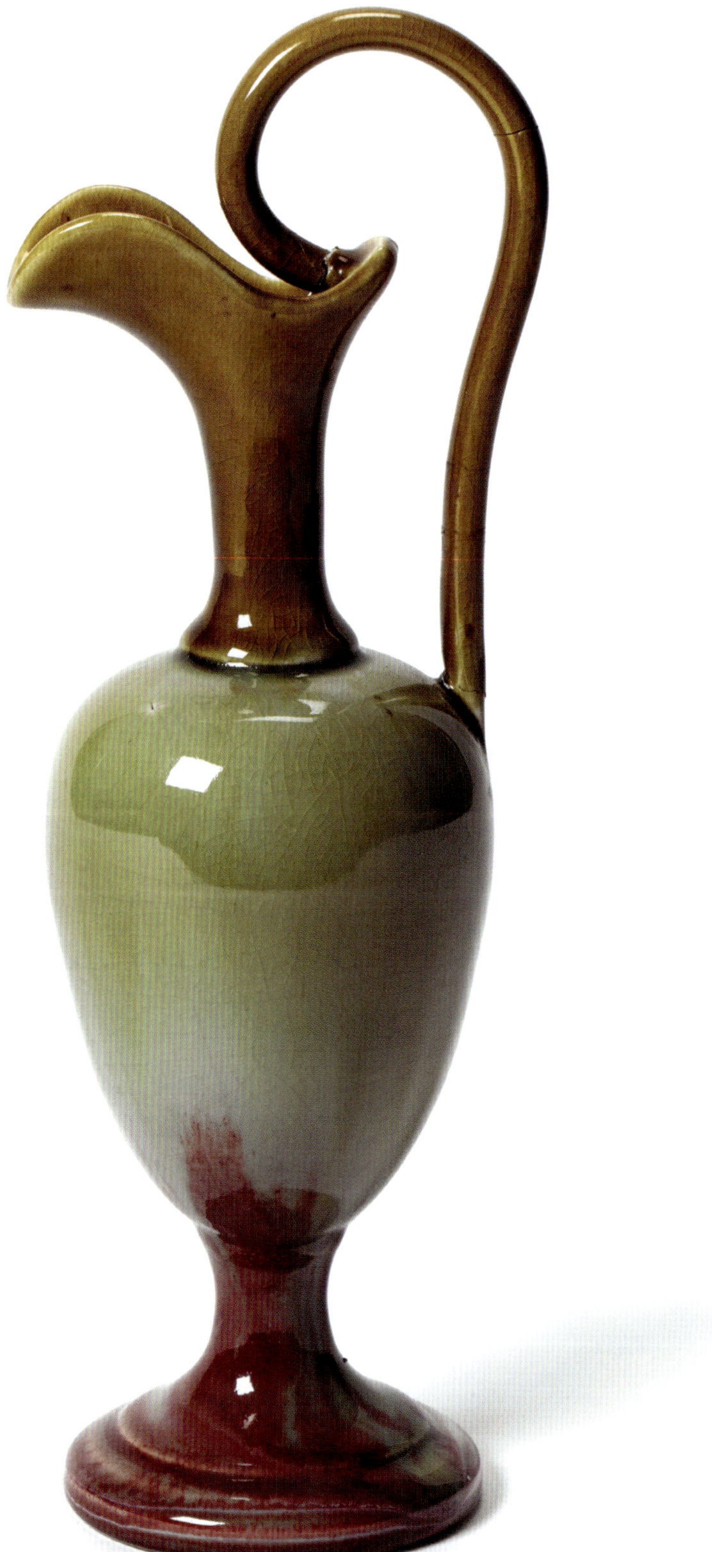

Fig. 48—Ewer, Classical style, red/olive green glaze; 25.5cm × 6cm. National Museum of Ireland, NMI 1886.119. Cat. no. 31.

In the study of decorative arts, the style of objects is a marker of their social context. In the essay 'Style as evidence', the art historian Jules Prown distinguished between 'verbal data' and the 'non-verbal data' conveyed by an object.[33] He introduced the concept that the 'non-verbal data' of objects provide valuable information to other disciplines that primarily use 'verbal data'.

In terms of the language of style in the nineteenth century, the Vodrey art pottery in the National Museum of Ireland reveals the taste of a middle- and upper-class consumer society that was both international and local. On the one hand, Vodrey's customers were interested in the Art Nouveau style from Paris; on the other hand, they were driven by a 'practical patriotism' that supported Irish home industries and the Celtic style. Nevertheless, our understanding of the late nineteenth-century perspective on Irish national identity must include the fact that the Celtic ceramics were exhibited alongside ceramics in the 'Moorish' style, raising questions about the meaning of styles in 1880s Dublin. ■

33 Prown 1980.

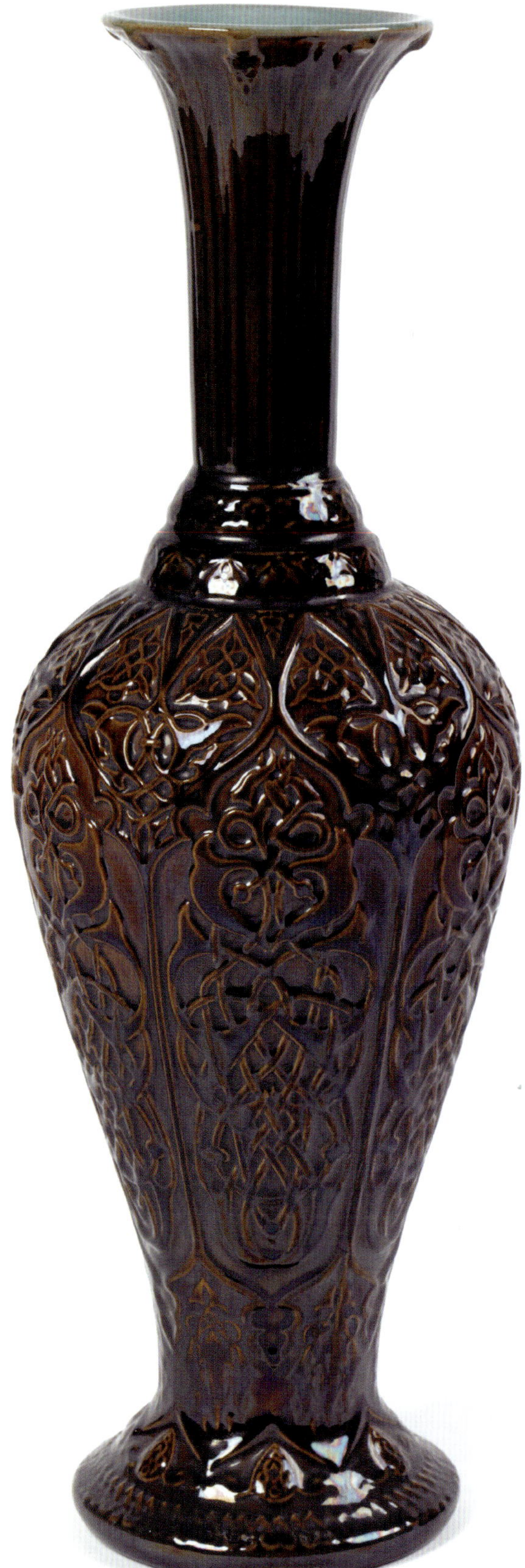

CHAPTER 14

Orientalism and the 'Moorish style'

Orientalism and the 'Moorish style'

The Moorish-style vases in the National Museum collection (Figs 49 and 50; cat. nos 23, 11 and 44) reveal that decoration of Irish middle-class homes in the later nineteenth century was influenced by Orientalism, a style popular throughout Europe. Orientalism can be traced back to the fashion for 'chinoiserie' in eighteenth-century interior decoration.[1] During the nineteenth century, this taste evolved amongst Arts and Crafts designers into an appreciation for crafts from a range of Eastern cultures, including China, India and Japan.[2] It was partly influenced by Owen Jones's classification of styles in *The grammar of ornament*,[3] described as 'a typical piece of Victorian taxonomy'.[4]

In interior design during the nineteenth century there was a fashion for decorative details and entire rooms in the 'Moorish' style,[5] a noted example being the Alhambra Music Hall in Leicester Square, London.[6] The *Cabinet Maker* trade magazine gave detailed instructions on designs for 'Moorish furniture'.[7] Objects like the vases in the Museum were placed in a room decorated in the Moorish style, frequently a men's smoking room. The original influence for such two-handled vases was an illustration in Owen Jones's book about a Moorish palace in Spain, *Plans, details, and sections of the Alhambra*.[8] It was imitated in glass and ceramics by several European manufacturers, including Theodore Deck and Edouard Honoré.[9]

1 MacKenzie 1995, 109–10, 113.

2 *Ibid.*, 117–18.

3 Jones (1856) described the characteristics of 'Arabian', 'Turkish', 'Moresque' and 'Persian' styles.

4 Mackenzie 1995, 118.

5 Cooper 1987 [1998], 16.

6 *Ibid.*

7 'How to make a Moresque flower table', *Cabinet Maker and Art Furnisher* 5 (November 1884), 93.

8 Jones and Goury 1842–5.

9 Baker and Richardson 1997, 93, 95, figs 5 and 6.

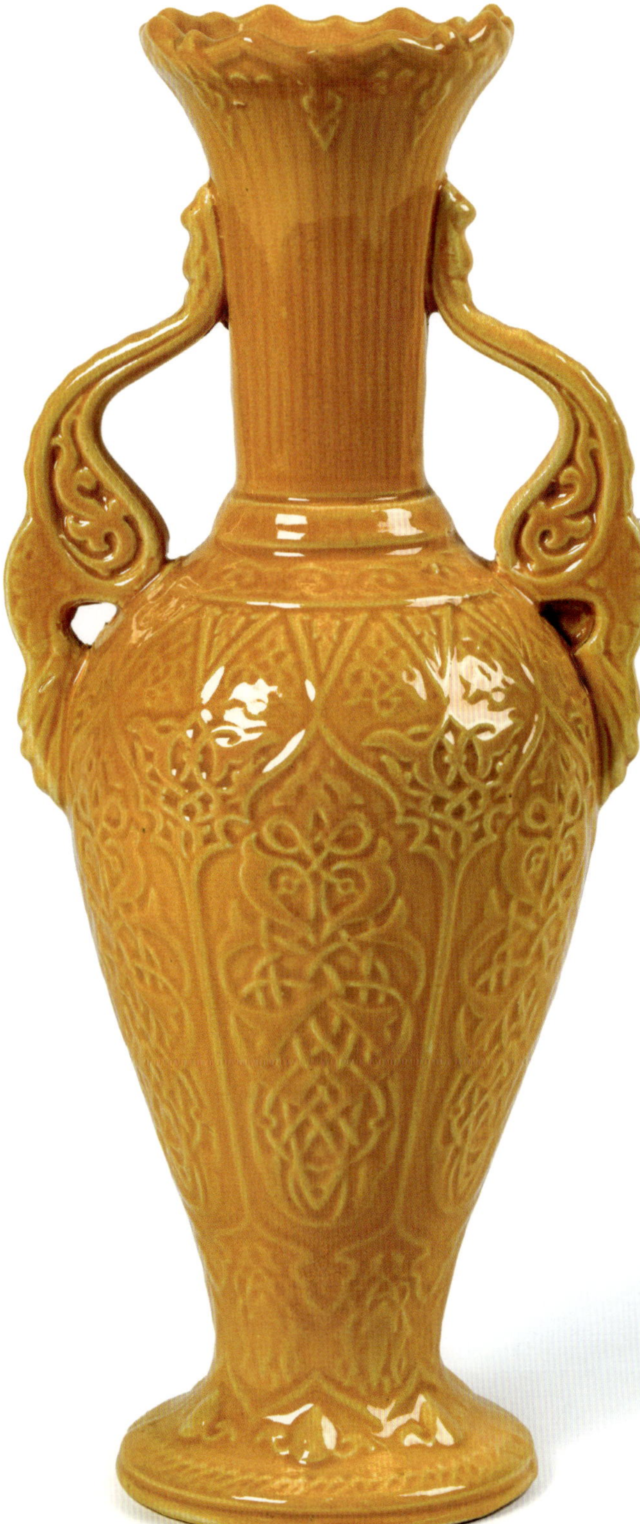

Fig. 49—Vase with handles, Moorish style, Alhambra influence; yellow glaze; 30cm x 11cm. NMI 1886.100. Cat. no. 23.

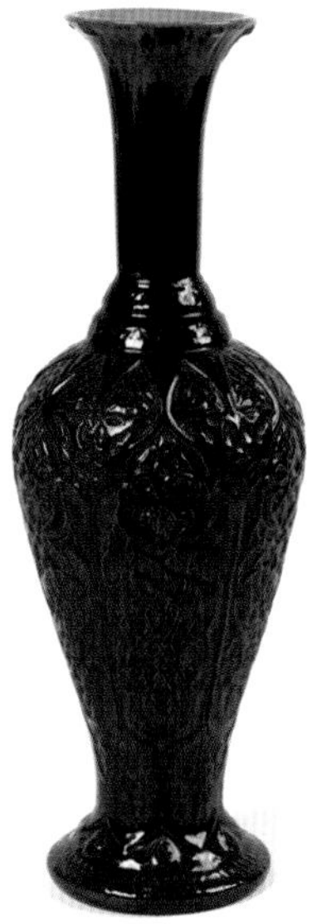

Fig. 50—Vase, Moorish style, Alhambra influence; dark blue outer glaze with turquoise inside, raised pattern gold/brown; 42cm × 13cm. NMI 1886.87. Cat. no. 11.

The actual source or prototype for Vodrey's Moorish designs was a vase by a French manufacturer, Voisin Lieu (1838–54),[10] now in the Victoria and Albert Museum. It was originally exhibited in the Museum of Practical Geology, which became part of the Department of Science and Art, London, in 1853.[11] In contrast to the Lieu vase in brown earthenware with a brown glaze, the two more decorative versions produced by Vodrey were in a dark blue with turquoise and a bright yellow glaze. In the case of the darker Moresque vase, the interior glaze is a colourful, brighter turquoise. In this object and other examples of Vodrey Dublin Pottery, like the flower-form vase (Fig. 43) shown earlier, the object opens at the mouth to reveal a lighter colour, simulating natural beauty.

The exhibition of Russell's ceramics in the 'Keltic' and 'Moorish' styles together at the 1885 Dublin Sketching Club exhibition indicates that these two styles could be placed side by side in the nineteenth-century interior,[12] introducing an alternate perspective on our perception of the Celtic style and Irish national identity. Why were these two styles, so different in geographical origin, considered compatible in late nineteenth-century Dublin interiors? In London the use of the Moorish style could have had imperialist implications, whereas in Dublin, an imperial dominion, its use could indicate identification with resistance to Empire in countries where the Moorish style originated. During a period of campaign for Home Rule in Ireland in the 1880s, India and Egypt were also striving for independence from imperialism.

Vodrey's Moorish vases exemplify a variety of sources in the design of a single object. Whilst the form was of Moorish or Arab origin, the yellow glaze indicates a Japanese or possibly a Chinese influence. In his article 'On ornamental design' (1874), Longfield commented on what he termed the 'resonance' of different styles from widely different cultures. He discussed the 'universality of form' and the relationship of Celtic forms to other styles of ornament, such as the Greek style.[13] These ideas were similar to those of the antiquarian George Petrie, who drew parallels between the Celtic style and Moorish designs.[14]

Whilst European design has been criticised for the colonialist and racist appropriation of Eastern cultural forms, it has also been noted that, at the height of colonial power, there was a corresponding

10 I am grateful to Jennifer Opie for this observation.

11 Burton 1999, 105.

12 *Catalogue of the Dublin Sketching Club, Twelfth Season* (1885–6), 21–2: 'Pottery by Charles Russell', nos 356–78.

13 Longfield 1874, 44.

14 George Petrie in *Saunders's News-Letter*, 9 December 1850. In *Ornamental Irish antiquities* by Waterhouse and Co. (1850, 9), Petrie's comments on the Tara Brooch were quoted as follows: 'The general form and character of this brooch is that usually recognized as peculiarly Irish, or, perhaps, properly; for it was to all events, common to Scotland; and, if we can trust to the authority of the author of "The Pillars of Hercules", it is also common to the Moorish tribes of Africa, and derived from thence; but, be that as it may, it is certainly of a very great and unknown antiquity in Ireland'.

admiration for Eastern design, albeit 'value-laden and sometimes culturally blinkered'.[15] Vodrey's yellow-glazed Moorish vase has winged handles like the famous Alhambra vase illustrated by Jones, who favoured the Moorish style and introduced the idea of cross-influences between North African art and the Celtic style.[16] It is likely that Russell exhibited the 'Keltic' and 'Moorish' styles together to assert the importance of the Celtic style alongside what was known to be Owen Jones's favoured style, a design statement in itself and open to further interpretation. ■

15 MacKenzie 1995, 107.

16 Jones and Goury 1842–5, 6.

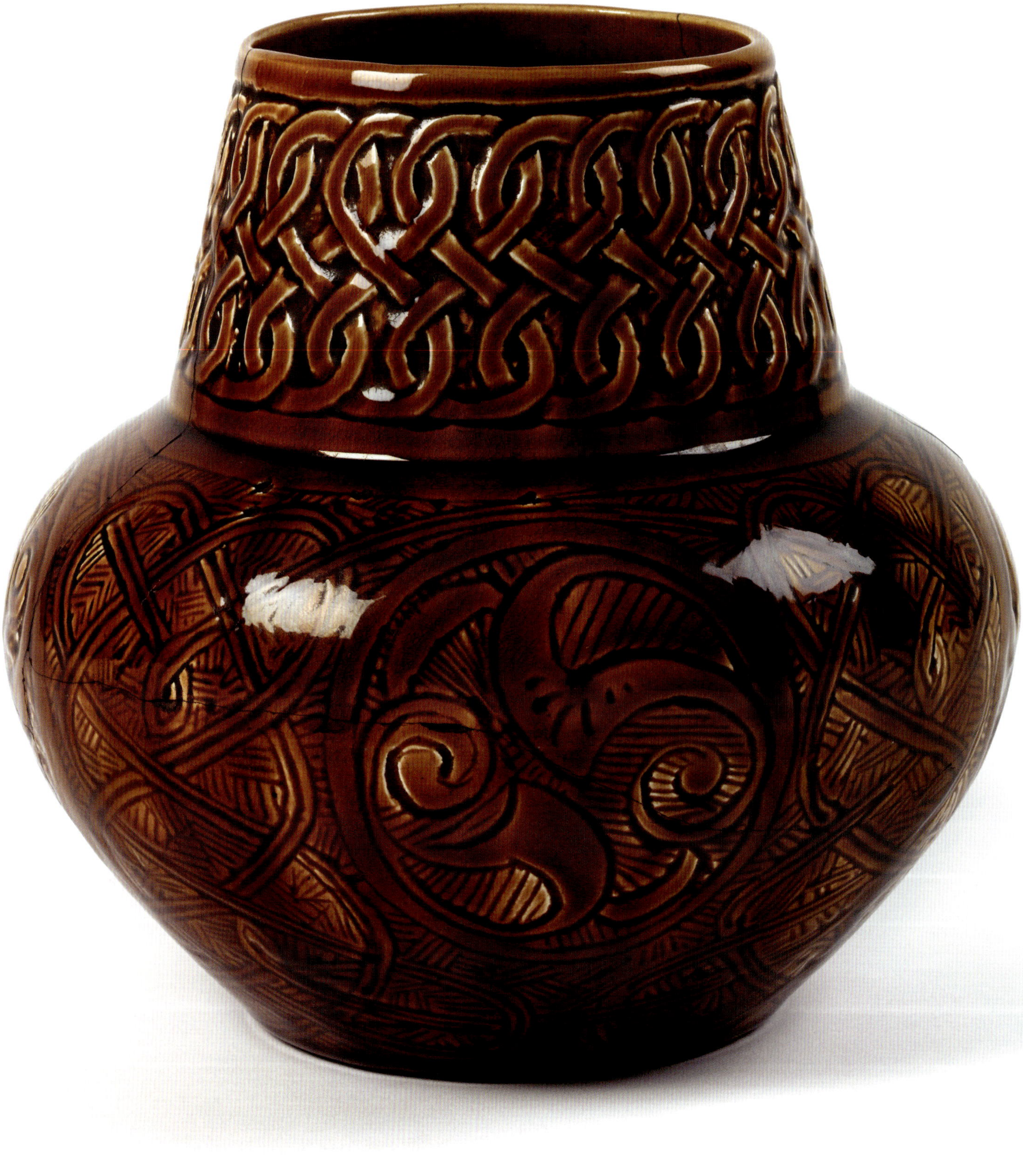

CHAPTER 15

Irish national identity and the 'Celtic Hall'

Irish national identity and the 'Celtic Hall'

In the contemporary Irish imagination, the Celtic style is still regarded as a distinctly national style related to our history and ethnicity. From the 1890s, Irish art and design were aligned to the Symbolist movement in Europe and have been described as a 'visual counterpart' to the literary revival led by the poet W.B. Yeats and the writer/philosopher George Russell (AE).[1] Gordon Bowe and Cumming's catalogue of objects from the Irish and Scottish Arts and Crafts movements revealed parallels between the cities of Dublin and Edinburgh, the shared Celtic heritage of forms being the basis for craft production in Dublin and Edinburgh from the 1880s to the early twentieth century.[2] The authors traced links between the poetic concepts of national identity and Arts and Crafts ideals of social reform, the range of crafts produced in a variety of media being described as 'visual manifestations of the contiguous Celtic revivals in the two cities'.[3]

However, when enthusiasm for the Celtic style first began in Ireland during the nineteenth century, interest in Celtic ornament was an aspect of revivalism in design and international fashionable taste. The jardinières produced by Vodrey were made for the interior of a late Victorian or 'Aesthetic' home and designed to contain a pot plant or spring bulbs. When Vodrey exhibited at the Irish Artisans' Exhibition of 1885, Celtic designs like the ruby-red jardinière from the National Museum collection (Fig. 51; cat. no. 10) were singled out for praise.

The Celtic pottery was described as 'Amongst the most attractive articles in the Vodrian Collection at the Irish Artisans' Exhibition'.[4] According to the artist F.S. Walker, the successful adaptation of Celtic design to pottery decoration was a positive sign for the development of 'Irish Art Industry'.[5] In the spirit of

1 Gordon Bowe 1991.

2 Gordon Bowe and Cumming 1998, 9–16.

3 *Ibid.*, 12–13.

4 Pentland 1885, 39.

5 Walker 1886, 168.

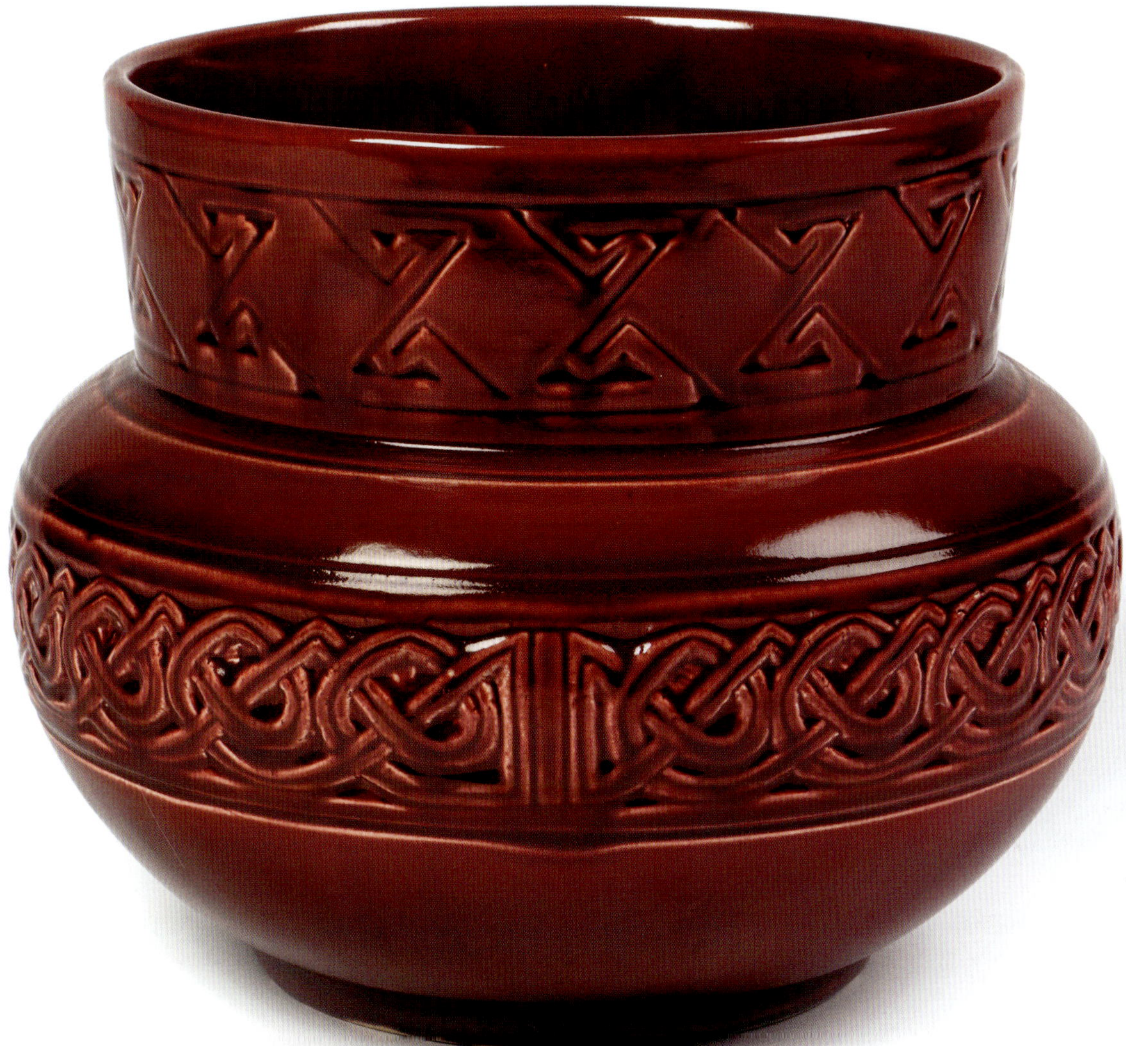

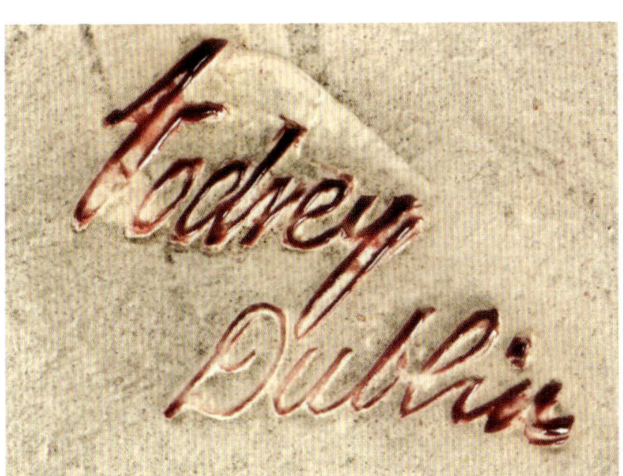

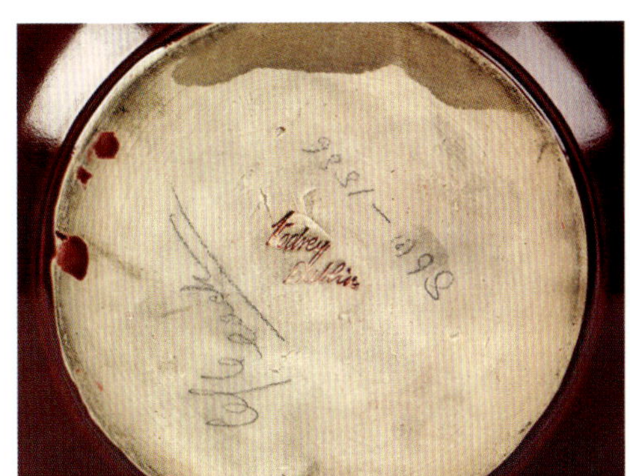

Figs 51—Jardinière with Celtic designs, ruby-red glaze; 23cm x 24cm. NMI 1886.86. Cat. no. 10.

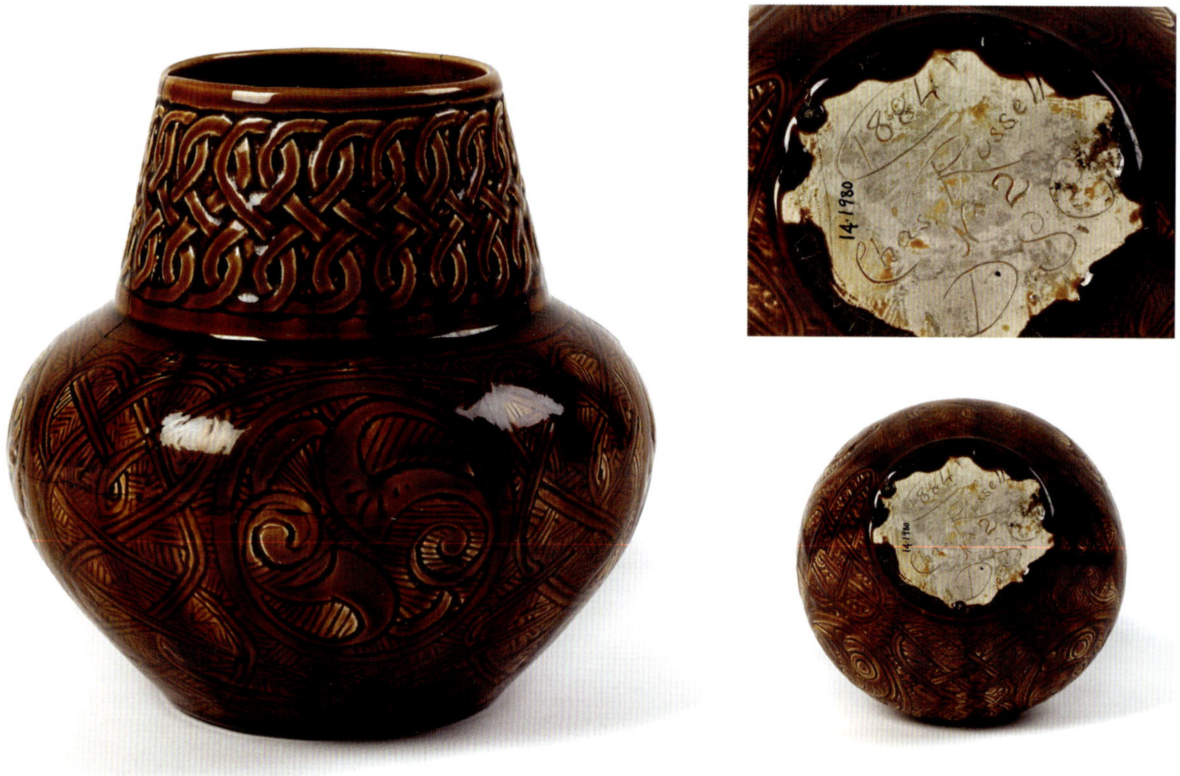

Fig. 52—Jardinière with Celtic designs, brown glaze, by Charles Russell and the Vodrey Dublin Pottery; 18cm × 18cm. Mark inscribed underneath: '1884 Chas Russell No. 2 DSC'. NMI 1980.14. Cat. no. 52.

romantic nationalism, he called for 'a great Public Hall' in Dublin, decorated by 'National Celtic ornament', which might be called the 'Celtic Hall'. These sentiments were echoed by other writers who encouraged the development of Irish art industries for economic revival and the possibility of the Celtic style being an expression of 'native character'.[6] They foreshadow the development of Irish dress design as a political statement and the use of the Celtic style in the early twentieth century to denote national identity.[7]

Celtic designs on ceramic objects produced by the Vodrey Dublin Pottery were based on Charles Russell's interpretations of Irish antiquities in the Royal Irish Academy collection and his drawings of the Book of Kells.[8] As we have seen from the earlier discussion of Russell's sketch-book, however, the ceramic process and Vodrey's production of the red jardinière involved several people, including those involved in slip-casting and mould-making, and this would have been directed by Frederick Vodrey.

Another large jardinière in the National Museum (Figs 52; cat. no. 52), signed by Russell and bearing the Vodrey Dublin Pottery mark, was illustrated by Paul Larmour, who pointed out that the decoration was based

6 Larmour (1992, 3–4) refers to an article by Professor Charles G. Leland, 'An opening for the unemployed in Ireland', *Longman's Magazine* 3 (13) (1883), 44–51, and to Stokes 1887, 5.

7 Ward 2014, 206, 209–10.

8 Peter Healy (pers. comm., December 2003), a grandson of Charles Russell, said that Russell spent many hours drawing from the Book of Kells in Trinity College and went there daily for a period.

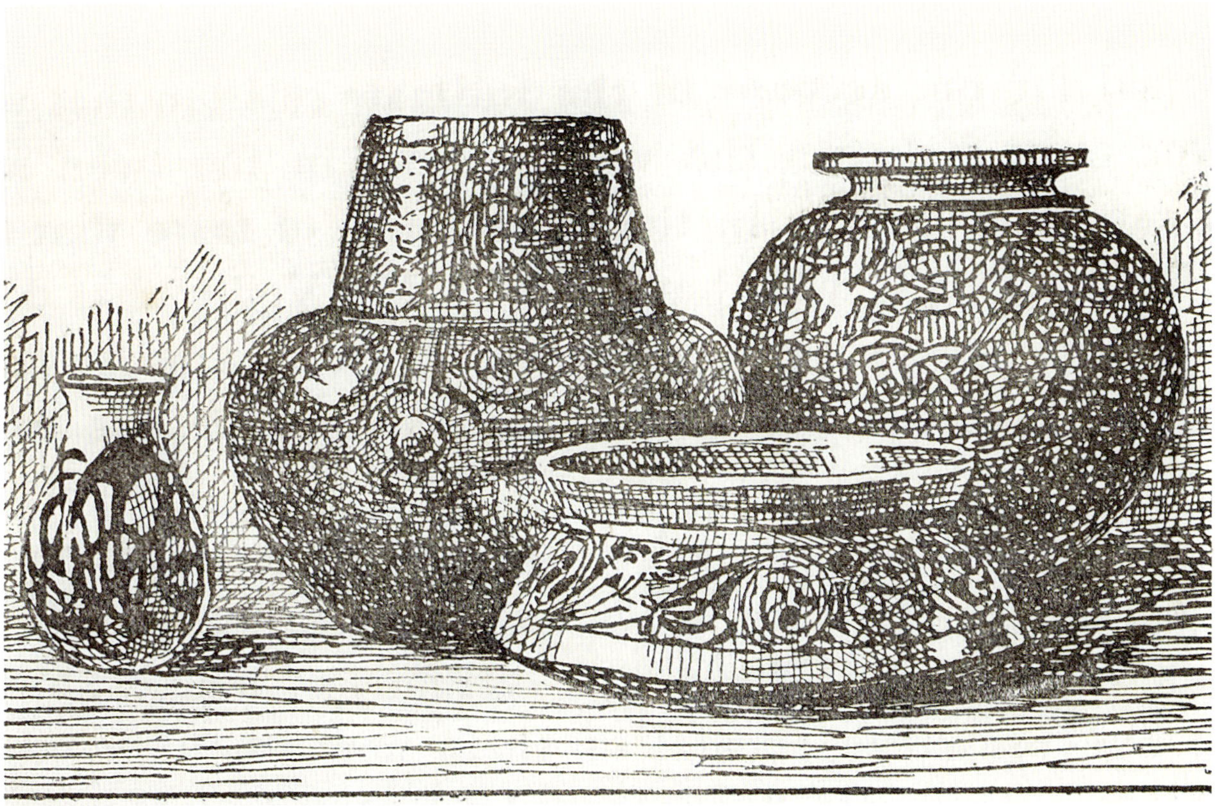

Fig. 53—Illustration from 'Of faience and its design in the Irish Artizans' Exhibition' (Pentland 1885, 40).

on the knop of a crozier fragment in the Petrie collection.[9] It is similar to one included in an illustration of Vodrey's art pottery with Pentland's article in the *Dublin University Review* (Fig. 53).

Walker's idea of the 'Celtic Hall' is a powerful concept that must have contributed to the development of Irish national identity. It coincided with the development of Celticism, the romantic revival of Celtic literature led by the English poet Matthew Arnold, which gave rise to the idea of the 'noble Celt'.[10] In *On the study of Celtic literature*, Arnold made several references to O'Curry and Moore, scholars of early Irish literature.[11]

During the nineteenth century the Celtic style, along with many other styles illustrated in Owen Jones's *The grammar of ornament*, was intrinsic to design theory and practice throughout Britain. Jones devoted a section to Celtic ornament, including examples from all the countries in the British Isles—England, Ireland, Scotland and Wales.[12] He embraced the Celtic 'style' of ornament as 'native', and referred to ancient pre-Christian sites, including Newgrange, Co. Meath, as 'our Druidical Temples'.[13] While Jones's examples of Celtic ornament were primarily from England or areas of what we consider

9 Larmour 1992, 6–7.

10 Brown 1996.

11 Arnold 1905 [1867], 38–40.

12 Jones 1856, 6.

13 *Ibid.*

modern Britain, he also drew on the Book of Kells and other Early Christian manuscripts, such as the Lindisfarne Gospels in Scotland.

The use of zoomorphic (animal) forms in 'the strange monstrous animals and birds, with long top-knot tongues, and tails, intertwining in almost endless knots' of 'Celtic decoration' was contrasted with the use of phyllomorphic (vegetable) forms in 'Classical decoration'.[14] *The grammar of ornament* provides a theoretical context for the designs produced by the Vodrey Dublin Pottery; the Celtic style had a popularity and commercial value outside Ireland besides its associations with cultural revival in Dublin.[15] Liberty's store in London retailed Celtic-style silver and art pottery from the 1890s,[16] and the production of ceramic designs influenced by revivalism and national identity was part of a Europe-wide trend in the ceramic industry.[17]

In Ireland, Vodrey's production of this Celtic-style art pottery must also be viewed in the context of antiquarianism and George Coffey's writings on the subject. Coffey was deeply interested in the universal origins of Celtic ornament and corresponded with other European scholars in the field. The study of Irish antiquities led by the Royal Irish Academy (RIA) was developed by Coffey when he was curator of the RIA collection and before he worked as Keeper of Antiquities at the National Museum. According to Crooke, the RIA antiquities, which were transferred to the new Museum of Science and Art,[18] were regarded as symbols of national identity.[19]

George Coffey described style as an expression of the characteristics of nationality in art and design.[20] His words echo views on the meaning of style in design at the time, and his *Guide to the Celtic antiquities ... in the National Museum* was praised in tones that show that it was regarded as a contribution to national identity. The *Journal of the Royal Society of Antiquaries of Ireland* described Coffey's work as

> 'calling attention to the nature and value of those early evidences of the piety, skill, and social advancement of our Celtic forefathers of which we possess such undeniable proofs in the rare, precious, and beautiful objects in the National Museum'.[21]

Within the context of the Celtic Revival in Ireland, the role of the antiquarian/archaeologist extended to a cultural agenda. Coffey's writings and his delivery of a lecture on Celtic ornament to the Dublin

14 Jones 1856, 6.

15 Anscombe 1995, 71.

16 Tilbrook and House 1976.

17 Csenkey and Steinart 2002.

18 Crooke (2000, 114) notes that there was a struggle between the members of the Academy and the Department of Science and Art for ownership of these objects.

19 *Ibid.*, 103–4. The author describes the purchase of Dean Dawson's collection of ancient Irish art in 1841 as an expression of 'romantic nationalism'. She quotes references to a 'patriotic object' and the idea that the purchase would be aiding 'a public and national design'. Further quotations from the Minutes of the Antiquities Committee in 1855 reveal that a sense of 'nationality' existed among the members of the RIA.

20 Coffey 1889, 407.

21 George Coffey Papers, National Library, MS 13,839, no. 516. Review in the Royal Society of Antiquaries' *Journal* (specific date not given).

Sketching Club (1897)[22] indicate the integration of design, antiquarianism, and the expression of national identity in Dublin during the later nineteenth century.

Whilst correspondence between Coffey and others reveals that he understood Celtic style in a broader context (being involved in discussions about the origins of style and ornament pursued by well-known European theorists such as Semper and Riegl),[23] he was also interested in establishing a national identity. Owing to personal connections with the struggle for Irish independence and the Irish Home Industry movement, Coffey provides a link between the Anglo-Irish ruling class and the aspirations of the rising nationalist middle class.[24]

Just as there was a tendency for the ruling class to appropriate culture in order to assert power in the nineteenth century,[25] the Celtic style later became an instrument of political ideals amongst nationalists. From the period of the Home Rule movement in the 1880s to the War of Independence in 1920–2, changes in the meaning of the Celtic style reflected political change and evolution in the concept of Irish national identity. In the early twentieth century the Celtic style became an emblem of Irishness and, along with images of the harp and shamrock, was a symbol of political independence.[26] This marked a shift away from designers' use of the Celtic style as one of the styles of ornament in Owen Jones's *The grammar of ornament*, and therefore a move away from late Victorian taste or 'Aestheticism'. ■

22 Minutes of the Dublin Sketching Club, 1897 (courtesy of Mr Peter Healy).

23 George Coffey Papers, National Library, MS 13, 839, no. 516. Review in the Royal Society of Antiquaries' *Journal* (specific date not given).

24 Interview with Dairine Coffey, granddaughter of George Coffey, 13 December 2004. George Coffey's wife, Jenny L 'Estrange, was part of 'Castle society'; they were founding members of the Irish Literary Theatre. Their son Dermot was married to Francesca Trench (known as Cesca or Siabh); although from a unionist background, she and her sister were involved in the nationalist movement.

25 Crooke 2000, 114.

26 Ward 2014.

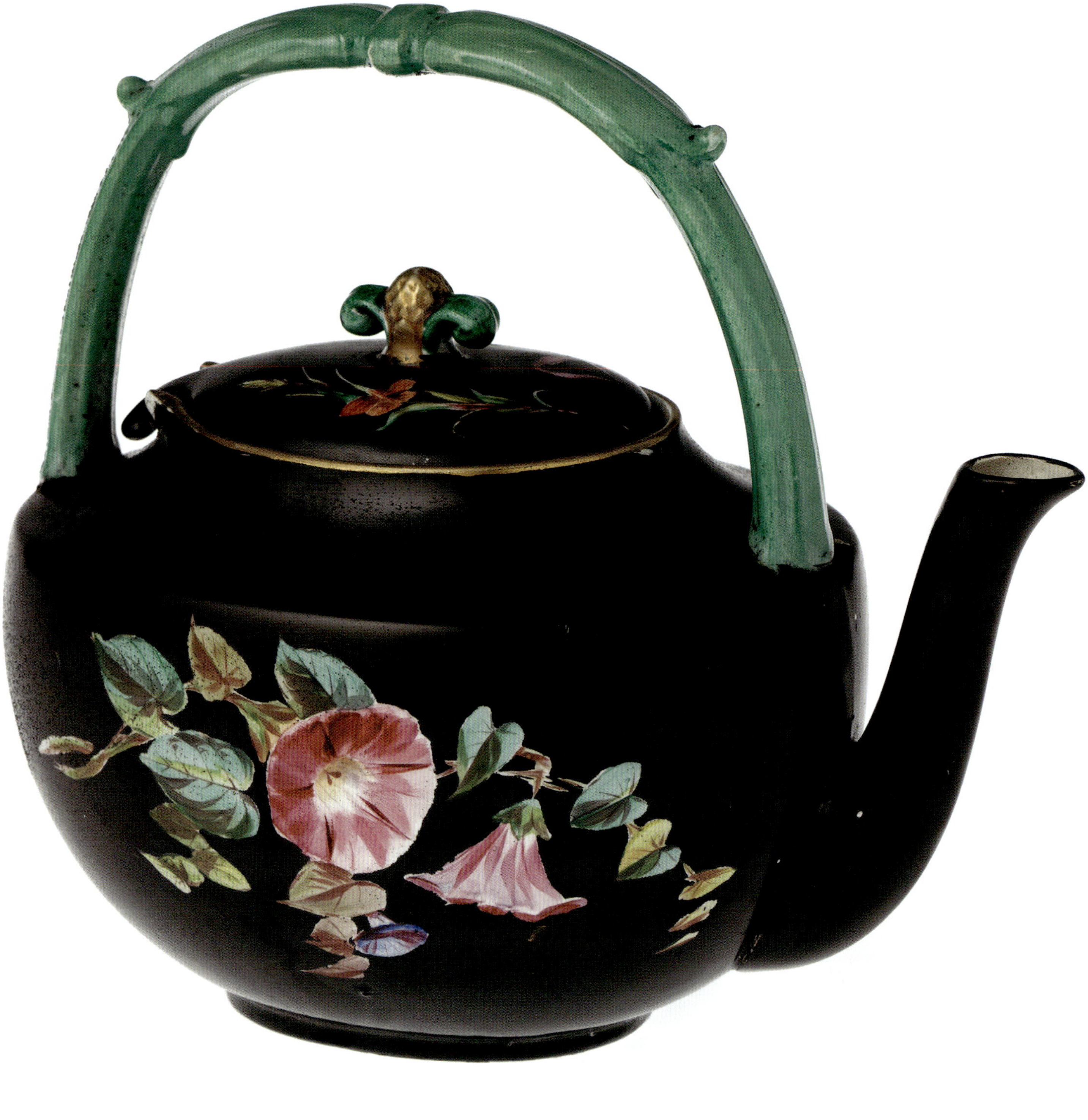

CHATPER 16

Conclusion

Conclusion

During the late nineteenth century there is evidence of upward mobility amongst the Irish middle class, reflected in the production and consumption of ceramics. The spread of fashionable taste and support for home industry from the upper-class élite to a wider customer base also influenced consumer demand. In addition, suburban expansion and the building of new homes gave rise to an increased demand for household furnishings, including ceramics, to which producers and retailers like W.H. Kerr and Frederick Vodrey responded. Kerr's interest in producing ceramics from Irish clays for commercial and also patriotic reasons—first as manager in Worcester and later for his own personal use—was a significant catalyst to the start of ceramic production in Ireland.

Whilst outside Ireland there was a distinction between producers of floral, hand-painted porcelain and those who produced monochrome earthenware or 'art pottery' catering for followers of social and artistic reform,[1] this differentiation did not apply in Dublin. Both types of art ceramics were produced by Frederick Vodrey because he was catering for a relatively small market within an intimate artistic community, where members of the DSC and students of the QI mingled. Vodrey's collaboration with artists like Mary Redmond and Charles Russell, and his association with the Dublin Sketching Club and the National Museum curators, gives us valuable insight into cultural activity in Dublin during the late nineteenth century.

In this story of 'Irish Art Pottery' there remain some open-ended questions—namely the association, if any, between Herbert Cooper and Frederick Vodrey, and the exact location of Vodrey's art pottery at the 'rere of' Moore Street, situated in Moore Lane, reportedly behind No. 19.[2] While the extent of the pottery workshop can only be fully established by future archaeological investigation, the question of whether Vodrey and Cooper worked together hinges on Westropp's single report that they did. It seems likely that Vodrey offered the facilities of firing and clay materials to the students at the Queen's Institute between

1 Blaszczyk 1994.

2 F. Vodrey's trade card, 1885. Cahill Litho., Printers & Co., Dublin. NMI 1886.125.

1872 and 1883, in the same way that his letter made these available to the Dublin Sketching Club. Similar to that small piece of documentary information, which points to Vodrey's collaboration with the DSC and was confirmed by Russell's descendants, there may also be evidence of Vodrey's links with the QI to be discovered in the future.

There are no further textual references to Vodrey Dublin Pottery after F.S. Walker's article in 1886, yet the style of some of the objects traced and documented suggests that Vodrey could have been producing art pottery into the early 1890s. Later developments in Irish ceramics indicate that his interest in producing art pottery with Irish clays and the creation of employment had an enduring influence; consumers fired by 'practical patriotism' were attracted because the ceramics were produced in Ireland and made of Irish clay. The written sources dealing with Frederick Vodrey and his art pottery in journals and newspaper advertisements present us with remnants of an important aspect of that wider phase in Irish material culture known as the Celtic Revival.

The ceramics produced by Vodrey are also of interest, firstly because they illustrate the principles of the design vocabulary in the nineteenth century and secondly because they are evidence of fashionable taste in Dublin, particularly the Aesthetic taste, confirming that in Ireland the Aesthetic style co-existed with the Celtic Revival style to create a unique cultural statement. The activity and writings of the National Museum curators Coffey and Longfield fostered an interest in design ideas, which prompted Vodrey to produce art pottery in response to consumer taste. The Celtic-style ceramics in the National Museum reflect the significance of cultural revival to Irish consumers in the late nineteenth century. Other examples show the wider range of taste and home decoration in Dublin *c.* 1870–90, from the botanical illustrations and organic Art Nouveau shapes to the simplified forms of emerging Modernism.

When the Queen's Institute closed in 1883, Herbert Cooper set up his own china-decorating business and continued to be well known for hand-painted porcelain until his retirement in 1907.[3] He also tutored students in his studio, where he employed some. Frederick Vodrey's 'Irish Art Pottery' ended sometime after his sudden death in 1897.[4] However, two writers who commented on the Irish pottery industry in the later 1890s—Lord Mayo and Eugene Sheerin—do not mention the ceramics from the Vodrey Dublin Pottery or the Queen's Institute. From these sources we can conclude that the production of pottery in Ireland had reverted to the state it was in during the early 1870s, before Vodrey's art pottery and the Queen's Institute classes began.

Writing in 1895, Lord Mayo, founder and president of the Irish Arts and Crafts Society, was critical of the lack of quality in ceramic designs in the Dublin shop windows.[5] The Belleek Pottery was the only Irish pottery that he mentioned.[6] In 1896 Eugene Sheerin, a well-known decorator in Belleek, also indicated that the Belleek Pottery in County Fermanagh was the only pottery of note in Ireland.[7] He called for the Irish Industries Association to recognise that 'Dublin would seem a good place in which to establish a

3 Curry 1993, 195.

4 Death certificate for Frederick Vodrey, 19 October 1897, at 29 Lower Abbey Street. Registrar's District No. 2, North City. Frederick Vodrey's occupation was given as 'Glass and China Merchant'.

5 Lord Mayo, 'Irish Arts and Crafts', *New Ireland Review* (January 1895), 673–80.

6 *Ibid.*, 678.

7 Eugene Sheerin, 'The pottery industry in Ireland', *New Ireland Review* (September 1896), 65–73.

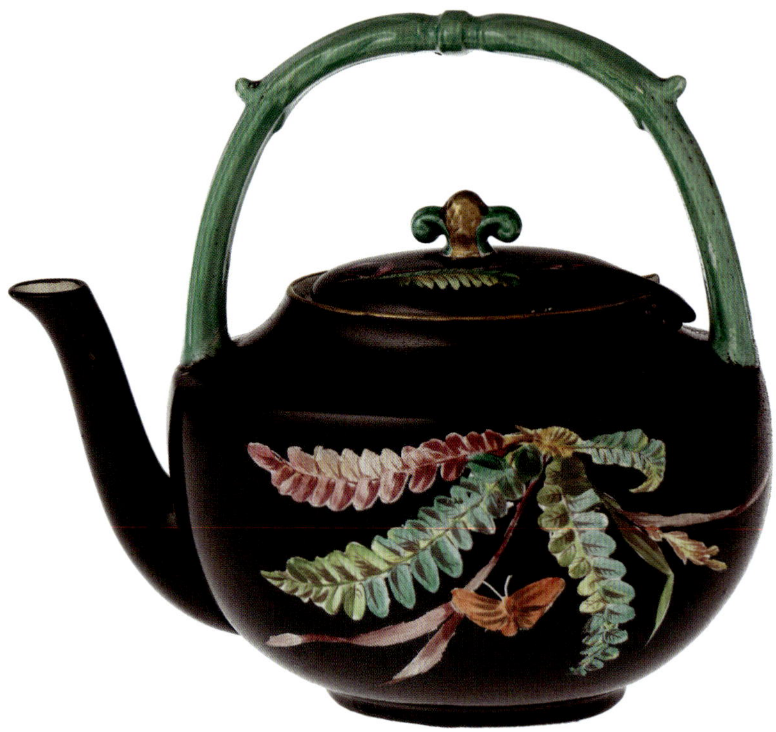

Fig. 54—Tea kettle, decorated with hand-painted flowers (convolvulus) on one side, and with flowers and fern on the other side; 20cm x 21cm. Signed 'H. Cooper Dublin'. The simulated bamboo handle shows the influence of Oriental ceramics from Japan and China. NMI 1946.44.1 & 2. Cat. no. 76.

high-class pottery'. His words echo Vodrey's comments to the Select Committee on Industries (1885), when he stated that Dublin was ideally situated for the development of a ceramic industry owing to proximity to the ports and easy access to raw materials—coal for firing the kilns, and the clay that would be needed for blending with Irish clays.[8]

The demise of Frederick Vodrey left a vacuum in the nascent Irish pottery industry, and there were no exhibitors of art pottery made in Ireland at the Dublin International Exhibition (1907), Belleek being the only exhibitor of Irish-made ceramics. Nevertheless, awareness of the potential for using Irish natural resources for ceramic manufacture continued, and the organisers of the 1907 exhibition asked the Della Robbia Pottery in England, which was established in 1894 and run along Arts and Crafts principles,[9] to provide a display of Celtic-style pottery made from Irish clay.[10] Coinciding with the 1907 exhibition, a report on *Irish Rural Life and Industry* discussed details of a proposed 'Scheme for an Irish Co-operative Pottery Works'.[11]

8 Select Committee on Industries (Ireland) 1885, 821.

9 Naylor 1971, 151.

10 The display of Della Robbia pottery was the centrepiece of an exhibit on the possible uses of Irish materials for industry (exhibit 159).

11 *Irish Rural Life and Industry—Report issued in connection with the Home Industries Section, Irish International Exhibition 1907*, 217–22. The proposed Scheme, written by W.P. Rix, Ceramic Specialist, includes a detailed plan and description of a pottery works and artisan dwellings for workers. The 'Ceramic Specialist' may have been Harold Rathbone.

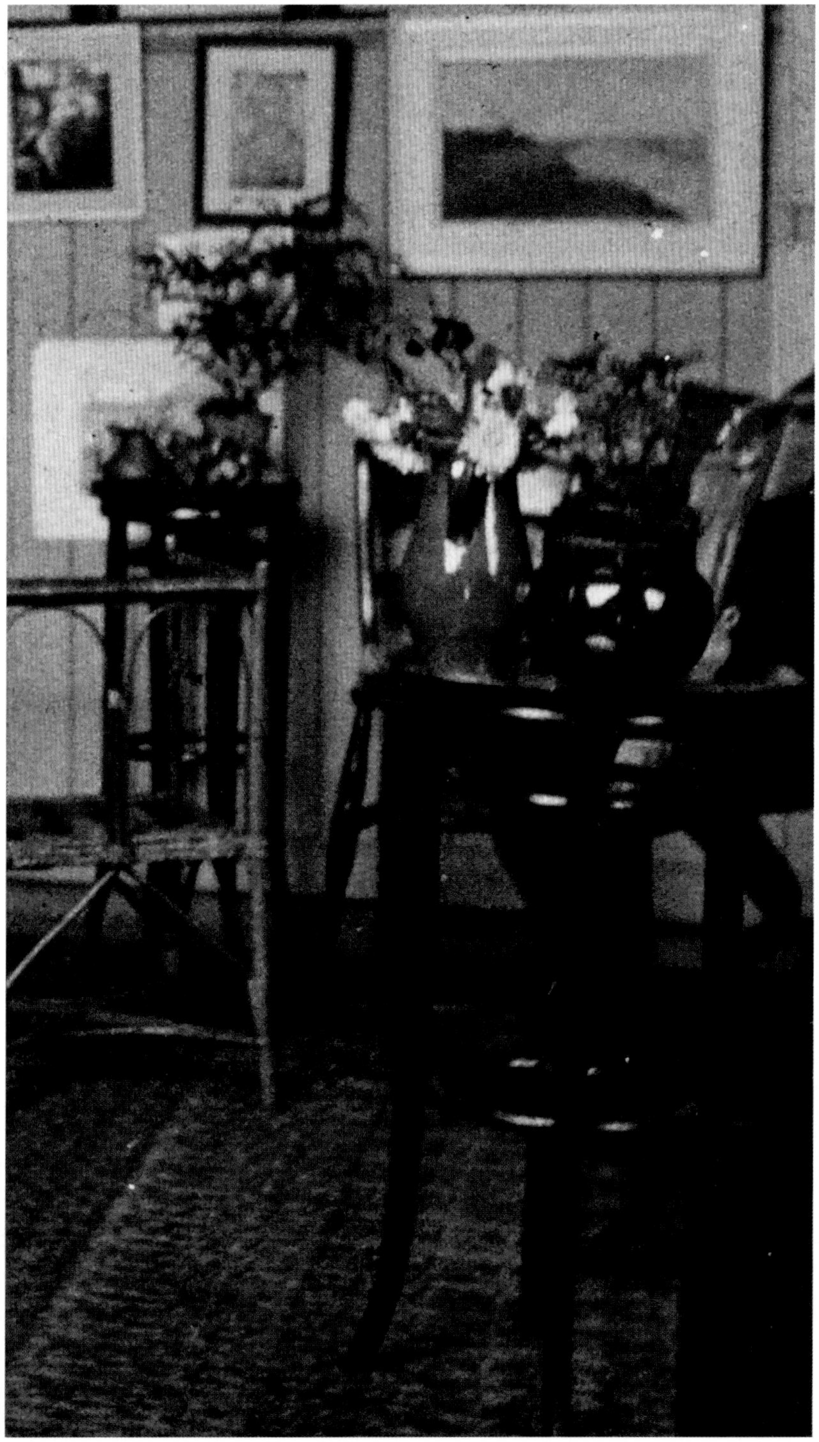

Fig. 55—Interior showing ceramic jug and jardinière, similar to Vodrey Dublin art pottery, Dublin, *c.* 1890. Photograph by T.F. Geoghegan (detail of Fig. 41).

The continuing quest to develop an Irish ceramic industry, from the time of the Royal Dublin Society's encouragement of small producers in 1825 to the 1907 proposal for an Irish Co-operative Pottery Works, was later picked up by the government in the early twentieth century. The ceramic industry in Ireland lay dormant for almost 30 years, apart from the established and successful Belleek Pottery in County Fermanagh. After the establishment of the Free State, Irish government policy was to 'encourage and locate modern industrialized ceramic factories outside Dublin', and this renewed interest in economic development led to the founding of the Carrigaline Pottery in County Cork (1928) and the Arklow Pottery in County Wicklow (1935). The Carrigaline Pottery made 'inexpensive tableware and ornaments as well as Art Deco items with variegated glazes'.[12] The Arklow Pottery established a modern production system based on original studio designs created by resident designers,[13] part of the government plan to develop industry.[14] It produced 'first domestic ware, later bone china, and in the 1950s art pottery'.[15]

The ceramics produced by Vodrey's art pottery from *c.* 1873 to 1890, and Herbert Cooper's decoration of porcelain wares with students at the Queen's Institute from 1872 to 1883, reveal the cultural dynamics of taste in Dublin during the late nineteenth century. While textual evidence shows that members of fashionable society in Dublin were keen followers of the Celtic Revival, the full range of styles evident in the objects shows that Irish consumers of 'all creeds and classes' were following international taste. Our study of these ceramic objects in the National Museum opens a window onto Irish society, revealing the upward mobility of the middle classes, the beginning of art education for women, the recognition of artisans' rights and the influence of national identity on Irish design. ■

12 Dunlevy 1988, 32.

13 Lamb 2017, 130–1.

14 Whitty 2003.

15 Dunlevy 1988, 32.

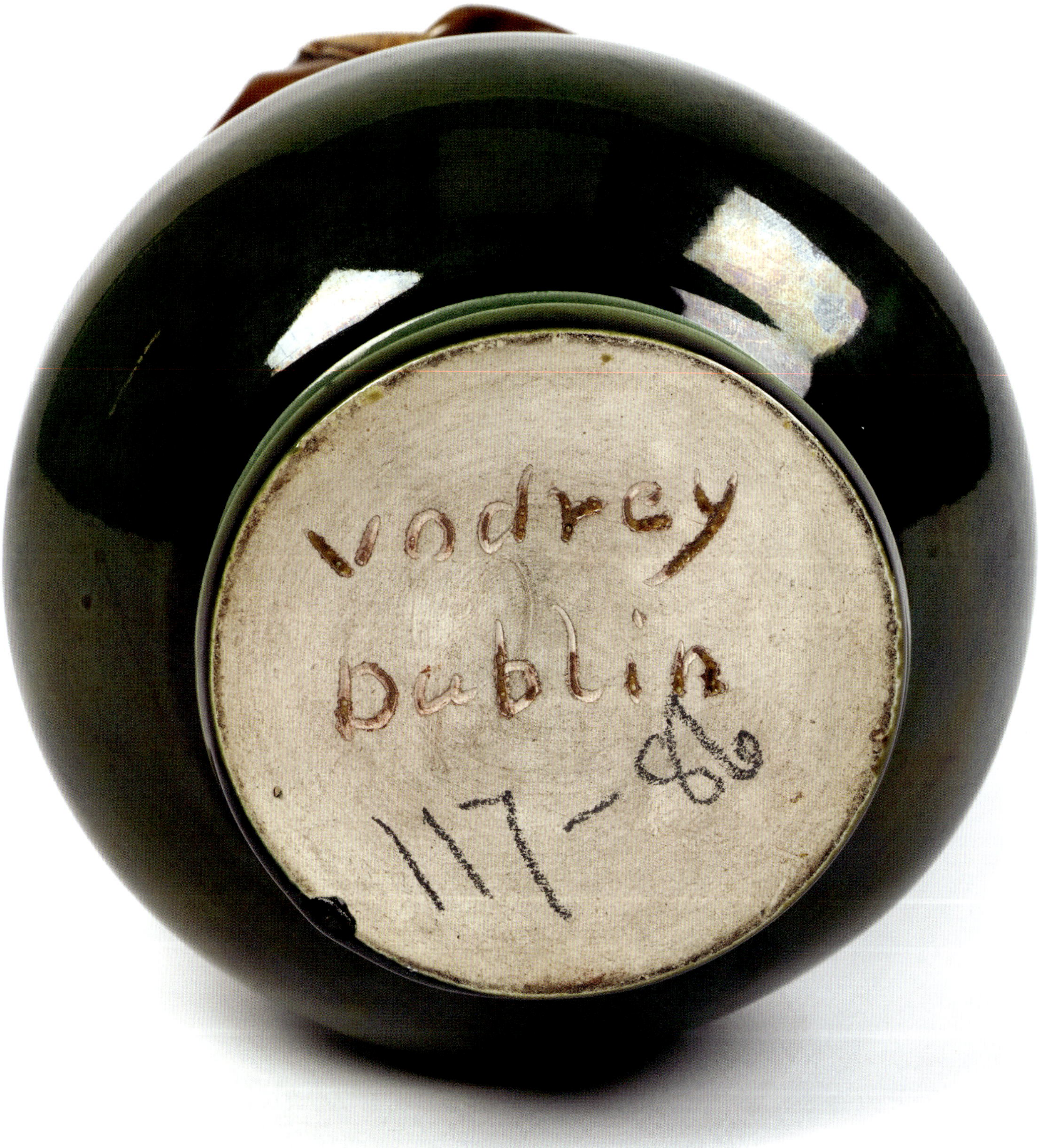
Vodrey
Dublin
117-86

Appendix

Marks found on Vodrey Dublin Pottery and chronology of style

The information gained from documentation of the objects of Vodrey Dublin Pottery in the National Museum, the Ulster Museum and private collections enables us to ascertain possible dates for different marks used by the pottery.[1] The marks identified could be assigned to specific years in the 1880s—1882, 1884 and 1886. There were four different marks in printed style and two marks in a hand-inscribed style; examples of all are illustrated here.

The Vodrey Pottery objects with the 1882 mark were mostly in white-glazed earthenware known as 'ivory raised flower ware', decorated with raised flowers and hand-painted with floral and gilt decoration (Fig. 13; cat. nos 39 and 40). These designs were probably the type exhibited at the 1882 National Exhibition in Dublin. According to Westropp, Vodrey was also producing wares in High Victorian styles such as the Classical or the Renaissance styles at the same time.[2]

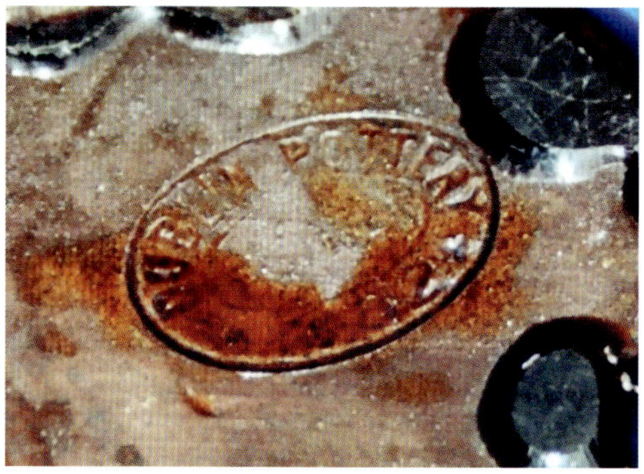

Fig. 56—'DUBLIN POTTERY VODREY 1882'.

The Renaissance style can be seen in a large ewer with a winged figure decorated in a ruby-coloured glaze, illustrated and dated *c.* 1880 by Westropp (cat. no. 38). The object, however, bears the more usual impressed mark, which is associated with *c.* 1886. Westropp may have based his dating on information received when the item was acquired by the Museum in the 1920s. It could be concluded that Vodrey was producing a range of styles, including Renaissance revival and High Victorian naturalism, at the time of the 1882 Dublin Exhibition, to which he had already introduced forms with a Japanese influence.

Vodrey's shift to the production of art pottery in the Japanese aesthetic appears to have been quite

1 Database included in Molloy 2007.

2 Westropp 1935.

Fig. 57—'DUBLIN POTTERY VODREY 1882'.

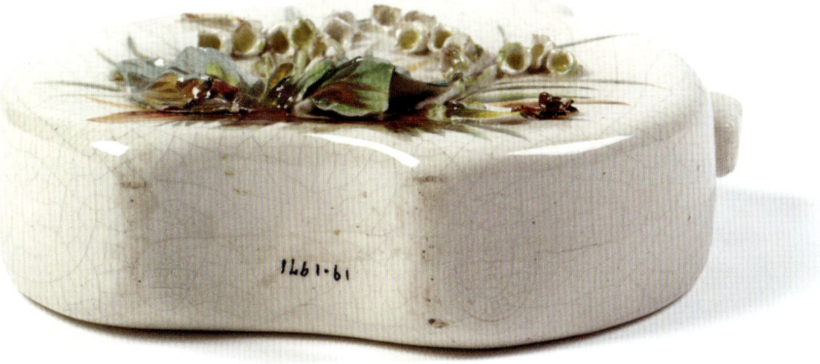

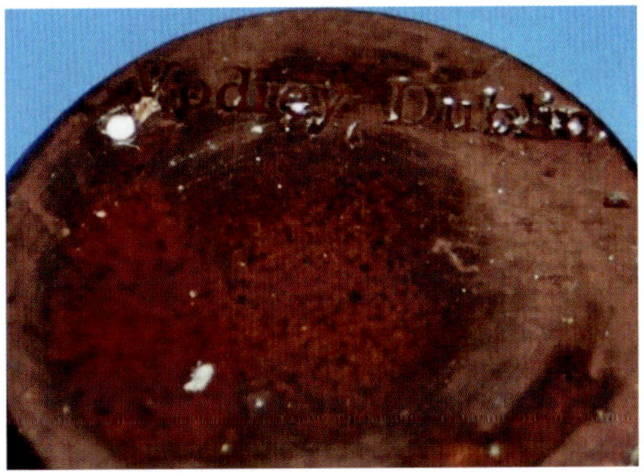

Fig. 58—'Vodrey, Dublin', c. 1884.

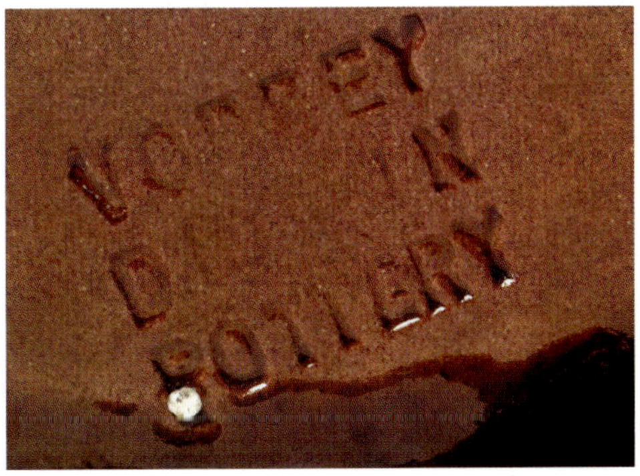

Fig. 59—'VODREY DUBLIN POTTERY', c. 1886.

rapid. It may have been as early as 1882. A gourd-shaped 'purse vase' in a private collection has the mark dated 1882,[3] indicating that by this date Vodrey was aware of Christopher Dresser's writings about Japan. The Japanese aesthetic is also represented by objects in the 1884 National Museum acquisition. Items like these were probably amongst the 'Vodrian Pottery' displayed at the 1883 Cork Exhibition.[4] The objects in the 1886 Museum acquisition indicate that by 1886 Vodrey was producing a wide range of ornamental ceramics in the Aesthetic taste.

3 The collector, Mr Peter Lamb, suggests that the shape of the object is based on a type of leather purse known in Japan.

4 *Cork Industrial Exhibition 1883. Report of the Executive Committee, Awards of the Jurors and Statements of Account* (1886), 395.

Fig. 60—'DUBLIN POTTERY VODREY', small impressed mark *c.* 1886–90.

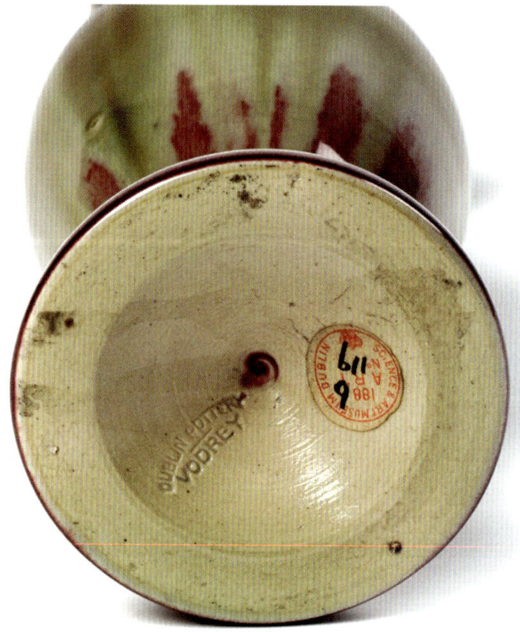

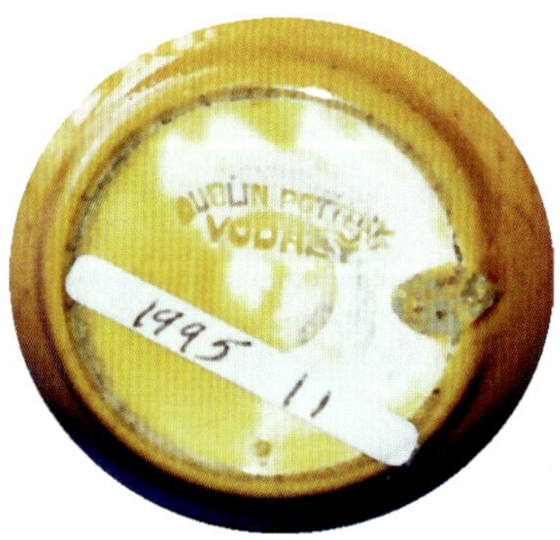

Fig. 61—'DUBLIN POTTERY VODREY', small impressed mark *c.* 1886–90.

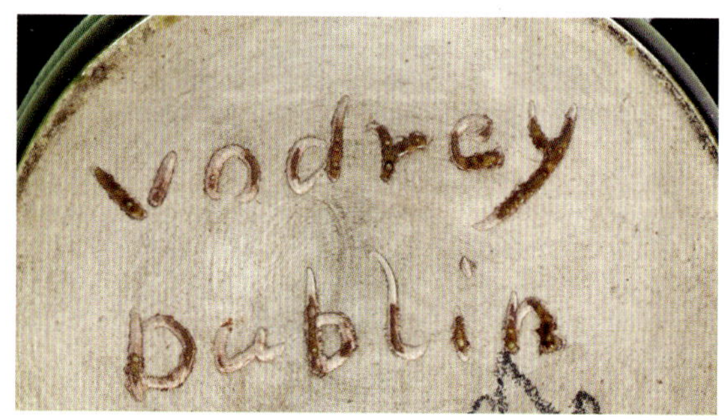

Fig. 62—'Vodrey Dublin' in the hand-inscribed style, *c.* 1886–90.

The yellow coffee cup and saucer in the National Museum (Fig. 4; cat. no. 21) and objects documented in private collections demonstrate that sets of tableware were produced by the Vodrey Dublin Pottery, as well as ornamental ceramics. In addition to the objects in the NMI collection, the functional wares documented include punch goblets, dessert plates and a teapot with sugar bowl and cream jug.[5] The ornamental wares reflect the Victorian interest in nature and plants in the interior and range from Art Nouveau-style vases to jardinières and small bulb pots. Some of the objects documented are stylistically later than the 1886 Museum objects, although they have the same range of marks seen in the 1886 Museum acquisition. Owing to stylistic differences, they could be dated a little later, *c.* 1890. ■

5 Database included in Molloy 2007.

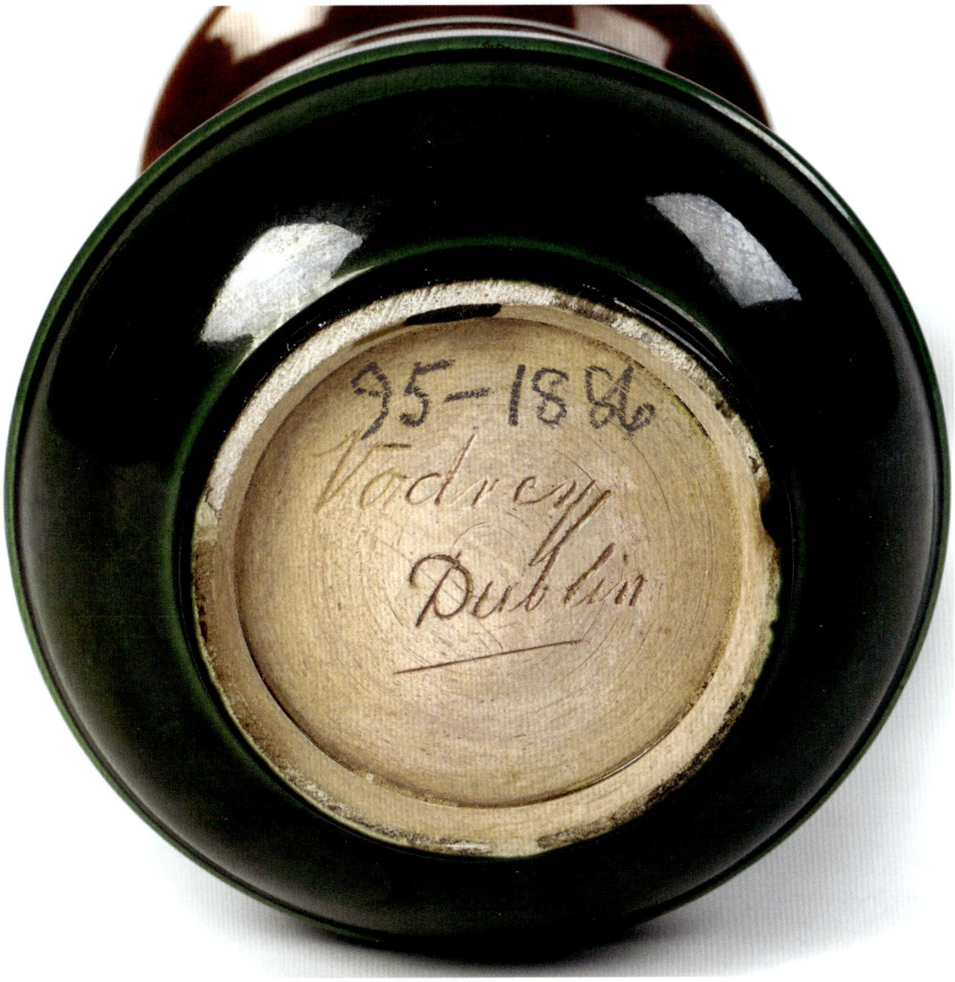

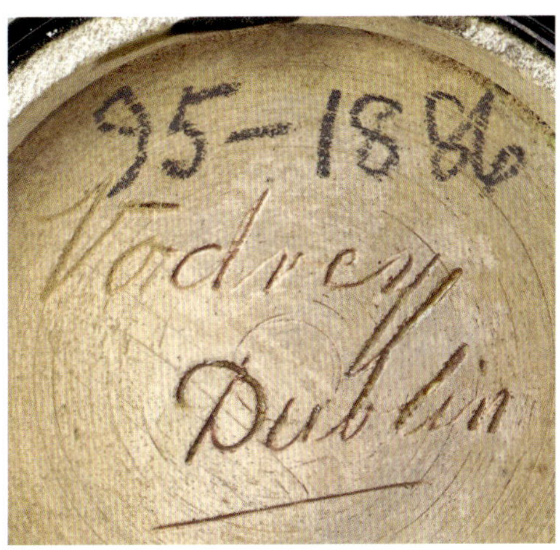

Fig. 63—'DUBLIN POTTERY VODREY', small impressed mark c. 1886–90.

List of figures

Fig. 23—Portrait of Frederick Vodrey by the Vodrey Dublin Pottery; bust profile in oval medallion, life-size, terracotta; signed on the back 'M Redmond 1884' and 'F Vodrey Jany [January] 1st 1884'. Impressed mark: 'DUBLIN POTTERY VODREY'. Photo courtesy of the Vodrey family, Canada.

Fig. 24—Christening mug with inscription 'Frederick Vodrey born 4th August 1845'. Hand-painted, gilt and floral decoration; Staffordshire. Photo courtesy of the Vodrey family, Canada.

Fig. 25—Cover of a booklet titled 'The Dublin Sketching Club November 1888'. Minute Book of the Dublin Sketching Club, 1885–91. Courtesy of the National Library of Ireland, MS Acc. 4786, Box 1.

Fig. 26—From a booklet titled 'Dublin Sketching Club 1888'; inside cover page, 'Descriptive notes and rules. November, 1888'. Minute Book of the Dublin Sketching Club, 1885–91. Courtesy of the National Library of Ireland, MS Acc. 4786, Box 1.

Fig. 27—Cover of booklet titled 'Dublin Sketching Club. List of Members August, 1889'. Minute Book of the Dublin Sketching Club, 1885–91. Courtesy of the National Library of Ireland, MS Acc. 4786, Box 1.

Fig. 28—Photograph of a Dublin Sketching Club excursion, Glen Duagh, Rockbrook, 25 May 1895. Minute Books of the Dublin Sketching Club. Courtesy of the National Library of Ireland, MS Acc. 4786, Boxes 1–3.

Fig. 29—Women sketching outdoors *c.* 1890. The style of dress worn by the women suggests the period *c.* 1888-95. From *Photographs of Irish scenery* by T.F. Geoghegan, 8 Lower Sackville Street, *c.* 1890. Courtesy of the National Library of Ireland, ALB 8:40.

Fig. 30—'Monkey and Rabbit' by Alexander Williams RHA. Vase, baluster shape, tapered ovoid body, mottled brown and blue glaze; applied decoration is hand-modelled, showing figure of a monkey hanging from a tree and holding a hare by the tail. Signed 'A. Williams' on the side, 'DSC' underneath, *c.* 1883; 21cm x 13cm. National Museum of Ireland, NMI 1913.13. Cat. no. 57.

Fig. 31—'Blackberry vase' by Charles Russell; inscribed 'DSC 1883' under base and 'C.R. IX 83' at bottom, to left of bramble branch; 1883; 20cm x 13.5cm. National Museum of Ireland, NMI 1980.13. Cat. no. 51.

Fig. 32—Drawing of Celtic interlace pattern from Charles Russell's sketch-book (facsimile). National Museum of Ireland, NMI AI/154/003.

Fig. 33—Vase, hand-painted with Celtic interlace and zoomorphic designs; 'C. Russell pinxii 6.11.85' inscribed underneath; green ground, yellow and burgundy, and the words 'Bliain sona nua agat'; 13cm x 8cm. National Museum of Ireland, NMI 1980.15. Cat. no. 53.

Fig. 34—Drawing/portrait of unidentified man (possibly Frederick Vodrey or his brother Thomas Vodrey) from Charles Russell's sketch-book (facsimile). National Museum of Ireland, NMI AI/154/003.

Fig. 35—Drawing of a Classical ewer from Charles Russell's sketch-book (facsimile). National Museum of Ireland, NMI AI/154/003.

Fig. 52—Jardinière with Celtic designs, brown glaze, by Charles Russell and the Vodrey Dublin Pottery; 18cm x 18cm. National Museum of Ireland, NMI 1980.14. Cat. no. 52.

Fig. 53—Illustration from J.H. Pentland, 'Of faience and its design in the Irish Artizans' Exhibition', *Dublin University Review* (August 1885), 40. Courtesy of the National Library of Ireland.

Fig. 54—Tea kettle with lid; black with simulated bamboo handle in green; decorated with hand-painted flowers (convolvulus) on one side and with flowers and fern on the other side; 20cm x 21cm. Signed 'H. Cooper Dublin'. National Museum of Ireland, NMI 1946.44.1 & 2. Cat. no. 76.

Fig. 55—Interior showing ceramic jug and jardinière, Dublin, *c.* 1890. Photograph by T.F. Geoghegan (detail of Fig. 39). Courtesy of the National Library of Ireland, ALB 8:40.

Fig. 56—Mark: impressed 'DUBLIN POTTERY VODREY 1882'.

Fig. 57—Mark: impressed 'DUBLIN POTTERY VODREY 1882'.

Fig. 58—Mark: impressed 'Vodrey, Dublin', *c.* 1884.

Fig. 59—Mark: impressed 'VODREY DUBLIN POTTERY', *c.* 1886.

Fig. 60—Mark: impressed 'DUBLIN POTTERY VODREY', *c.* 1886–90.

Fig. 61—Mark: impressed 'DUBLIN POTTERY VODREY', *c.* 1886–90.

Fig. 62—Mark: 'Vodrey Dublin' in the hand-inscribed style, *c.* 1886–90.

Fig. 63—Mark: impressed 'DUBLIN POTTERY VODREY', *c.* 1886–90.

List of archival items

- Frederick Vodrey's trade card for the Irish Artisans' Exhibition, Dublin, 1885: 'Artistic and Domestic Pottery'. National Museum of Ireland, NMI 1886.125.

- Medal/badge for Queen's Institute, bronze, Dublin, 1861, by John Woodhouse. Depicts bust of Queen Victoria; inner circle inscribed 'DOCTRINUM ATQUE INDUSTRIAM EMOLLIT ARS', outer circle/ arms of Maltese cross inscribed with the words 'QUEEN'S INSTITUTE DUBLIN FOUNDED 1861'. National Museum of Ireland, NMI HC RIA 131.

- Charles Russell's sketch-book (facsimile). National Museum of Ireland, NMI AI/154/003.

- Certificate awarded to Frederick Vodrey at the Exhibition of Irish Arts and Manufactures, Dublin, 1882: 'This is to Certify that the Jury of Section *Ceramic* Class *J* has awarded Commendation to Mr Frederick Vodrey of Mary Street and Moore Street, Dublin, for Vases, Jugs, teapots made from Irish clay and for Rich Painting thereon. Given at Dublin, the 30th Day of December 1882'; signed by Chairman *Mr Charles Dawson, Lord Mayor*. National Museum of Ireland, NMI DC:2017.13. Presented by the Vodrey family, Canada.

- Certificate awarded to Frederick Vodrey at the Cork Industrial and Fine Art Exhibition, 1883 (for glass-engraving by Franz Tieze): 'The Certificate of Merit has been awarded to Frederick Vodrey Dublin. For Glass Engraving'. National Museum of Ireland, NMI DC.2017:14. Presented by the Vodrey family, Canada.

- Certificate awarded to Frederick Vodrey at the Cork Industrial and Fine Art Exhibition, 1883, for 'faience': 'This is to Certify that a Medal has been awarded to Frederick Vodrey of Mary St. Dublin for Vodrian Pottery'. National Museum of Ireland, NMI DC:2017.15. Presented by the Vodrey family, Canada.

- Medal for 'ornamental faience' awarded to Frederick Vodrey at the Cork Industrial Exhibition, 1883. Provenance: Vodrey family, Canada.

- Certificate awarded to Frederick Vodrey at the Irish Artisans' Exhibition, 1885: 'First Class Certificate awarded to F. Vodrey'. National Museum of Ireland, NMI DC:2017.16. Presented by the Vodrey family, Canada.

- Minute Books of the Dublin Sketching Club. National Library of Ireland, MS ACC. 4786, Boxes 1–3.

- Catalogues of the Dublin Sketching Club Annual Exhibitions (facsimile copies). National Gallery of Ireland Archives, 708.15 DUB/SKE Box 186. Some originals are also in a bound volume in the National Library of Ireland, AA 68.

Bibliography

Anderson, A. 2009 'Chinamania': collecting Old Blue for the house beautiful, *c.* 1860–1900. In J. Potvin and A. Myzelev (eds), *Material cultures, 1740–1920: the meanings and pleasures of collecting*, 109–28. Routledge, London and New York.

Anon. *c.* 1888 *Industries of Dublin. Historical, statistical, biographical. An account of the leading business men, commercial interests, wealth and growth.* Spencer Blackett, London.

Anscombe, E. 1995 A sense of place: Knox, Manx nationalism and the Celtic Revival. In S.A. Martin (ed.), *Archibald Knox*, 70-71. Academy Editions, London.

Armstrong-Duffy, S. 1984 Late nineteenth-century sketching clubs in Ireland. Unpublished BA thesis, Trinity College Dublin.

Armstrong-Duffy, S. 1987 The role of women in sketching clubs in the late nineteenth century. In W. Ryan-Smolin, E. Mayes and J. Rogers (eds), *Irish women artists from the eighteenth century to the present day*, 12–14. National Gallery of Ireland and the Douglas Hyde Gallery, Dublin.

Armstrong-Duffy, S. 1993 Time on their hands. *Women's Art Magazine* **32** (May/June), 12–14.

Arnold, M. 1905 [1867] *On the study of Celtic literature.* Smith, Elder and Co., London.

Aslin, E. 1981 *The Aesthetic Movement—prelude to Art Nouveau* (rev. edn). Excalibur Books, New York.

Aslin, E. 1986 *E.W. Godwin, furniture and interior decoration.* John Murray, London.

Atterbury, P. and Henson, J. 1993 *Ruskin Pottery: the pottery of Edward Richard Taylor and William Howson Taylor, 1898–1935.* Baxendale Press, Somerset.

Audsley, G.A. and Bowes, J.L. 1875 *Keramic art of Japan.* Henry Sotheran and Co., Liverpool.

Baker, M. and Richardson, B. 1997 *A grand design: the art of the Victoria and Albert Museum.* V&A Museum Publications, London.

Bantry White, H. 1911 History of the science and art institutions, Dublin. *Museum Bulletin* **1** (4), 7–34. National Museum of Science and Art, Dublin.

Bartlett, J.A. 1993 *British ceramic art 1870–1940.* Schiffer Publishing, Atglen, PA.

Béaslaí, P. 1958 *The story of the Catholic Commercial Club, Dublin, 1881–1954*. Powell Press, Dublin.

Bergesen, V. and Godden, G. 1991 *Encyclopaedia of British art pottery 1870–1920*. Barrie and Jenkins, London.

Bielenberg, A. 2018 The Irish economy, 1815–1880: agricultural transition, the communications revolution, and the limits of industrialisation. In T. Bartlett (ed.), *The Cambridge History of Ireland*, III, 200–2. Cambridge University Press, Cambridge.

Blaszczyk, R.L. 1994 The aesthetic moment. *Winterthur Portfolio* **29** (2/3), 121–53 (doi:10.1086/496658).

Blaszczyk, R.L. 2000 *Imagining consumers: design and innovation from Wedgwood to Corning*. John Hopkins University Press, Baltimore and London.

Bloomfield, J.C. 1882–3 The development of Irish industries. *Society of Arts Journal* **31**, 432–9.

Bourke, M. 2011 *The story of Irish museums 1790–2000*. Cork University Press, Cork.

Boyce, G. 1991 *Nationalism in Ireland* (rev. edn). Routledge, London and New York.

Boydell, M. and Doyle, P. 1994 *Reflections: Dublin engraved glass in the late nineteenth century*. National Museum of Ireland, Dublin.

Brown, T. (ed.) 1996 *Celticism*. Amsterdam Studies on Cultural Identity. Studia Imagologica, Amsterdam.

Buckley, C. 1990 *Potters and paintresses: women designers in the pottery industry*. The Women's Press, London.

Burton, A. 1999 *Vision and accident: the story of the Victoria and Albert Museum*. V&A Museum Publications, London.

Butler, P. 2000 *Irish botanical illustrators and flower painters*. Antique Collectors' Club, Woodbridge.

Calloway, S. and Federle Orr, L. (eds) 2011 *The cult of beauty: the Aesthetic Movement 1860–1900*. V&A Publishing, London.

Coffey, G. 1889 *The proposed technical instruction bill, and the science and art department: a paper read before the Statistical Society of Ireland, February, 1889*. Edward Ponsonby, Dublin.

Coffey, G. 1909 *Guide to the Celtic antiquities of the Christian period preserved in the National Museum, Dublin: Royal Irish Academy collection*. Hodges, Figgis and Co., Dublin/Williams and Norgate, London.

Cooper, J. 1987 *Victorian and Edwardian furniture and interiors from the Gothic Revival to Art Nouveau* [rev. edn 1998]. Thames and Hudson, London.

Cox, L. 1947 Isaac Watts Knowles. *Bulletin of the American Ceramic Society* **21** (8), 154–6.

Crooke, E. 2000 *Politics, archaeology, and the creation of a National Museum of Ireland: an expression of national life*. Irish Academic Press, Dublin.

Crowley, C. (ed.) 2017 *Frederick William Burton: for the love of art*. National Gallery of Ireland, Dublin.

Crowley, D. and Taylor, L. (eds) 2000 *The lost arts of Europe: the Haslemere Museum collection of European Peasant Art*. Haslemere Education Museum, Haslemere.

Csenkey, E. and Steinart, A. (eds) 2002 *Hungarian ceramics from the Zsolnay factory 1853–2001*. Yale University Press, New Haven.

Curry, K. 1993 Painting on porcelain. *Irish Arts Review* **4**, 192–5.

Curry, K. 2001 William Dargan and the Worcester Shakespeare service. *Irish Arts Review* **17**, 71–9.

Daly, M.E. 1984 *Dublin, the deposed capital: a social and economic history, 1860–1914*. Cork University Press, Cork.

Daly, M.E. 1998 The growth of Victorian Dublin. In M.E. Daly, M. Hearn and P. Pearson, *Dublin's Victorian houses*, 1998:3-47. A. & A. Farmar, Dublin.

Daly, M.E., Hearn, M. and Pearson, P. 1998 *Dublin's Victorian houses*. A. & A. Farmar, Dublin.

Degenhardt, R.K. 1993 *Belleek: the complete collector's guide and illustrated reference* (rev. edn). Wallace-Homestead Book Company, Des Moines, IA.

Dennis, R. 1887 *Industrial Ireland: a practical and non-political view of Ireland for the Irish*. John Murray, London.

Dresser, C. 1882 *Japan: its architecture, art and art manufactures*. Longmans, Green and Co., London.

Drudy, P.J. (ed.) 1982 *Ireland: land, politics and people*. Cambridge University Press, Cambridge.

Dunlevy, M. 1988 *Ceramics in Ireland*. National Museum of Ireland, Dublin.

Durant, S. 1986 *Ornament: a survey of decoration since 1830*. Macdonald, London and Sydney.

Eastlake, C.L. 1868 *Hints on household taste in furniture, upholstery and other details*. Longmans and Co., London.

Elliott, G. 2000 *The design process in British ceramic manufacture 1750–1850*. Staffordshire University Press, Stoke-on-Trent.

Farmar, T. 1991 *Ordinary lives: three generations of Irish middle-class experience*. Gill and Macmillan, Dublin.

Farmar, T. 2010 *Privileged lives: a social history of middle-class Ireland 1882–1989*. A. & A. Farmar, Dublin.

Fine, B. and Leopold, E. 1998 *The world of consumption*. Routledge, London and New York.

Fitzpatrick, T.E. 1886 *Existing manufactures of Ireland with suggestions for their development*. Thomas Moore, Dublin.

Fitzsimon, B.T. and Murphy, J.H. 2004 *The Irish Revival reappraised*. Four Courts Press, Dublin.

Forty, A. 1986 *Objects of desire: design and society 1750–1980*. Cameron Books, London. Reprinted by Thames and Hudson, 1987.

Gates, W.C. 1984 *The city of hills and kilns: life and work in East Liverpool, Ohio*. East Liverpool Historical Society, East Liverpool.

Gere, C. and Hoskins, L. 2000 *The house beautiful: Oscar Wilde and the Aesthetic interior*. Lund Humphries in association with the Geffrye Museum, London.

Godson, L. 2003 Catholicism and material culture in Ireland 1840–1880. *Circa* **103**, 38–44.

Girouard, M. 1977 *Sweetness and light: the Queen Anne Movement 1860–1900*. Clarendon Press, Oxford.

Gordon Bowe, N. 1990 Symbolism in turn-of-the-century Irish art. *Irish Arts Review* **6**, 133–44.

Gordon Bowe, N. 1991 The Irish Arts and Crafts Movement (1886–1925). *Irish Arts Review Yearbook 1990–1991*, 172–85.

Gordon Bowe, N. (ed.) 1993 *Art and the national dream: the search for vernacular expression in turn-of-the-century design*. Irish Academic Press, Dublin.

Gordon Bowe, N. and Cumming, E. 1998 *The Arts and Crafts movements in Dublin and Edinburgh, 1885–1925*. Irish Academic Press, Dublin.

Greenhalgh, P. 1988 *Ephemeral vistas: the Expositions Universelles, Great Exhibitions and World's Fairs 1851–1939*. Manchester University Press, Manchester.

Grossick, G. (ed.) 1977 *The lower middle-class in Britain 1870–1914*. Croom Helm, London.

Halen, W. 1990 *Christopher Dresser*. Phaidon, London.

Harrod, T. 2000 'For love and not for money': reviving peasant art in Britain 1880–1930. In D. Crowley and L. Taylor (eds), *The lost arts of Europe: the Haslemere Museum collection of European Peasant Art*, 13–24. Haslemere Education Museum, Haslemere.

Haslam, M. 1975 *English Art Pottery 1865–1916*. Antique Collectors' Club, Woodbridge.

Hearn, M. 1998 How Victorian families lived. In M.E. Daly, M. Hearn and P. Pearson, *Dublin's Victorian houses*, 1998:59-128. A. & A. Farmar, Dublin.

Helland, J. 2007 *British and Irish home arts and industries 1880–1914: marketing craft, making fashion*. Irish Academic Press, Dublin.

Hudson, J.W. 1851 *The history of adult education in which is comprised a full and complete history of the Mechanics' and Literary Institutions, Athenaeums, Philosophical, and Mental and Christian Improvement Society, Literary Unions, Schools of Design etc., of Great Britain, Ireland, America, etc. etc.* Longmans, London.

Hutchinson, J. 1987 *The dynamics of cultural nationalism: the Gaelic Revival and the creation of the Irish nation state*. Allen and Unwin, London.

Jewitt, L. 1878 *The ceramic art of Great Britain from prehistoric times to the present day*. Virtue and Co., London.

Jones, O. 1856 *The grammar of ornament, illustrated by examples from various styles of ornament*. Day and Son, London.

Jones, O. and Goury, J. 1842–5 *Plans, details and sections of the Alhambra* (2 vols). Owen Jones, London.

Kane, Sir R. 1844 *The industrial resources of Ireland*. Hodges and Smith, Dublin.

Lamb, P. 2017 *The life and work of John Ffrench, Irish ceramic artist (1928–2010)*. Gandon Editions, Kinsale.

Langham, M. 2001 *Belleek Irish porcelain: an illustrated guide to over two thousand pieces*. Quiller Press, London.

Larmour, P. 1992 *The Irish Arts and Crafts movement*. Friar's Bush Press, Belfast.

Longfield, T.H. 1874 On ornamental design. *The Irish Builder* **16** (1 February 1874), 44–6.

Longfield, T.H. 1875 Ornamental design. *The Builder* **33** (13 March 1875), 237–9.

Lyons, H. 2005 *Christopher Dresser, the people's designer, 1834–1904*. Antique Collectors' Club, London.

McBride, L.W. 1991 *The greening of Dublin Castle: the transformation of bureaucratic and judicial personnel in Ireland 1892–1922*. Catholic University of America Press, Chicago.

McBrinn, J. 2009 Collecting the sublime and the beautiful: from romanticism to revolution in Celtic Revival jewellery. In J. Potvin and A. Myzelev (eds), *Material cultures, 1740–1920: the meanings and pleasures of collecting*, **209-226**. Routledge, London, and New York.

McCarthy, F. 2014 *Anarchy and beauty: William Morris and his legacy 1860–1960*. Yale University Press, New Haven and London.

McCrum, E. 1993 Commerce and the Celtic Revival: Irish jewellery of the nineteenth century. *Éire-Ireland* **28** (4), 36–52.

MacKenzie, J.M. 1995 *Orientalism: history, theory, and the arts*. Manchester University Press, Manchester.

MacLeod, C. 1972 *Glass in the National Museum of Ireland by Thomas and Richard Pugh*. Stationery Office, Dublin.

Maguire, J.F. 1853 *The Industrial Movement in Ireland as illustrated by the National Exhibition of 1852*. John O'Brien, Cork/J. McGlashan, Dublin/Simpkin, Marshall and Co., London.

Molloy, A. 1987 Vodrian pottery. *Irish Arts Review* **4** (1), 33–6.

Molloy, A. 2007 Frederick Vodrey (1845–97): artisan entrepreneur in the Irish economic and cultural revival. Unpublished Ph.D thesis, Royal College of Art, London.

Molloy, A. 2013 Vodrey Dublin pottery: commodification of Celtic style as a symbol of Irish national identity in the 1880s. *Journal of Design History* **27** (1), 38–57 (https//doi:10.1093/jdh/ept019).

Molloy, A. 2014 Commodification of Celtic style as a symbol of Irish national identity in the 1880s. *Journal of Design History* **27** (1), 38–57.

Molloy, A. 2020 Ornament and revivalism—1880s art ceramics and the creation of a ceramic collection at the National Museum of Ireland. *Irish Studies Review* **28** (4), 498–522 (https//doi.org/10.1080/09670882.2020.1833274).

Moody, T.W. and Martin, F.X. (eds) 2001 *The course of Irish history* (revised and enlarged edn). Mercier Press, Cork.

Murphy, P. 2010 *Nineteenth century sculpture: native genius reaffirmed*. Yale University Press, New Haven and London.

Murray, A. 1903 *A history of the commercial and financial relations between England and Ireland*. P.S. King, London.

Naylor, G. 1971 *The Arts and Crafts movement*. Studio Vista, London.

Pearsall, W.B. 1886 Sketching from nature. *The Irish Builder* **28** (628) (15 February 1886), 51–2.

Pearson, P. 2002 *Decorative Dublin*. O'Brien Press, Dublin.

Pentland, H.J. 1885 Of faience and its design in the Irish Artizans' Exhibition. *Dublin University Review* (August 1885), 33–41.

Pevsner, N. 2008 [1936] *Pioneers of modern design, from William Morris to Walter Gropius* (revised and expanded edn). Yale University Press, New Haven.

Prown, J.D. 1980 Style as evidence. *Winterthur Portfolio* **15**, 97–210.

Prown, J.D. 1982 Mind in matter: an introduction to material culture theory and method. *Winterthur Portfolio* **17**, 1–20.

Rains, S. 2010 *Commodity culture and social class in Dublin 1850–1916*. Irish Academic Press, Dublin.

Reynolds, M. 1984 Vodrian pottery. *Crafts Council of Ireland Newsletter* (May/June 1984), 4–5.

Rolleston, T.W. (ed.). 1889 *The prose writings of Thomas Davis*. Walter Scott, London.

Royal Commission on Technical Instruction 1884 *Report of the Royal Commission on Technical Instruction, 1884*, Vol. IV. Eyre and Spottiswoode, London.

Ryan-Smolin, W., Mayes, E. and Rogers, J. 1987 *Irish women artists from the eighteenth century to the present day*. National Gallery of Ireland and the Douglas Hyde Gallery, Dublin.

Schafter, D. 2003 *The order of ornament, the structure of style: theoretical foundations of modern art and architecture*. Cambridge University Press, London.

Select Committee on Industries (Ireland) 1885 *Report of the Select Committee on Industries (Ireland)*. Hansard, London.

Sheehy, J. 1980 *The rediscovery of Ireland's past: the Celtic Revival 1830–1930*. Thames and Hudson, London.

Sheehy, J. 1987 The training and professional life of Irish women artists before the twentieth century. In W. Ryan-Smolin, E. Mayes and J. Rogers (eds), *Irish women artists from the eighteenth century to the present day*, 1987:7-9. National Gallery of Ireland and the Douglas Hyde Gallery, Dublin.

Smith, A.D. 1971 *Theories of nationalism*. Camelot Press, London.

Snoddy, T. 2002 *Dictionary of Irish artists: 20th century* (rev. edn). Merlin Publishing, Dublin.

Stewart, A. 1985 *Royal Hibernian Academy: index of exhibitors and their works 1826–1979*, Vol. 1. Manton, Dublin.

Stewart, A.M. 1997 *Irish art societies and sketching clubs: index of exhibitors, 1870–1980*, Vol. I. Four Courts Press, Dublin.

Stokes, M. 1887 *Early Christian art in Ireland*. Chapman and Hall, London.

Teehan, J. 1995 Neo Celtic art. In W. Halen, *Dragons from the north: Norwegian silver around 1900, including an article on the Neoceltic art in Ireland*, 41–8. Oslo Museum of Applied Art, Oslo.

Tilbrook, A.J. and House, G. (eds) 1976 *The designs of Archibald Knox for Liberty & Co.* Ornament Press, London.

Turpin, J. 1983 The South Kensington System and the Dublin Metropolitan School of Art 1877–1900. *Dublin Historical Record* **36** (2), 42–64.

Vincentelli, M. 2000 *Women and ceramics: gendered vessels*. Manchester University Press, Manchester.

Walker, F.S. 1886 Suggestions for the development of Irish art industry. *Dublin University Review* (February 1886), 168–71.

Wallace, P.F. and Kenny, M. 1970 *Pottery in Ireland through the ages*. National Museum of Ireland, Dublin.

Ward, A. 2014 Dress and national identity: women's clothing and the Celtic Revival. *Costume* **48** (2), 193–212.

Westropp, M.S.D. 1913 Notes on the pottery manufacture in Ireland. *Proceedings of the Royal Irish Academy* **32**C, 1–27.

Westropp, M.S.D. 1935 *General guide to the art collections' pottery and porcelain*. National Museum of Ireland, Dublin.

Whipp, R. 1990 *Patterns of labour: work and social change in the pottery industry*. Routledge, London and New York.

White, H.B. 1911 History of the Science and Art Institutions, Dublin. *Museum Bulletin: National Museum of Science and Art, Dublin* **1** (4), 7–34.

Whitty, A. 2003 Arklow pottery. *Irish Arts Review* **20** (1), 122–6.

Widar, H. 1990 *Christopher Dresser*. Phaidon, London.

Williams, J. 1994 *A companion guide to architecture in Ireland 1837–1921* (with a foreword by Mark Girouard). Irish Academic Press, Dublin.

Wood, C. 1978 *Dictionary of Victorian painters* (2nd edn). Antique Collectors' Club, London.

Catalogues of Art and Industry exhibitions

Cork Industrial Exhibition 1883. Report of the Executive Committee, Awards of the Jurors and Statements of Account (Purcell and Co., Cork, 1886).

Irish Artisans' Exhibition Complete Official Catalogue (2nd edn) (John Falconer, Cork, 1885).

Record of the Irish Exhibition of Irish Arts and Manufactures 1882 (John Falconer, Dublin, 1883).

Manuscript sources

Biographical Index of Irish Architects, Irish Architectural Archive.

Family archives and artefacts of F. Vodrey, courtesy of Rosemary and Mitch Vodrey, Winnipeg, Maureen and Robert Vodrey, Ottawa, and Sue Vodrey Harbottle, Vancouver.

Family papers of F. Vodrey, courtesy of Mr Jack Vodrey.

Family papers of Jabez Vodrey descendants, East Liverpool, Ohio, USA.

George Coffey Papers, National Library of Ireland, MS 13, 839, no. 516.

National Museum of Ireland Archives, Box 218, 1908 (Longfield acquisition).

Register of Objects, National Museum of Ireland.

Russell/Healy family archive, courtesy of Mr Peter Healy.

Catalogue

Catalogue

Vodrey Dublin Pottery, National Museum of Ireland[1]

1. Vase, blue, white, brown, green.
Spherical shape, mottled glaze.
11.5cm x 10.5cm.
Vodrey Dublin; *c.* 1884.
Purchased from F. Vodrey for three shillings and sixpence.
NMI 1884.418.

2. Vase, green, white, brown.
Squat bulbous shape, wheel-turned, Japanese style. Red clay (possibly from Coalisland or Sheldon, England) visible under glaze.
11.5cm x 10cm.
Vodrey Dublin; *c.* 1884.
Purchased from F. Vodrey for three shillings and sixpence.
NMI 1884.419.

3. Vase, brown, green, cherry red.
Ovoid body, dimpled, thrown, Japanese style.
9cm x 7.5cm.
Vodrey Dublin; *c.* 1884.
Purchased from F. Vodrey for two shillings and sixpence.
NMI 1884.420.

4. Jardinière, various tones of dark green.
Raised beaded decoration, wheel-turned.
18cm x 17cm.
Vodrey Dublin (handwritten style); *c.* 1886.
NMI 1886.80.

5. Vase, turquoise inside, green outside.
Large squat spherical shape, wheel-turned.
20cm x 19cm.
DUBLIN POTTERY VODREY (small impressed mark, capital letters); *c.* 1886.
NMI 1886.81.

6. Frog ornament/ paperweight, green.
Splayed legs and arms. Influence of C. Dresser and *Japonisme.*
6cm x 8cm.
DUBLIN POTTERY VODREY (small impressed mark, capital letters in an elliptical oval); *c.* 1886.
NMI 1886.82.

7. Frog/container for matches, green.
Seated, open mouth. Influence of C. Dresser and *Japonisme.*
17cm x 15cm.
Vodrey Dublin (incised in

1 The following numbers of Vodrey Dublin Pottery from the 1886 acquisition of 'Forty-seven specimens of glazed pottery Modern Irish (Vodrey Dublin' have yet to be identified: 1886.93; 99; 106; 107; 108; 113; 114.

handwritten style, three times); *c.* 1886.
NMI 1886.83.

8. Vase, ruby red.
Flower form, lustred effect, Art Nouveau style.
21.5cm x 11.5cm.
Vodrey Dublin (handwritten style); *c.* 1886.
NMI 1886.84.

9. Vase, turquoise, green/yellow, gold/yellow.
Long neck, bottle shape, spherical body, extensive glaze cracks, wheel-turned; influence of *Japonisme.*
15cm x 5.5cm.
DUBLIN POTTERY VODREY (small impressed mark, capital letters); *c.* 1886.
DC.1886.85.

10. Jardinière, ruby red.
Z-type decoration on neck, band of Celtic interlace on body, Celtic style, moulded.
24cm x 23cm.
Vodrey Dublin (handwritten style); *c.* 1886.
Molloy 1987; 2014; 2020; Larmour 1992.
NMI 1886.86.

11. Vase, dark green outside and turquoise inside.
Incised 'arabesque' decoration, moulded, Moorish style.
42cm x 13.5cm.
VODREY DUBLIN POTTERY (large impressed mark in capital letters); *c.* 1886.
Molloy 1987.
NMI 1886.87.

12. Vase, brown, turquoise and white.
Tapered ovoid body, short, collared neck, flecked glaze, Classical style.
24cm x 15cm.
DUBLIN POTTERY VODREY (small impressed mark, capital letters in an elliptical oval); *c.* 1886.
NMI 1886.88.

13. Vase, brown/black at top, grey with tints of mauve and blue.
Tapered ovoid shape, subtle glaze colours, Classical style.
25.5cm x 5.5cm.
DUBLIN POTTERY VODREY (small impressed mark, capital letters); *c.* 1886.
Molloy 1987.
DC.1886.89.

14. Vase, green, gold, brown.
Long neck, spherical body; influence of C. Dresser and *Japonisme.*
20cm x 11cm.
DUBLIN POTTERY VODREY (small impressed mark, capital letters); *c.* 1886.
NMI 1886.90.

15. Pitcher, ruby red.
Medieval form, possibly Japanese or Chinese inspiration.
21.5cm x 11cm.
DUBLIN POTTERY VODREY (small impressed mark, capital letters); *c.* 1886.
Wallace and Kenny 1970.
NMI 1886.91.

16. Vase, brown, white and green.
Spherical body, four sides dimpled, four handles, moulded.
19cm x 17cm.
Dublin Pottery (impressed, unclear); 1886.
NMI 1886.92.

17. Punch goblet, ruby red.
Short stem, wheel-turned.
6cm x 8.5cm.
DUBLIN POTTERY VODREY (small impressed mark, capital letters).
Date unknown.
DC.1886.93.

18. Vase, gold brown, dark green.
Long neck, ovoid body, flared frilly rim, wheel-turned, Art Nouveau style.
17.5cm x 9.5cm.
DUBLIN POTTERY VODREY (small impressed mark, capital letters); 1886.
NMI 1886.94.

19 Vase, gold, brown, black, olive green, dark green.
Long neck, flared rim, straight-sided ovoid body.
19cm x 4cm.
Vodrey Dublin (handwritten style); *c.* 1886.
NMI 1886.95.

20. Vase, olive green, brown.
Gourd shape; influence of C. Dresser.
17cm x 9cm.
DUBLIN POTTERY VODREY (small impressed mark, capital letters).
Molloy 2020.
NMI 1886.96.

21. Vase, green/brown, gold/brown.
Tapered ovoid shape, deep collared neck, Classical style.
23cm x 11.5cm.
Vodrey Dublin (handwritten style); *c.* 1886.
NMI 1886.97.

22. Vase, green, brown.
Long neck, slender ovoid body, wheel-turned, flared rim in the shape of a flower, hand-modelled, Art Nouveau style.
21.5cm x 9.5cm.
Vorde(?) (mark not clear, handwritten style); *c.* 1886.
NMI 1886.98.

23. Vase, yellow.
Two-handled vase, 'Alhambra type', moulded, incised arabesque pattern, Moorish style.
30cm x 11cm.
DUBLIN POTTERY VODREY (small impressed mark in capitals); *c.* 1886.
Molloy 2014.
NMI 1886.100.

24. Cup and saucer, white.
White glaze with applied floral decoration.
Cup: height 6.5cm.
Saucer: diameter 12cm.
DUBLIN POTTERY VODREY (small impressed mark, capital letters).
Mark on the saucer only, none on the cup. The saucer also has the letters SEALE impressed.
c. 1882.
DC.1886.101.

25. Coffee cup and saucer, yellow.
The cup handle has a double strand, saucer is flat with sloping rim, wheel-turned.
Cup: height 6.5cm.
Saucer: diameter 11cm.
DUBLIN POTTERY VODREY (small impressed mark, capital letters, on undersides of both the cup and the saucer); *c.* 1886.
NMI 1886.103.

26. Vase, yellow.
Bottle shape, short neck, similar to a Japanese saké bottle, *Japonisme*.
30cm x 10.5cm.
DUBLIN POTTERY VODREY (small impressed mark, capital letters); *c.* 1886.
Dunlevy 1988, 31; Gordon Bowe and Cumming 1998.
NMI 1886.105.

27. Vase, ruby red.
Urn shape, right-angled handles, Classical style.
35cm x 16cm.
c. 1886.
NMI 1886.110.

28. Ewer, dark green.
Handle is right-angled, ovoid body, short neck; influence of C. Dresser.
17.5cm x 9cm.
DUBLIN POTTERY VODREY;
c. 1886.
NMI 1886.111.

29. Vase, brown, gold and purple streaks.
Spherical body, square chunky base; influence of C. Dresser.
24cm x 4.5cm.
VODREY DUBLIN POTTERY (large impressed mark in capital letters);
c. 1886.
NMI 1886.112.

30. Vase, brown, green, yellow.
Long neck, flower-shaped rim, hand-thrown, Art Nouveau style.
15cm x 10cm.
Vodrey Dublin (handwritten style, different from usual handwritten mark, possibly a one-off piece); *c.* 1886.
NMI 1886.117.

31. Ewer, olive green, ruby red.
Classical form, with handle; spout is gold/brown; the ruby-red and green glazes merge where the ovoid body meets the foot of the ewer; wheel-turned.
25.5cm x 6cm.
DUBLIN POTTERY VODREY (small impressed mark in capitals); *c.* 1886.
Molloy 1987; 2020.
NMI 1886.119.

32. Candlestick, olive green, pale green, cherry red streaked with white.
Raised decoration—dots, dashes, slashes.
Height 18cm.
DUBLIN POTTERY VODREY (small impressed mark, capital letters);
c. 1886.
NMI 1886.121.

33. Jardinière, brown, white, green.
Three-legged skillet or cauldron shape; glaze is mainly brown with green and white blobs or splashes.
21cm x 24cm.
VODREY DUBLIN POTTERY (large impressed mark in capital letters);
c. 1886.
NMI 1886.122.

34. Urn, olive green, cherry red.
Two-handled, slender shape, wheel-turned, with lump that corresponds to chip on no. 35 below (owing to being fired together), Classical style.
23cm x 6.2cm.
DUBLIN POTTERY VODREY (small impressed mark, capital letters);
1886.
NMI 1886.124.

35. Urn, olive green, cherry red.
Two-handled, slender shape, wheel-turned, with chip that corresponds to lump on no. 34 above, Classical style.
23cm x 6.2cm.
DUBLIN POTTERY VODREY (small impressed mark, capital letters); 1886.
NMI 1886.125.

36. Vase, brown.
Ovoid body, dimpled.
20.5cm x 22cm.
VODREY DUBLIN POTTERY;
c. 1886.
Reynolds 1984.
NMI 1886.126.

37. Vase, white, pink, blue, green.
Wide neck, bulbous body, applied floral decoration (convolvulus).
14cm x 7cm.
DUBLIN POTTERY VODREY 1882 (in oval stamp).
Gift from K. Dobbyn, esq.
Similar to a vase illustrated by Nanci Hatte in the magazine *Antiques* (28 May 1975).
NMI 1921.115.

38. Ewer, ruby red.
Renaissance style. Spout in the shape of a winged female, raised floral and scrolls, shells and festoons.
32.5cm x 15cm.
DUBLIN POTTERY VODREY (small impressed mark, capital letters); 1886.
Westropp 1935.
NMI 72.1927.

39. Vase (flower-holder), white and green.
Square with applied floral decoration (lily of the valley), one of a pair.
13cm x 13cm.
DUBLIN POTTERY VODREY 1882 (belt-impressed; earliest identified mark).
Purchased from Austin Greene/ Greene Antique Galleries.
NMI 1971.19.

40. Vase (flower-holder), white and green.
Square with applied floral decoration (lily of the valley), one of a pair.
13cm x 13cm.
DUBLIN POTTERY VODREY 1882 (belt-impressed; earliest identified mark).
Purchased from Austin Greene/ Greene Antique Galleries.
NMI 1971.20.

41. Vase, red.
Baluster shape, deep collar, miniature, Classical shape.
11.5cm x 9cm.
DUBLIN POTTERY VODREY (small impressed mark, capital letters).
Date unknown.
Adams Salerooms 2002.
NMI 2002.64.

42. Vase, green.
Long neck, fluted, vegetal shape with ridges.
20cm x 6cm.
DUBLIN POTTERY VODREY (small impressed mark, capital letters).
Date unknown.
Adams Salerooms 2002.
NMI 2002.66.

43. Vase, gold yellow, ruby red.
Tapered ovoid shape, dimpled, double handles on three sides, Classical shape.
11cm x 8cm.
DUBLIN POTTERY VODREY (small impressed mark, capital letters).
Date unknown.
Donated in 2003 by Mairead Johnston, daughter of Ray Johnston, who bought it in Rathmines in the 1980s.
NMI 2003.

44. Vase, yellow.
Two-handled vase, 'Alhambra type', moulded, incised arabesque pattern, Moorish style.
30cm x 10cm.
DUBLIN POTTERY VODREY (small impressed mark in capitals); *c.* 1886.
Purchased 25 September 2008 from Michael O'Connell, Capoley, Portlaoise, Co. Laois.
NMI 2008.27.

45. Frog match-holder, red.
Seated with open mouth.
Height 15.5cm; width 16cm; diameter 14cm.
Marked twice underneath 'Vodrey Dublin'.
Purchased 23 April 2010 from Whyte's Auctioneers, 38 Molesworth Street, Dublin.
NMI 2010. 28.

46. Teapot and lid, red, gold.
Spherical shape, high-hipped. Chinese influence.
Finely potted, white/yellow clay body. Ruby-red glaze inside, rich gold and red on sides.
Part of a set with creamer/milk jug (no. 47) and sugar bowl (no. 48) below.

22cm x 24cm.
DUBLIN POTTERY VODREY (small impressed mark, capital letters);
c. 1890.
Donated in memory of Eithne and Jim Bolger.
DC.2023.49.

47. Creamer/milk jug, red.
Part of a set with teapot (no. 46) and sugar bowl (no. 48).
Handle in the form of a branch, Chinese influence.
9.5cm x 6cm.
DUBLIN POTTERY VODREY (small impressed mark, capital letters).
DC.2023.50.

48. Sugar bowl, red.
Part of a set with teapot (no. 46) and creamer/milk jug (no. 47) above.
Large in relation to teapot and creamer/milk jug. Three-legged 'skillet' shape with angular arms.
9.5cm x 9.5cm.
DUBLIN POTTERY VODREY (small impressed mark, capital letters).
DC.2023.51.

49. Vase, red, varied tones.
Spherical body, collared neck, long stem.
12.5cm x 9.5cm.
DUBLIN POTTERY VODREY (small impressed mark, capital letters).

Civic Museum, Dublin.

Vodrey Dublin Pottery, National Museum of Ireland: Paddy Healy/Olive Russell bequest

50. Vase, blue ground, green, pink, yellow.
Elliptical body, zoomorphic snake decoration, underglaze painting, Celtic style.
8cm x 8cm.
Impressed DUBLIN POTTERY VODREY, inscribed 'C Russell 31-10-85'; 1885.
Larmour 1992.
NMI 1980.6.

51. Vase, black and green.
'Blackberry vase', baluster shape, tapered ovoid body, applied decoration of hand-modelled blackberries and leaves.
20cm x 13.5cm.
Inscribed 'DSC 1883' under base and 'CR IX 83' at bottom, to left of bramble branch; 1883.
NMI 1980.13.

52. Jardinière, brown.
Large spherical body, deep neck band, Celtic-style interlace designs based on the knop of Petrie Collection crozier (Larmour 1992).
18cm x 18cm.
Inscribed '1884 Chas. Russell no. 2 DSC'; 1884.
Presented by Mr Paddy Healy.
Molloy 2014; Larmour 1992.
NMI 1980.14.

53. Vase, green, yellow, burgundy.
Globular body, Celtic style, zoomorphic snake decoration, burgundy band with yellow border, words hand-painted in old Irish script, 'Bliain sona nua agat'.
13cm x 8cm.
Impressed DUBLIN POTTERY VODREY, inscribed 'Russell pinxii 6-11-85', 'Keltic' painted in blue; 1885.
Larmour 1992.
NMI 1980.15.

54. Vase, brown, green.
Flower form, long neck, ovoid body, Art Nouveau style.
22cm x 11cm.
VODREY DUBLIN POTTERY (small impressed mark, capital letters).
Object was damaged and repaired.
NMI 1981.1.

55. Cylindrical vase, mottled blue and yellow glaze.
Spray of flowers and leaves applied.
23.5cm x 11.7cm.
'WPB August 81' incised on bottom left below flowers, possibly William Booth Pearsall.
NMI 1981.2.

56. Vase, purple and green.
Cylindrical shape with applied decoration of fern fronds.
24.5cm x 12cm.
No mark or signature. Probably by Charles Russell.
NMI 1981.3.

Dublin Sketching Club (DSC) ceramics in the National Museum of Ireland (see also nos 51, 52, 55 and 56 above)

57. Vase, mottled brown and blue.
Baluster-shape tapered ovoid body. Applied decoration is hand-modelled: figure of a monkey hanging from a tree and holding a hare by the tail.
21cm x 13cm.
'DSC' underneath. Signed 'A. Williams' on the side.
c. 1883.
NMI 1913.13.

58. Vase, blue, green, brown.
Square shape, hand-painted with ship and seascape on the front, and with abstract grasses on the back.
19cm x 16.5cm.
No marks; attributed to Herbert Cooper. 'Dublin' written underneath, indistinctly in blue.
NMI 1913.14.

59. Vase, turquoise and yellow.
Cylindrical shape, moulded, decorated with bird, bamboo branch and leaves; crack on side.
22cm x 12cm.
No mark; attributed to DSC.
NMI 1913.15.

60. Vase, brown, yellow, turquoise.
Cylindrical shape, moulded, thickly potted.
16cm x 6.5cm.
No mark; attributed to DSC.
NMI 1913.16.

61. Plaque, turquoise, brown.
Round medallion shape with applied maple leaf decoration.
Diameter 15.5cm.
Initials 'W.S.' below the leaf.
Attributed to DSC.
NMI 1913.17.

62. Vase, brown.
Cylindrical shape, flower decoration.
15.2cm x 6.7cm.
Inscribed 'DSC 1884' underneath; 'H. Cooper' inscribed on the side.
NMI 1966.3.

Vodrey Dublin Pottery in the Ulster Museum

(1886 acquisitions by Dept of Science and Art; numbers identified 1886.102, 1886.109, 1886.116, 1886.118)

63. Vase, brown, turquoise.
Long neck, globular body, thrown; influence of C. Dresser, *Japonisme.*
20.5cm x 11.5cm.
DUBLIN POTTERY VODREY (small impressed mark, capital letters); *c.* 1886.
Ulster Museum 225.1910. (Museum of Science & Art label 1886.102.)

64. Bonbon dish, brown, white.
Circular shape, wavy sides and rim, hand-modelled, brown glaze decorated with white splotches.
Object has a paper label (oval elliptical shape) with the words 'VODRIAN POTTERY DUBLIN'; space for the number and price is left blank.
17.8cm x 15.5cm.
DUBLIN POTTERY VODREY (small impressed mark, capital letters).
Possibly *c. 1883 owing to the term 'Vodrian Pottery' on the label.*
Ulster Museum 225.1910. (Museum of Science & Art label 1886.109.)

65. Vase, gold, brown.
Long neck, globular body, wheel-turned; influence of C. Dresser, *Japonisme.*
17.5cm x 9cm.
DUBLIN POTTERY VODREY *(small impressed mark, capital letters); c. 1886.*
Ulster Museum 225.1910. (Museum of Science & Art label 1886.116.)

66. Vase, green, brown.
Large flower form, bulbous body, and flared rim, wheel-turned, Art Nouveau style.
19cm x 14cm.
Vodrey (handwritten style); *c.* 1886.
Ulster Museum 225.1910. (Museum of Science & Art label 1886.118.)

67. Vase, gold, brown.
Long neck, globular body, wheel-turned; influence of C. Dresser, *Japonisme.*
17.5cm x 9cm.
DUBLIN POTTERY VODREY (small impressed mark, capital letters); *c.* 1886.
Ulster Museum 225.1910. (Museum of Science & Art label 1886.116.)

Ulster Museum (possibly 1886 acquisitions by Dept of Science and Art)

68. Urn, ruby red.
Two-handled, moulded, Classical style.
26.5cm x 6.5cm.
DUBLIN POTTERY VODREY(small impressed mark, capital letters);
c. 1886.
Ulster Museum 225.1910.

69. Vase, blue, purple, turquoise.
Bottle shape (identical shape to a vase in the National Museum, no. 26 above), subtle flecked glaze with indigo blue and turquoise, possibly lustred, moulded; *Japonisme.*
32cm x 6.5cm.
DUBLIN POTTERY VODREY
(small impressed mark, capital letters); *c.* 1886.
Ulster Museum 225.1910.

70. Ewer, ruby red, olive green.
The handle is right-angled, the rim is like a wavy flowesr, wheel-turned; influence of C. Dresser, Art Nouveau style.
16.5cm x 10.5cm.
Vodrey Dublin (handwritten style).
c. 1886.
Ulster Museum 225.1910.

Herbert Cooper and the Queen's Institute

71. Plate, porcelain.
Glazed decoration in orange, yellow, blue, gilt. Hand-painted in Imari style, with birds, flowers, butterflies and scrolls.
Diameter 20cm.
Indistinct mark on back: 'H Cooper'.
Label for Museum of Science and Art.
NMI 1909.1311.

72. Plaque.
Water-lily pad, flower and leaf.
Green, white, gilt.
23cm x 23cm.
No marks; attributed to Herbert Cooper.
NMI 1913.27.

73.Tea service, porcelain, yellow, gilt.
Teapot and lid; two cups and saucers; oval tray; cream jug with lid; sugar bowl, two-handled with lid.
Decorated with flowers and fruit on a yellow ground.
Monogram 'C.O.G.' on the teapot, sugar bowl and cups. Each piece signed underneath with 'W.H. Kerr, Queen's Institute Dublin' or 'W.H. Kerr, Dublin'.
c. 1870–1.
According to Curry (1993), Kerr was involved with Herbert Cooper and the QI until 1871. Curry also writes that all porcelain blanks painted during the First Period of the QI were from the Worcester Royal Porcelain factory and provided by Kerr.
NMI 1940.2.
The overall registration number for this tea set is NMI DC:1940.2. The individual items are then numbered as follows:
DC:1940.2.1.1, sugar bowl
DC:1940.2.1.2, lid (for sugar bowl)
DC:1940.2.2.1, cup
DC:1940.2.2.2, saucer
DC:1940.2.3.1, cup
DC:1940.2.3.2, saucer
DC:1940.2.4.1, teapot—H 13cm
DC:1940.2.4.2, lid (for teapot)
DC:1940.2.5.1, jug
DC:1940.2.5.2, lid (for jug)
DC:1940.2.6, tray—L 39cm

74. Plaque, porcelain.
Glazed white and hand-painted with roses in red, yellow and white. Gilt rim. Base with raised centre perforated with four holes for hanging.
Dimensions: 45cm approx. (object on display in Museum galleries).
Attributed to Herbert Cooper.
NMI 1946.42.

75. Vase, porcelain, pale blue, red, white, green, gilt.
Baluster shape with circular foot and rim; painted with flowers.
Attributed to Herbert Cooper.
NMI 1946.43.

76. Tea kettle with lid, black, green, pink, gilt.
Body is painted with a black background, decorated with a butterfly and fern on one side and flowers (convolvulus) on the other side. Lid is also painted with flowers and fern on the black. Handle, in the form of a bamboo branch, is painted green.
20cm x 21cm.
'H. Cooper Dublin' painted in black.
NMI 1946.44.1. and NMI 1946.44.2.

77. Plate, porcelain, blue glaze, white floral decoration; one of two with same monogram (see no. 78 below).
Hand-painted white flowers, purple leaves and grasses on blue background. Monogram 'EP' in the centre. Distinctive artist's mark, 'MP', painted in red on the back.
Diameter 23cm.
Label on the back reads 'Hand Painted by Hon Mrs Eastes nee Miss Plunkett'.
Attributed to Herbert Cooper Studio, *c.* 1883–1909.
NMI 1965.7.

78. Plate, porcelain, pink glaze, white floral decoration; one of two with same monogram (see no. 77 above).
Hand-painted white roses and grasses on pink background.
Monogram 'EP' in the centre.
Distinctive artist's mark, 'MP', on back.
Diameter 23cm.
Label on the back reads 'Hand Painted by Hon Mrs Eastes nee M. Plunkett'.
Attributed to Herbert Cooper Studio, *c.* 1883–1909.
NMI 1965.8.

79. Plate, turquoise, gilt.
Turquoise ground with gilt rim.
Decorated with hand-painted flowers (violets, roses, and sweet pea) in rectangle card shapes. Plate was broken and mended.
Diameter 23cm.
Signed 'H.C., Q.I., Dublin' and with a shamrock.
NMI 1972.45.

80. Teapot stand, porcelain, glazed white, gilded rim edge.
Heavy circular rim curved up; foot pressed out. Hand-painted with daisies and violets. 'H. Cooper' painted underneath.
Diameter 16.5cm.
Impressed mark of crown over 'H & C' for Hammersley & Co. *c.* 1890.
NMI 1973.18.

81. Moustache cup.
Shape with moulded ionic capitals, C-scroll handle. Hand-painted red berries on one side, pink flowers on the other side.
12cm x 7cm.
Stamped 'Hammersley & Co. England', with design no. 150153, registered in 1891.
According to Curry (1993), blanks from Hammersley & Co. were painted at Herbert Cooper's Studio, 27 Molesworth Street, from 1888 to 1907.
NMI 1973.51.

82. Moustache cup.
Shape with moulded ionic capitals, C-scroll handle. Hand-painted, floral spray, possibly sweet pea flowers.
Registered design no. 150153 underneath, with 'H Cooper Dublin' painted in purple.
NMI 1973.53.

83. Moustache cup.
Shape with moulded ionic capitals, C-scroll handle. Hand-painted flowers of pink foxgloves and white heather on one side, orange flowers on the other side.
12cm x 7cm.
Stamped 'Hammersley & Co. England', with design no. 150153, registered in 1891.
NMI 1973.55.

84. Saucer, porcelain, glazed white, gilded.
Hand-painted with blue floral spray.
Rim with moulded ionic capitals (design no. 150153, registered in 1890). 'Dublin 1892' painted in purple underneath.
Diameter 15.5cm.
Impressed mark of crown over 'H & C' for Hammersley & Co.; *c.* 1890.
NMI 1973.57.

85. Bowl, porcelain, glazed white, gilded on rim and foot.
Shape has moulded ionic capitals (design no. 150153, registered in 1890). Hand-painted with primroses around the sides. 'H Cooper Dublin 1893' painted in purple underneath.
Possibly for sugar or a finger-bowl.
Height 6cm, diameter 11.6cm.
NMI 1973.64.

86. Cream jug.
Hand-painted with pink floral decoration, gilt on rim and handle.
Shape has moulded ionic capitals; C-scroll handle attributed to Hammersley & Co., England.
11.5cm x 8cm.
'H Cooper' painted in brown underneath; *c.* 1890–2.
NMI 1973.66.

87. Teapot stand, porcelain, glazed white.
Heavy circular rim curved up; foot pressed out. Hand-painted with yellow rose, leaves and buds. 'H. Cooper' painted underneath.

Diameter 16.5cm.
Impressed mark of crown over 'H & C' for Hammersley & Co.
c. 1890.
Stand badly broken and fixed with metal rivets before purchase.
NMI 1974.17.

88. Tea plate, porcelain, glazed white, gilded.
Rim with moulded ionic capitals (design no. 150153, registered in 1890). Hand-painted with primroses and beetle. 'Dublin 1892' painted underneath.
Diameter 16cm.
c. 1890.
NMI 1974.40.

89. Tea plate, china, white.
Hand-painted with butterflies, grass and shamrock. Moulded with ionic columns around the rim; design of type attributed to Hammersley & Co., no. 150153, registered in 1890.
Diameter 16cm.
'H. Cooper Dublin' painted underneath.
c. 1891.
NMI 1974.41.

90. Set of dessert plates (eleven).
Hand-painted, floral with gilt rim. A different botanical illustration on each plate; the Latin name of the plant is hand-painted on the back: *Adiantum vernis, Trilonia cloivesil, Begonia rex, Aenides bookii, Doochia lunulate, Epidendrum vitellinum, Pteris trgyrea, Woodwardia areolate, Nephrolepis exaltata, Fuchsia, Lalia superliens.* 'W.H. Kerr Dublin' painted underneath.
Diameter 23cm.
Impressed mark underneath for Kerr and Binns's Worcester period (but with crown on top and WORCESTER below); *c.* 1870–1.
NMI 1977.12.1–1977.12.11.

91. Tea and coffee set, bone china: eleven coffee cups, ten teacups, twelve saucers and one slop bowl.
Cups and saucers are each decorated with different hand-painted flowers, including primroses, lily of the valley, forget-me-nots and honeysuckle. Saucers are decorated with lily of the valley, ferns and swallows. The slop bowl has roses all around. Saucers are also painted in the centre with monogram 'EHM' (unidentified) in gold; 'H. Cooper 27 Molesworth St. Dublin' painted underneath.
Teacup height 5.5cm; coffee cup height 6.5cm; saucer diameter 13cm; slop bowl 15cm x 8cm.
c. 1883–1907.
NMI 1977.65.

92. Sugar bowl.
Hemispherical shape, with moulded ring handles and high foot rim. Hand-painted with apple blossom and forget-me-not flowers on a yellow background.
7.5cm x 10.5cm.
Signed underneath 'H Cooper Dublin' with shamrock.
NMI 1978.8.

93. Cup, yellow, pink.
Bowl shape, gilt on ornate handle and foot. Hand-painted with pink wild rose spray on yellow background.
11cm x 5.5cm.
Signed 'H Cooper, Dublin'. Board of Trade registration mark 22 June 1870. Shape attributed to Hammersley & Co.
NMI 1978.9.

94. Coffee cup.
Regency-style shape. Rim hand-painted with band of Sèvres turquoise and gilt decoration; floral sprays on the body—pansies, roses, convolvulus and fern. 'HC. QI Dublin' painted underneath.
6cm x 3cm.
NMI 1981.22.

95. Bottle/flask, earthenware, yellow with gilt details on feet and rim.
Circular-shape body, two feet; influence of *Japonisme.* Central circular panels painted with a wagtail and blackberry bush on one side, and with butterflies and shamrock on the other side.
13.5cm x 12cm.
Original label: 'Made of Pure clay found at Athlone and fired in primitive kiln at the Queen's Institute 1882. Presented by H. Cooper'.
NMI 1996.4.

96. Plaque, earthenware.
Hand-painted with kingfisher, Prunus blossom, water lily on pond. Some raised enamel painting.
Influence of *Japonisme.*
Diameter 41cm.
Signed 'HC Queen's Institute' with a shamrock.
c. 1871–83.
Purchased in 1996 from Maureen Johnston.
NMI 1996.6.

97. Plate, cream, gilt; one of a pair (see no. 98 below).
Hand-painted with dragonfly, water lily and bullrushes. Monogram 'GEL'.
Diameter 22.5cm.
Unmarked.; *c. 1883–1907.*
NMI 2006.30.

98. Plate, cream, gilt; one of a pair (see no. 97 above).
Hand-painted with orange and purple wallflowers and white dog rose. Monogram 'GEL'.
Diameter 22.5cm.
Signed 'H Cooper 27 Molesworth St Dublin'.; *c. 1883–1907.*
NMI 2006.31.

99. Plate, porcelain, glazed white with raised gold rim; floral decoration, purple, pink and green.
Hand-painted botanical illustration of iris flower, leaves and bulb. The botanical name *Epidendrum* is painted in red on back. 'WH Kerr Dublin' also painted in red on back.
Diameter 22cm.
c. 1871–83.
NMI 2006.32.

100. Plate, porcelain, glazed white with raised gold rim, plant illustration in purple, pink and green.
Hand-painted botanical illustration of ferns. The botanical names *Hypolepis amaurorachis* and *Scolopendrium* vulgare are painted in red on back. 'WH Kerr Dublin' also painted in red on back.
Diameter 22cm.
c. 1871–83.
NMI 2006.33.

101. Cup and saucer, porcelain, glazed yellow, white, green.
Hand-painted daisies and leaves on a yellow background. Cup has a square raised foot. Saucer rim is gilt.
Cup height 4.5cm; saucer diameter 14cm.
Signed on the back: '1886 Rose Skehan'.
Attributed to Queen's Institute/ Herbert Cooper's studio.
NMI 2006.45 (A) and (B).

102. Cup and saucer, porcelain, glazed yellow, green, pink, burgundy.
Hand-painted shamrock leaves and flower on a yellow background. Cup has a square raised foot. Saucer rim is gilt.
Cup height 4.5cm; saucer diameter 14cm.
Signed on the back: 'R.S. 1886'.
Attributed to Queen's Institute/ Herbert Cooper's studio.
NMI 2006.46 (A) and (B).

103. Coffee cup, porcelain, glazed cream background and burgundy.
Coffee-can shape with ring handle. Blackberry fruits and leaves painted in purple/burgundy on a cream ground. Gilt rim, foot and handle. Similar design (a set) to nos 104 and 111 below.
Height 6cm, width 5.5cm.
Attributed to Queen's Institute/ Herbert Cooper's studio.
NMI 2006.48 (A).

104. Saucer, porcelain, glazed cream background and burgundy.
Hand-painted with blackberry fruits and leaves in purple/burgundy on a cream ground. Gilded rim. Similar design to no. 103 above and no. 111 below.
Diameter 14cm.
Attributed to Queen's Institute/ Herbert Cooper's studio.
NMI 2006.48 (B).

105. Coffee cup, porcelain, glazed white, green, grey, burgundy.
Funnel shape. Hand-painted shamrock leaves. Gilt on rim, foot and handle. 'H Cooper' painted in blue underneath, with a six-petalled flower.
Height 7.5cm, width 4.5cm.
NMI 2006.56.

105. Coffee cup, porcelain, glazed white, green, blue, pink.
Coffee-can shape. Hand-painted shamrock leaves on one side and blue butterfly with pink flowers on the other side. Gilt on rim, foot and handle. 'QI Dublin' (very indistinct) painted in gold underneath, with a shamrock leaf.
Height 6.5cm, width 5.5cm.
c. 1871–83.
NMI 2006.57.

106. Side plate, porcelain, glazed yellow, white, pink, and green.
Hand-painted with pansies and leaves. Shape a Hammersley & Co. registered design—moulded columns around undulating rim, gilded.
Diameter 17.5cm.
Hammersley & Co. mark impressed on back.
Attributed to Queen's Institute/ Herbert Cooper's studio.
c. 1890.
NMI 2006.59.

107. Side plate, porcelain, white, red, pink and blue.
Hand-painted with small red flowers and pink butterfly, rust and blue spots on a white ground. Shape a Hammersley & Co. registered design—moulded columns around undulating rim, gilded.
Diameter 17.5cm.
Hammersley & Co. mark impressed on back.
Attributed to Herbert Cooper's studio.
c. 1890.
NMI 2006.60.

108. Side plate, porcelain, white, wine, blue.
Hand-painted with buds and flowers. Shape is a Hammersley & Co. registered design—moulded columns around undulating rim, gilded.
Diameter 17.5cm.
Hammersley & Co. impressed mark on back.
Attributed to Queen's Institute/ Herbert Cooper's studio.
c. 1890.
NMI 2006.61.

109. Side plate, porcelain, white, yellow.
Hand-painted with white roses on a yellow ground. Shape is a Hammersley & Co. registered design—moulded columns around undulating rim, gilded.
Diameter 17.5cm.
Hammersley & Co. impressed mark on back.
Attributed to Queen's Institute/ Herbert Cooper's studio.
c. 1890.
NMI 2006.62.

110. Side plate, porcelain, white, pink.
Hand-painted with pink roses on a yellow ground. Shape is a Hammersley & Co. registered design—moulded columns around undulating rim, gilded.
Diameter 17.5cm.
Hammersley & Co. impressed mark on back.
Attributed to Queen's Institute/ Herbert Cooper's studio.
c. 1890.
NMI 2006. 63.

111. Side plate, porcelain, glazed cream background and burgundy.
Blackberry fruits and leaves painted in purple/burgundy on a cream ground. Gilt rim. Similar design to nos 103 and 104 above.
Diameter 14.5cm.
Attributed to Queen's Institute/ Herbert Cooper's studio.
NMI 2006.64.

112. Saucer, porcelain, glazed yellow, white, green, burgundy; plant illustration in purple, white and green.
Hand-painted flowers (possibly clematis) and fern leaf on a yellow background.
Diameter 15cm.
Signed on the back: 'M Shehan 1886'.
Attributed to Queen's Institute.
NMI 2006.65.

113. Saucer, porcelain, glazed yellow, white, green, burgundy; plant illustration in purple, pink and green.
Hand-painted fuschia flowers on a yellow background.
Diameter 15cm.
Signed on the back: 'M Skehan 1886'.
Attributed to Queen's Institute/ Herbert Cooper's studio.
NMI 2006.66.

114. Side plate, porcelain, glazed, white, pink and green.
Hand-painted with roses and leaves. Shape is a Hammersley & Co. registered design—moulded columns around undulating rim, gilded.
Diameter 17.5cm.
Hammersley & Co. impressed mark on back.
Attributed to Queen's Institute/ Herbert Cooper's studio.
c. 1890.
NMI 2006.73.

115. Side plate, porcelain, glazed white, pink and green.
Hand-painted with dahlias and

leaves. Shape is a Hammersley & Co. registered design—moulded columns around undulating rim, gilded.
Diameter 17.5cm.
Hammersley & Co. impressed mark on back.
Attributed to Queen's Institute/ Herbert Cooper's studio.
c. 1890.
NMI 2006.74.

116. Side plate, porcelain, glazed white, pink and green.
Hand-painted with violet flowers and leaves. Shape is a Hammersley & Co. registered design—moulded columns around undulating rim, gilded.
Diameter 17.5cm.
Hammersley & Co. impressed mark on back.
Attributed to Queen's Institute/ Herbert Cooper's studio.
c. 1890.
NMI 2006.75.

117. Side plate, porcelain, glazed white and green.
Hand-painted with white roses and leaves. Shape is a Hammersley & Co. registered design—moulded columns around undulating rim, gilded.
Diameter 17.5cm.
Hammersley & Co. impressed mark on back.
Attributed to Queen's Institute/ Herbert Cooper's studio.
c. 1890.
NMI 2006.76.